Juxtaposing Narrative and Fiction
Explorations in Postmodern Novels

Juxtaposing Narrative and Fiction

Explorations in Postmodern Novels

Lata Mishra

GNOSIS

Nurturing the Aspirations

Worldwide Circulation through Authorspress Global Network
First Published in 2013
by
GNOSIS
(An Imprint of Authorspress)

Editorial
Q-2A Hauz Khas Enclave
New Delhi-110 016

Marketing
E-35/103, Jawahar Park
Laxmi Nagar, Delhi-110 092

e-mails: authorspress@rediffmail.com; authorspress@hotmail.com
Website: www.authorspressbooks.com

Juxtaposing Narrative and Fiction:
Explorations in Postmodern Novels
ISBN: 978-93-81030-38-7

Printed in India at Shri Krishna Offset Press, Delhi

Preface

The present anthology, *Juxtaposing Narrative and Fiction:Explorations in Postmodern Novels,* looks into varying theoretical assumptions, political ideologies and discourses that have boosted diverse viewpoints on fiction and narratives. The postmodern condition in literature is preoccupied with the idea of representation of life: knowledge, history, and reality through the employment of the metanarrative. The narrator uses the narrative function to constitute a fictive world. The fictive world may comprise fictive characters and events.

Postmodernist fictions have shown a return to the narrative. Postmodernists, being critical and relativists in nature, deconstruct the concept of an absolute signified and thus reject the totalizing modernist claims. The narrative style that has evolved and developed in contemporary culture is characterized by the postmodern technique of an amalgamation of various narrative voices within the story. In the third person narrative the supposed dissociation between the author and the narrator could be more aptly described as the absence of a narrator. A narrative theory based on a linguistic theory considers communication as the constitutive and ever present function of language.

Postmodernists view texts as a product of the endless play of language which precedes the author. Meaning is generated in language not through terms which are naturally imbued with absolute meaning, but through difference. Lyotard claimed that culture is formed through narrative knowledge in fiction. It may be argued that in order to understand the literature of other cultures, an attempt ought to be made to enter into a cultural discourse governed by different assumptions than those of one's own. With the arrival of a postcolonial world and the development of deconstruction theory, the idea of universal value or an absolute presence has faded.

This anthology comprises research papers that explore the theoretical concerns of postmodernism and provide new insights into the works of major postmodernist writers who have opened the narrative up to new possibilities. They explore the relationship between postmodern narrative and postmodern theory. These writers seem to emphasize on a self-contained fictional environment rather than realism.

Lata Mishra

Contributors

Anand Balwant Patil, Retd. Director of the School of Languages and Literature, Swami Ramanand Teerth Marathwada University, Nanded, Maharashtra.

Sambit Panigrahi, Lecturer, Department of English, Ravenshaw University, Cuttack, Odisha.

Garima Kalita, Associate Professor, Department of English, Cotton College, Guwahati, Assam.

Hemang A. Desai, Head of English Department, N.V. Patel College of Pure & Applied Sciences, Vallabh Vidyanagar, Gujarat.

Vijay Singh Thakur, Assistant Professor, Department of Languages and Translation, Dhofar University, Salalah, Sultanate of Oman.

Sathikulameen, Research Scholar, Department of English, University of Madras, Chennai, Tamil Nadu.

Sudhir K. Arora, Associate Professor, Department of English, Maharaja Harishchandra, P. G. College, Moradabad, Uttar Pradesh.

Bhagabat Nayak, Head, Department of English, Kujang College, Kujang, Jagatsinghpur, Odisha.

Jamsheed Ahmad, Research Scholar, Department of English, Aligarh Muslim University, Aligarh, Uttar Pradesh.

Arindam Ghosh, Research Scholar, Department of English & Other Modern European Languages, Bhasha-Bhavana, Visva-Bharati, Santiniketan, West Bengal.

M. Rosary Royar, Department of English, Fatima College, Madurai, Tamil Nadu.

G.A. Ghanshyam Head, Department of English, Government M.L. Shukla College Seepat, Bilaspur Chhattigarh.

Marie Aruna Josephine, Assistant Professor, Department of English, Government Arts College, Puducherry.

Bilal A. Shah, Assistant Professor of English, Department of Higher Education, Government of Jammu and Kashmir.

Sandeep Kumar Sharma, Lecturer in English, D. M. College, Moga, Punjab.

Jayshree Singh, Assistant Professor, Department of English, Bhupal Nobles Post-Graduate Girls' College, Udaipur, Rajasthan.

M. Preetha, Research Scholar, Department of English, Avinashilingam Deemed University for Women, Coimbatore, Tamil Nadu.

Rajesh B. Sharma, Department of English & Modern European languages, Lucknow University, Lucknow, Uttar Pradesh.

Lata Mishra, Department of English Studies and Research Government K.R.G. (P.G.) Autonomous College, Gwalior, Madhya Pradesh.

Contents

1

Emerging Trends in Postmodern Indian Novel in English

Anand Balwant Patil

The spatial dimensions of emerging literatures have been a constant reference throughout this paper, which makes it thus a more than a fitting subject to discuss here. At the beginning of my paper I examine diverse cartographies of literary emergence, which pinpoint this process in the Third World, or, to be more exact, within some areas... those delimited by the economic terms emerging markets and emerging economics. A Rostowian literary scale and an essentially inter-systematic model of emergence was derived from these positions: the emergence of a dependent ex-colonial system in a metropolit —an hegemonic backdrop-C'esar Dominguez, "Literary Emergence as a case study of Theory in Comparative Literature" Trans. from the Spanish by Carla Dechant and Mark D. Wiersma. *Comparative Literature and Culture Web Journal* 802, (2006).

The concept of emerging Indian literature(s) is often used but rarely theorized in Indian criticism. The objective of this paper is to construct a new theory to explain the emergence of 'postmodern Indian novel in English.' Here "Emerging Literature" and "Literary Emergence" demand an interdisciplinary and pluralist model. Is Indian novel twice born with two faces like Janus or thrice born with three faces like Guru Datta? Is it autonomous and 'independent' or mere 'extension' of the European culture and imperialism? Is it really postcolonial or postmodern? What is meant by "postmodern" in the Indian context? Is it a movement, trend or mere tendency? How far is it Indian as well as Bharatiya? From where did this concept of 'postmodern novel' travel to India? Has modernism died altogether? What is its relationship with the Indian novels in constitutionally recognized languages? Has it anything to do with Euramerican market?

A number of such questions are to be answered with comparative perspectives. According to the OD 'emergent' means 'new and still developing'. It is 'nascent' which breaks the surface. "Trend" is defined as "a general tendency in the way a situation is changing. This historiographic and supranational problem became the main theme of the XI Congress of the International Comparative books. In fact, the adjective 'modern' or 'new' was used to describe different changes since our colonial contact with Europe (see Patil 1999) Everything Western was 'modern' and Indian 'backward', inferior in the nineteenth century. For example, the avatars of emerging 'Anglo-Indian literature', later 'Indo-Anglian' and after independence 'Commonwealth literature' and today Indian writing in English or New Literature are labels which exhibit developmentally linked with Europe. Thus the present topic is large enough and cannot be studied with sample texts in isolation.

A comparative study of the novelists, who are more exposed to the Western models and culture, if carried out with other formerly colonized countries, will display more complex postmodern intertextuality. On the contrary, those who have less cultural contact with the West are still stuck in modernism of the twentieth century. Edward Said has devoted *Culture and Imperialism* (1994) to the analysis of modern novel as the product of European culture and imperialism. Later Homi K. Bhabha edited *Nation and Narration* (1995) to explore whether the nation itself narrates in its voice or in 'his/her Masters Voice'. It is the result of literary enculturation that diaspora fiction such as Bapsi Sidhwa's *Ice-Candy Man* (1988) and Salman Rushdie's *Midnight's*

Children (Booker Prize, 1981) pioneered the trend of postmodern novels in India and was successfully extended by two more Booker Prizes: Arundhati Roy's *The God of All Things* and Aravind Adiga's *The White Tiger* (2008). What trends can be traced in the contemporary Indian English novel?

I have juxtaposed the following sample texts from the corpus of the small minority novels in English which was ridiculed as a "tourist fiction' before the Indian Man Booker Awardee appeared on the horizon. These texts are selected at random and will be discussed in the chronological order:

1. Kiran Nagarkar. *Ravan and Eddie.* Delhi: Penguin Books, 1995 (Sahitya Akademi Delhi Awardee)
2. Anita Nair. *The Better Man.* Delhi: Penguin Books, 1999.
3. Chetan Bhagat, *Five Point Someone: What not to do at IIT.* Delhi: Rupa & Co. 2004
4. Aravind Adiga. *The White Tiger.* Delhi Noida: Harper and Collins, 2008, (Man Booker Award)

In order to gain methodical comparative perspectives on these samples, we have to juxtapose two major concepts related to the theme of the seminar: Modernism and Postmodernism. There will be ample scope for other papers to be discussed in this frame of reference. J. A. Cuddon writes about modernism:

> A comprehensive but vague term for a movement (or tendency) which began to get underway in the closing years of the 19th century and which has had a wide influence internationally during much of the 20th c. The term pertains to all the creative arts, especially poetry, fiction, drama, painting, music and architecture... In fact, such movements, of their nature, do not just start and stop; the evolution is gradual. The impetus and energy of one diminishes (but continues) at the momentum of another burgeons (515).

Such modernist tendencies are active in different countries at different periods of time. In India it became most prominent after independence. It can be described as 'an armed version of colonialism'. But this aspect is mostly ignored in Indian 'monoliterary' impressionist as well as elitist literary criticism conveniently. Basically it was a European and transcontinental movement, and its principal centres of activity were the capital cities. Most of the above-mentioned novelists seem to be products of Indian cities, and their location of cultural capital is also an important factor. We will trace the degrees of their revolt against established rules, indigenous traditions and conventions. What are their ways of looking at 'man's position and function in the universe?' How do they experiment with forms and styles? Various aspects of modernism are revealed in a number of theories, which we will apply to the sample texts, such as constructionism, structuralism, new humanism, stream of consciousness, symbolism, and imagism and so on. Modernism was defined as 'the experience of constant change, perpetual crises.

> Post-modernism is a general (and sometimes controversial) term used to refer to changes, developments and tendencies which have taken place (and are taking place) in literature, art, music, architecture philosophy, etc. since the 1940s or 1950s. Post-Modernism is different from modernism (q.v.) even a reaction against it. It is no easier to define than many other-isms. Like them, it is morphous by nature (Cuddon, 689)

When we discuss postmodernism, it does not mean that modernism is completely over. A clear demarcation between two is not possible. Some of its features can be sorted on as anti-traditional, anti-authority etc. This list includes hybridization, indeterminacy, fragmentation, decolonization, irony, presentable-unpresentable, selflessness, immanence, performance, carnivalization and construction. In *The Postmodern Condition* Jean-Francois Lyotard writes about "missing contents" and the "unpresentable" in the literature of modernity. Thus Western narratives are delegitimzed. 'Pluralism' is a watchword in it. David Harvey, in *The Condition of Postmodernity* (1989), pointed out that it is "a next stage of (capitalist) modernity, only faster and more complex".There are many parallel movements or tendencies and post colonialism is more relevant to Indian literature(s).

'Postcolonial' does not mean merely 'after' colonialism, but it hints at 'because of', 'against', and resistance is implied in it. The Marxists describe both postmodernism and postcolonialism as "fads, folders of a consumer society" in late capitalism. Colonialism is supposed to be the "unbridgeable racial chasm", and "the structural domination of the empire and different forms". The postcolonial criticism claims to be an anti-imperialist emancipator project. It exposes the politicized dimension of both commonwealth and regional literature studies. I found it very useful in diagnosing cultural amnesia, dependence complex, ambivalences, stereotypes, mimicry, hybridity, plagiarism, remolding, 'faking' etc, in Indian literature. Very often it means 'inclusive' of or the colonial and the 'other'. It is a very complex label and is likely to mislead the ill-informed reader. Of course, it is 'a space clearing gesture' which provides an opportunity to test whether 'subalterns can speak.' It has its own limitations but critics agree that postcolonial literatures share a "foregrounding (of) the tension with the imperial powers". Moreover, as Djelal Kadir observes, the politics of representation displays that authors are all "otherwise" awake but to the otherness within as well as mindful of the other as other. It will be more interesting to examine how Indian writers write back to the indigenous as well as alien empires.

The first page of *Ravan and Eddie* exhibits how Kiran Nagarkar's first novel is considered a landmark in post-independence Indian literature. Black, bawdy and disturbingly funny, the discontinuous, hopscotch flow of the novel is said to redefine the twentieth century Marathi novel. It is a modernist cultural product of the Westernized elite class in Mumbai. A vein of absurdism and satire runs through it. This is an extension of Beckettian, Sartrean, Kafkaesque, Camusque or Kunderian modernist fiction. Nagarkar's subversive confessions in

'Acknowledgements' reveal some clues to the nature and scope of his *Ravan and Eddie* which he had started as a Hindi screen play "with something farcical, bawdy or self-deprecatory". Later the film director 'dropped' his two heroes but Nagarkar "owed *Ravan and Eddie* to him". His English screenplay on them was too long and he wrote "70 pages of a novel in Marathi on them". To some extent, it is a dark comedy set in the Central Works Department Chawl No. 17 in Bombay where the Hindus and Catholics live together. It starts around 1947. The Catholics from Goa and Hindus from 'India' are portrayed by subverting the *Bible* and the *Ramayana* respectively.

The multilingualism and multiculturalism add a new dimension of Indianness to this modern narrative. In a way it is a bildungsroman that tells a hilarious story of Ravan, a Maratha Hindu, and Eddie, a Roman Catholic. The blurb exhibits a comment "novel about two larger-than-life heroes and their bawdy, Rabelaisian adventures in postcolonial urban India". Why do Indian modern authors prefer protagonists from outside their sub-caste-culture groups? For instance, in Kiran Desai's *The Inheritance of Loss* or Aravind Adiga's *The White Tiger* the other high caste non-brahmin protagonists are juxtaposed. It is an important topic for a cultural study. This strong emerging trend is perhaps the part of colonial 'self-other' dichotomy. The 'epilogue' confirms that it is a linear modernist narrative with simple lengthy dialogues, dramatized episodes, and realistic settings but without much ado about stream of consciousness and flashbacks. The epilogue opens and ends as follows:

> The matriculation exam in those days was after the eleventh grade. Like a lot of other students from municipal and not-so-fancy parochial schools, Ravan and Eddie never went past the tenth grade. There were scenes, bitter fights, Shankar rao turned his back upon the proceedings but Violet broke her vow of stubborn 'no comment' ... It was a duet. Two volatile martial arts in a state of continuous equilibrium. Two warriors and two life-long enemies locked in the ritual of battle (n. p. after 328)

Nagarkar's narrative displays deliberate radical break with some of the traditional bases in the cosmopolitan centre like 'Bombay' in the postcolonial period. It questions the certain theses that supported traditional modes of social organisations, religion, morality, ways of conceiving self, minority-majority complexes etc. It is neither too avant-garde nor too experimental to be acceptable for the Western readers. A golden mean is struck in indianizing it. Except limited intertextuality of film titles, letters and two scriptures, there is not a postmodernist break from modernist 'high art'. The mass culture is neither carnivalized nor elitism overthrown. However, a good and comparative consciousness of colonialism, religion-caste, sect, culture, linguistic bias and other aspects of co-existence is shown in this fictional representation. It is not free from poetics of culture, but the author, God, maintains a neutral poise, to a great extent, in representing 'others'. He has kept his own major sub-caste groups outside the boundaries of the text. Perhaps this is one of the reasons that he could make his novel 'hilarious', 'bawdy', 'wicked' and 'irreverent'.

Indian criticism has always ignored such issues connected with the politics of representation. Self and 'other' dichotomy play a significant role in it and it emphasizes the poetics of culture too much. That is why 'postcolonial' subversive, anti-Euro-American or 'postmodern' self-reflective historiographic fiction, as defined by anti-colonialists such as Fanon, Achebe, Said, Benita Parry, Ngugi, Linda Hutcheon and others, is yet to 'emerge' in India in the real sense of those terms. It is too culture conditioned as well as determined by the late capitalistic and imperialistic Western markets, as pointed out by Dominguez. He has shown how *Princeton Encyclopedia of Poetry and Poetics* (1965) and Erich Auerbach's essay titled "Philologie der Wltliteratur" (1952) emphasized "national" character of non-Western emerging literatures but not their "origins" : "National wills are stronger and louder than ever, yet in every case they promote the same standards and forms for modern life... European cultures... still retain their individualities" (Auerbach 2).

Thus *Ravan and Eddie* is an 'extension' of "European culture, standards and forms for modern life" in the Westernized financial capital of India. It is rather difficult to determine whether the 'Hindu Nation' makes its own narration through it. Very few indigenous structural elements can be traced in it. It can be compared with the diasporic postmodern novels of NRIs such as Salman Rushdie, Meena Alexander and others for measuring the freedom the writer enjoys, the role of 'distant nativism' and production of postmodernity in fiction.

The location of an author and the place of publication, publisher and reviewers play a major role in its shaping of spirit and structure. Meera Nair's *The Better Man* is also published by Penguin which shows the effect of globalization on not only the literary market but also on the whole literate in India. Nair lives in Bangalore but her first novel is set in a remote village, Kaikurussi in Kerala just like R. K. Narayan's Malgudi.

The Better Man can be easily classified as a rural/regional novel in Indian neo-casteist postcolonial categorization. The novelist slowly unfolds the complex process of "the remaking of a man in quiet manner". She skilfully fathoms the deepest recesses of man's psyche and the power politics, as well as cultural conflicts in a village. On the whole, it is about every human's attempt to find a degree of inner peace and happiness. Its narrative technique is in the Conradian mode. For example, it opens with a long and complete monologue by the painter-one-screw-loose Bhasi, addressed to Mukundan Nair, the protagonist in the first chapter: "A Reason to Be". All 24 chapters are significantly titled. The first person auto-photo self narrative shifts to the third person in the next chapter titled "Reluctant Native" which opens as follows:

> Once upon a time Mukundan had a life that in no way resembled the hell he had been exiled to. As a government employee all his working years had been negligible and the comforts many... (13)

Thus the 'plot' unfolds in the conventional indigenous technique of Gunadhya's story. On its next page there is a rich intertextuality of foreign English authors and books: James Hadley Chase, Sidney Sheldon, Wilbur Smith, Irving Stone, Agatha Christie, R. K. Narayan, Pearl S. Buck, Nevil Shute, David Copperfield. The exceptional single name of the Indian novelist also shows the high degree of Anglicization and the nature of the fictional product of alien culture and imperialism. The plot is very complex and 'well-made', but it is not a 'drawing-room novel' Mukundan's father Achuthan, Kutty Paru Kutty, painter Bhasi, Anjana and Shanta are, to use E. M. Forster's concept, round characters. Krishnan, the Power House Ram Krishnan, Shankaran Nair and others are 'types'. The story is full of violence and suspense. The open ending reminds us of the scene of exploding the temple in Ayan Rand's *The Fountain Head.* Mukundan goes alone to explode the community hall constructed on the piece of land owned by the migrant painter. The novel ends with philosophisizing of the epiphany experienced by Mukundan. "This was the moment that had eluded him all his life. When he would become a man. A better man than he ever had been. Mukundan felt his destiny flicker, leap, and change its course" (361).

Like *Ravan and Eddie,* its epilogue displays its formal affinity with the modern Euro American fiction. However, Meera Nair has provided fine threads of Indian mythical intertextuality and karma theory. But Indian folk or classical forms and structures are absent in it. There is a great gulf that separates Nair's 'Bharat', Bhagat's 'Shining India' and Adiga's 'Bharat-cum-IT India".

Compared to Chetan Bhagat's clichés and Kiran Nagarkar's touches of irony and humour, Nair's language is more experimental and style loaded with analysis of events and moods. For example, the protagonist's monologue is constructed in the full chapter No 27 and carries a very symbolic title "Fireflies are not stars". It is just like Hamlet's dilemma of action. Before taking the decision to explode the community hall, he broods over his actions in the past and their immediate outcomes. Finally he concludes:

> Man cannot change the movement of the planets with the sweep of his hand. Every man is guided by a force that is individual and unfathomable. Man can heal, but a little. Man can aid self-discovery, but only little. No man is master of another man's destiny. For man is not God. And fireflies are not stars (330).

Five Point Someone is the new best seller from the award-winning author who is the product of an "IT culture". It is a first novel by the author employed in Hong Kong's filmy 'karate', Bruce Lee's fights and so on. Except the exposure of the inside stories in IITs in India, which are believed to be top most seats of learning for the cream of intellects in India, there is nothing that is postmodern in it. It is an episodic plain and linear modernist narrative like the 'campus fiction' of Kingsley Amis in England. But it contains a little bit of self-reflective element in its tone of telling a story in contemporary catch words and IIT linguistic codes and registers. It opens with the following para in the first chapter:

> Before I really begin this book, let me first tell you what this book is not. It is not a guide on how to live through college. In the contrary, it is probably an example of how screwed up your college years can get if you don't think strait. But this is my take on it, you are free to agree or disagree... So stuff it boys-it is my story. I am the one writing it and I get to tell it the way I want it. (p.1)

This reads like the opening of Stern's *Tristram Shandy*, but Bhagat's imagination is more culture conditioned by the orthodoxy of his own subculture group. He is not so outspoken and satirical as Sterne is. Its setting is IIT campus without any specific locale. The timespan is four years of training in it. It is meant to entertain more than instruct. The author lacks literary competence and the poor intertextuality makes it a 'popular novel'. Technically it is an ordinary plain narrative and yet we have to take a serious note of its colloquial language and 'smart' dialogues. As the languages of Western Pop music market has overpowered our songs and music, such 'compu-novels' in English are likely to dislocate the Indian regional language novels. Already the translations of alien "bestsellers" have weaned the readers away from them. Such best-sellers with some autobiographical elements and captivating plot, simple characters and dramatized filmy dialogues, 'friendly tone' and 'dollops' of humour make a fun filled trip to 'IIT' very successful for the ordinary readers. Such bestsellers and translations will soon pave the path for the Indian postmodern novel in near future. Does not the class/caste/culture determine these four categories exhibited by sample texts?

Literary postmodernism's reception depends on the literary as well as intertextual competence of the Indian readers. At present we cannot expect the oppositional trend in a sense implied in the concept of 'postcolonialism'. There is no total break from the hegemonic system because most of the Indian writers writing in English belong to Indian intra-hegemonic subsystems. So the process of emerging trend of postmodernism and postcolonialism needs to be discussed from both an intra-and inter-'systemic standpoint'. The last para of Bhagat's 'acknowledgements' also predicts the future of postmodernism in Indian literature. He observes: "And lastly, it is only when one writes a book that one realizes the true power of MS Word, from grammar checks to replace alls. It is simple-without this software, this book could not be written." (n.p.)

In the middle of the previous century the death of the author-God was declared. It is not only the creativity and competence of both the author and reader that will shape the future 'postmodern' Indian novel but also computers will shape its theories and spirit. As defined earlier, the true postmodernist experimental novels with paradises, subversion, fragmentation, hybridization etc. are not yet born due to culture conditional Indian socio-political structures. Yet the global technological revolution is bound to make metamorphosis in our literate. In this respect the future can be predicted with the help of some critic's observations. Gregory G. Coloms and Mark Turner open their article "Computers, Literary Theory and Theory of Meaning" as:

> Computing has become a form of life, like using toaster or TVs making phone calls, driving cars. It is for so many of us a practical necessity, part of the technological background that enables our intellectual and professional activity.... It is already clear that computing will greatly change those literary studies that depend on powers information storage and retrieval. Computing will bring within the powers of any adept undergraduate a body of information —and an appearance of learning-that would make Erasmus look down from high heaven and weep for envy.

This drastic change called postmodernism which produced Adiga's first novel was rightly foreseen by a historian about whom Patricia Waugh writes:

> So the historian Arnold Toynbee was the first to use the term outside the specific literary critical sense when he announced in the fifties that we were entering the postmodern age: the fourth and final phase of Western history and one dominated by irrationalism and helplessness. (*A Study of History*, 1947) In the world, not only self but also consciousness is discovered to be adrift increasingly unable to anchor itself to any universal ground of justice, truth or reason, and is itself 'decentreed' (to use a term favoured by post-structuralists), no longer agent, origin, author, but a junction through which impersonal forces pass and intersect-Dover Beach, perhaps displaced by an international airport lounge (7.8)

This prophecy has come true in Adiga's "new" epistolary but e-mail like structure of *The White Tiger*. The seven letters are structured in seven days and nights. They are written from "the desk of 'The White Tiger', a thinking man and an entrepreneur, living in the world's centre of technology and outsourcing Electronics city phase I (Just off Hosur main Road), Bangalore India They are ironically addressed to fell the "plot" His Excellency Wen Jiabao, The Premier's office, Beijing, Capital of the Freedom-Loving nation of China". The addressee's pseudo-names Ashok Sharma, the White Tiger and e-mail address of this 'boss' are given at the end. This 'make believe' of the car-driver cum entrepreneur cum murderer is so skilfully contrived that it subverts the structure of the modernist novel from the very beginning to the open ending. The satire opens as follows:

> Mr. Premier,
>
> Sir,
>
> Neither you nor I speak English, but there are some things that can be said only in English. My ex-employer the late Mr. Ashoka's ex-wife, Pinky Madam, Taught me one of these things, and at 11:32 p.m. today, which was about ten minutes ago, when the lady on All India Radio announced, 'Premier Jiabao is coming to Bangalore next week.' I said that thing at once. (5)

Apparently plain prose narrative turns the concepts of form of letter, time, space, 'truth' 'reality' etc. topsy-turvy. This aesthetics of fiction suggests a break with previous structures of modernity. This is very close to mimicry. The murder of a rich high-caste Thakur by the low-caste Halwai driver is otherwise a horror story that fits well into the patterns of both the Hindi film and dalit writing. The process of deformation of cultural genres continues till the end. The intertextuality of imaginary texts: Exciting Tales of Exotic China, the titles of American business book —Ten secrets of business success or become an entreprenfur in seven DAYS! (6) An ad of the search of the murderer. (12) Lessons for Young Boys from The life of Mahatma Gandhi's, DP's appeal about Ashok Thakur's murder case search of the criminal (30) spread over many pages) Iqbal, Rumi, Mirza Galib (40), Sign board of the hospital (48) news ad (54), Gandhi's photo (52), Price list 'Jackpot' English liquor shop with a signboard (72-74) which reminds of Robinson Crusoe, & Tristram Shandy, a dialogue between God and Devil (87), Slogans (99, 101) Murder Weekly's title of a thriller, and its insets (125,152, 210) legal statement (168), repeated single sentence in italic 'what a fucking joke' on several pages, parents' letter (190), ad sticker (230), guide booklet structure (228-229), split dialogue between Evil and Good in mind of Balaram (246), machine drawn ticket showing weight and telling fortune (248), grandfather's letter (262) a rhyming couplet in italic (367), single lines from stream of consciousness spread all over the text, for example, (265, 268), Iqbal, zoo story, letter (270-278), use of CD (281), news on the internet (281), slogan 'Government work is Gods work (297), Balaram's motto and ads (501-3) subversion of history in italic (504) Murder Weekly (515), and innumerable subtle allusions, puns, etc. display Adiga's literary competence. Of course, his experiences as a journalist and education in Europe and America has made a great difference between his fictional post modernity and Arundhati Roy's literary intertextuality in *The God of Small Things*.

Had Adiga not shown his craftsmanship in mimicry, subversions, mixture of high and low cultures, blend of genres a-historical twists, broad varieties of critical perspectives, de-definition, fragmentation, ambiguities and 'factual discourses', plagiarisms, displacements, montages, openness and brokenness, delegitimation of codes, demystification of knowledge, self-reflection, irony, unpresentable scenes, self-multiplication, growing capacity of mind to generalized human nature, irrealist constructs, growing intervention of mind in nature and culture, the conflicting versions of Balram's worlds in the making, absurd actions, problematizing forces in Indian society and many other features of, in Linda Hutcheon's words, self-reflective historiographic metafiction, Adiga's novel would have been thrown in the dustbin as a popular or detective novel.

Thus, the initial emergence of postmodernism is linked with globalization, boom of Latin American magic realism and recession of European literature. Gabriel Gracia Marquez provided models for Günter Grass and later Salman Rushdie complimented both these Nobel laureates and acknowledged his indebtedness to them. Our Arundhati Roy and Kiran Desai are the grand-daughters of these Euro-Latin-American masters. But the recent debate over *Slumdog Millionaire* and *The White Tiger* as means of parading Indian poverty in the advanced countries for the material gain needs to gain comparative perspectives over the politics of International cultural hegemony, market monopoly and finance as argued by Dominique. He writes:

> In this sense, the fact that research on emerging literatures initiated in the 1980s is highly significant coming precisely at a time when emerging economics and emerging markets (see Mate's de Castro) became popular to refer to the rise in stock markets in certain countries, mainly in the third world, as opposed to the more traditional stock markets of New York, London, Frankfurt, and Tokyo...(3)

This is the basic frame of reference for the study of postmodernism in Indian literature. But the postcolonial contexts should not be cut out of it. Different social institutions such as family, caste structures, methods of literary organizations, or educational models, immigration and diaspora mediation etc. are responsible for the transmission of the dominant culture. It is not an accident that these novelists, who hail from high elite varna/castes class, mediate former colonizer's culture, imperialism and postmodernism. Through alien forms and cultural structures they not only retain their traditional hegemony but also avoid such indigenous conflicting elements which resist the domination of alien cultures. As far as Adiga's *The White Tiger* is concerned, there are very few postmodern structural elements than those found in profusion in novels of Arundhati Roy and Kiran Desai. It can be labelled as a 'neo-dalit tourist fiction'. It is an illusion that our gramin (rural) and dalit literature translated into English is recognized as extraordinary original literature in the Western world. It is mere extension/expansion of "their" Western literature and they use it as sources for studies in anthropology, commerce, sociology and comparative cultural studies. For example, Brooks World Poverty Institute undertakes such projects to study culture, poverty, etc. in the Third World. It is interesting to note its director's views on *The White Tiger* as a primary source of study of Indian poverty. It is not a co-incidence that prestigious Man Booker and Golden Globe awards travel to India in the same year. Even Big Bacchanji is upset by this international politics.

Once upon a time our cotton was sent to Manchester and India purchased their clothes. Now they publish our bestsellers and we buy their cultural products. Denis Rogers, the director of BWPI responded to the use/misuse of *The White Tiger* from the Western point of view:

> "Bestsellers such as Indian writer Aravind Adiga's The White Tiger and Indian-Canadian Rohintion Mistry's A Fine Balance," he said, "convey complex ideas in a most powerful way.... We are not arguing that poets should replace finance Ministers,"said BWPI Research Director, "But we are stressing that novelists make distinctive and important contribution to the broader store house of knowledge on the process, experience and consequences of 'development." (*Times of India, Pune Mirror* 8-11-08: 131)

It is good that politics of literature has re-entered into Indian literate. Whatever be the politics of global literary market, it is the fact that diaspora and rich elites will import postmodernism as modernism entered India with colonial history. Why anticolonialism has not taken roots at international or Euroamerican levels and survived only at the domestic-intra level is another serious problem Our fiction is thematically a 'twice-born' fiction, but its structure or form has remained Western. Western culture dominates its texture. All the four sample texts discussed here show hardly any rich indigenous intertextuality or elements of mass-folk-low culture as such. If the gap widens too much, Indian regional literature(s) will be "appropriated" Hence post-colonialism and postmodernism need to be carefully co-opted in a different kind of Indian 'multiculturalism: It is not an American 'melting pot' at present. The crux of the matter lies with one contemporary dilemma: Will Indian literature and culture produce Talibani terrorist Osama Bin Laden or Utopian dreamer Barack Obama who wrote his *Dreams from My Father* (!995)?

The last paragraph of Ralph Cohen's "Introduction" to his anthology of essays titled *The Future of Literary Theory* (1989, xx) defends my position:

> If I am asked why her essay begins this anthology, I reply that Cixous, novelist and dramatist and critic, writes theory out of a lyric sense of the place writing has in her life and how, despite the fact that writing has in her life and how, despite the fact that writing can create for her a paradise or hell, it makes survival possible. Theory is for her a personal public commitment to ethical and literary values. How better to begin a collection of essays on what literary theory can or ought to be?

Let me conclude this speech with Lewis Wolpert's (1929-) single sentence from *Unnatural Nature of Science* (1996); as in *Oxford Quotations and Proverbs*:

"As one explores phenomena or ideas at the frontiers of scientific knowledge it is the unexpected that provides the clues to guide further work."

Works Cited

Adiga, Aravind. *The White Tiger*. Delhi-Noida: Harper and Collins, 2008.

Bhabha, Homi, K. (ed.) *Nation and Narration*. London. Routledge, 1995.

Bhagat, Chetan. *Five Point Someone: What Not to do at llT*, Delhi: Rupa & co., 2004.

Colomb, Gregory G. and Mark Turner (1998), "Computer, Literary Theory and Theory of Meaning" in Ralph Cohen (ed.). *The Future of Literary Theory*, London: Routledge, 307-410.

Cuddon, J. A. *The Penguin Dictionary of Literary Terms and Literary Theories*. Harmondsworth: Penguin Books, 1999.

Nagarkar, Kiran. *Ravan and Eddie*. Delhi: Penguin Books, 1995.

Nair, Anita. *The Better Man*. Delhi: Penguin Books, 1993 rpt., 1999.

Patil, Anand. *Western Influence on Marathi Drama*. Panaji, God: Rajhauns Vitaran, 1993.

______. *Perspectives and Progression*. New Delhi: Creative Books, 2005.

Said, Edward. *Culture and Imperialism*. London: Chatto and Indus. 1994.

Waugh, Patrica. *Practicing Postmodernism*. London: Arvind., 1992.

Young, Robert. *Postcolonialism Theory: A Very Short Introduction*. London: Routledge. 2003.

2

Dead Author, Sovereign Language and Interpretative Reader: A Postmodernist Approach to Italo Calvino's *If on a Winter's Night a Traveller*

Sambit Panigrahi

In the realm of postmodern thought, there is a marked shift from the pre-existing dominance of the author to the all-pervasive ubiquity of the text. The text is no more seen as an entity that is the sole creation of the author-God, the uncontested creative genius. It is, on the contrary, a product of the endless play of language which precedes the human subject, or the author. The author remains no more than a "shaman" (as Roland Barthes would have it), a mediator through which the infinite play of language precipitates into the text. In this arena of shifting perspectives, it is also found that it is not the author who renders meaning to the text; rather, it is the reader who gives meaning to the text through his act of reading. The text therefore slips out of the dictatorial hands of the author and generates its own meaning which is deciphered and interpreted by the reader.

Replete with postmodernist undertones, Calvino's *If on a Winter's Night a Traveller* marks the decimation of boundaries and effectuates a shift from the reign of the absoluteness of 'reason' to the realm of a 'reason-less' and 'logic-less' chaotic disarray. The excessive ascendancy granted to man over the rest of the world by The Enlightenment starts crumbling in the postmodern realm of existence. In this scenario, man is made to diffuse into the 'boundary-less' mélange of the innumerable constituents (both animate and inanimate) of the world. Such an anti-anthropocentric tendency augured by postmodernism finds finest manifestations in the "death of the author" where the author is completely assimilated into the labyrinth of language. Structured in a maverick fashion, this novel of Calvino ridicules the pre-existing notion that the author is the omniscient creator of the text and the sole decider and regulator of its meaning. What Calvino's work presents, instead, is the eclectic idea that the author is no more than an invisible point through which the infinite play of language precipitates into the text.

At the same time, the novel also ascertains that it is not the author who fixes meaning to the text; rather, it is the reader who deciphers the meaning of the text through his reading and subsequent interpretative act. On closer observation, therefore, this novel of Calvino seems to asseverate the diminishing glory of the author at the same time endorsing the increasing importance of the reader. In addition, this novel of Calvino declares the all-pervasiveness of language where it is believed that our perception of the world is mediated only through language. Viewed in this context, this article seeks to explicitly discuss the typical postmodern issues of the "death of the author," the role of the reader and the prime importance of language in the construction of reality, with reference to Italo Calvino's magnum-opus *If on a Winter's Night a Traveller.*

Repudiating the authorial omnipotence in a text, Italo Calvino's *If on a Winter's Night a Traveller* avers that writing is an impersonal act whose scope extends beyond the authorial imperium. The waning significance of the author is readily traceable in the very first chapter through the reader's failure to locate the "unmistakable tone of the author" and his concomitant conviction that the book is "readable . . . independently of what . . . [is] expected of the author" (Calvino 9). The depersonalisation of the author is more evidently noticeable in the chapter "If on a

Winter's Night a Traveller" where a purposefully created confusion between the identities of the author, the reader and the character of the novel (the traveller in the train) baffles us and we are not able to dissever them as distinct individualities.

These three discrete personalities dramatically merge into a single person (the traveller) with their separate persona or the "I [s]" (Calvino 15) thoroughly fragmented and mixed up confusedly amongst each other. Adding to the ripping apart of the author's individuality to an array of multiple fractions, the narrator in "Chapter five" describes that the "author has become plural" so that "no body can be delegated to represent anybody" (Calvino 96). Such disintegration of the authorial presence and its synchronic blurring of the author/reader/text barricades are resonant of the Roland Barthes concept of the "death of the author." No more considered as the sole architect of the text, the author is now an unseen occurrence, an "anonymous presence against an even more anonymous background" (Calvino 14). Giving a serious jolt to the author's preconceived ingenuity, the reader in "Chapter Two," witnesses him as a copier, not as a creator. Divulging his "virtuoso tricks" of copying, the reader informs us that instead of saying anything new, he merely keeps on repeating the same thing "word for word" (Calvino 25). For his sheer inability to write afresh, the text remains a copied representation of other pre-existing texts as the narrator admits: "Of course: there are themes that recur, the text is interwoven with these reprises . . ." (Calvino 25).

Writing, bereft of authorial encumbrance, then remains an impersonal act. The narrator-author in "Chapter Eight" befittingly denounces any anthropocentric trace, whether social or cultural or psychological, that contributes to the shaping up of his individual subjectivity. They might, apprehends the author, curtail his limitless writing prowess. Depersonalizing the process of writing, the narrator aptly demonstrates: "Style, taste, individual philosophy, subjectivity, cultural background, real experience, psychology, talent, tricks of the trade: all the elements that make what I write the recognizable as mine seem to me a cage that restricts my possibilities" (Calvino 171). This is part of what Brian McHale would call "procedural writing"[1] (183) that according to him "involves . . . surrender of authorial control over the production of the text, as a means of evading or overriding the constraints of literary and cultural norms and personal psychology" (184).

The author, in an attempt of self-assassination, intends to take his redundant "presence" away from the space in between "the white page and writing of words" (Calvino 171). His confessions are worth quoting here: "How well I would write if I were not here! If between the white page and the writing of words and stories that take shape and disappear without any one's ever writing them there were not interposed that uncomfortable partition which is my person!" (Calvino 171). Reinforcing further the "desacrilization of the image of the Author" (Barthes 148) and the impersonality of writing, the author imagines himself as only "a hand, a severed hand that grasps a pen and writes" (Calvino 171), a practice akin to the surrealist "automatic writing"[2] (Barthes 148). Interestingly however, he wants to erase his personality not for being the spokesman of trans-individual entities like the "collective unconscious" and "the spirit of the times;" but "to transmit the writable that waits to be written, the tellable that nobody tells" (Calvino 171). He writes only for the sake of the act of writing, not to represent any socio-cultural milieu, whether physical or psychological, that builds his persona. There is a death of subjectivity with the act of writing.

Echoing a similar idea in his monumental essay, "The Death of the Author," Roland Barthes says: "Writing is that neutral, composite, oblique space where our subject slips away, the negative where all identity is lost, staring with the very identity of the body of writing" (146-147). Making the author a mingling point in the ocean of language and citing the example of the French symbolist Mallarme who could foresee his own death in his act of writing, Barthes continues: "For him, for us too, it is language which speaks, not the author; to write is, through a prerequisite impersonality . . . to reach that point where only language acts, 'performs', and not 'me'" (147). French philosopher Michel Foucault, In his monumental essay "What is an Author," describes the text, in a maverick tone, to be the murderer of the author as he construes: "The work, which once had the duty of providing immortality [to the author], now possesses the right to kill, to be its author's murderer . . ." (175).

"Chapter two" of *If on a Winter's Night a Traveller*, while underpinning the notion of the author's demise, affirms that the book is not the progeny of the authorial motif, rather a mechanistic assemblage of the minimal constituent fragments of language. The flinging of the defective copy onto the floor by the reader in this chapter results in the crumbling of the composite book into the elementary shards of language. This linguistic disintegration of the book is accurately expressed in the following lines by the narrator:

> You fling the book on the floor . . . let sentences, words, morphemes, phonemes gush forth, beyond recomposition into discourse . . . hurl the book and reduce it into photons, undulatory vibrations, polarized spectra; through the wall, let the book crumble into molecules and atoms passing between atom and atom of the reinforced concrete, breaking up into electrons, neutrons, neutrinos, elementary particles more and more minute; through the telephone wires, let it be reduced to electronic impulses, into flow of information, shaken by redundancies and noises, and let it be degraded into a swirling entropy. You would like to throw it out of the house, out of the block, beyond the neighbourhood, beyond the city limits, beyond the state confines, beyond the regional administration, beyond the national community, beyond the Common Market, beyond Western culture, beyond the continental shelf, beyond the atmosphere, the biosphere, the stratosphere, the field of gravity, the solar system, the galaxy, the cumulous of galaxies . . . where it would be received by nonbeing, or, rather, the not-being . . . (Calvino 26)

In this process of linguistic disintegration, evidently, the linguistic modules of the book including "sentences, words, morphemes, phonemes" break further into even finer fragments like molecules, atoms, protons, electrons, neutrons that gush forth and move beyond "the neighbourhood," "the city limits," "the state confines," "the regional administration," "the national community," "the common market" and "the Western culture" to be received by the "nonbeing" or "not-being" (Calvino 26). Manifestly, the linguistic components of the book stretch beyond the confinements of human subjects and human organizations as mentioned above thereby thoroughly undermining any probable human domination over language. The deliberate use of the expressions like "nonbeing" or "not-being" hint at the disassociation of the text from any subjective trace of the author's "being." The truth of the text, therefore, is not the truth of the author, rather, of language where the text is the product of a linguistic discourse. Echoing a similar view, Julia Kristeva, in her essay "The Ethics of Linguistics," says: ". . . the problem of truth in linguistic discourse became dissociated from any notion of the speaking subject [the author]" (208). Such a disregard for the author or the speaking subject is part of what Hans Bertens would call "linguistic determinism" (59), i.e. the idea that claims that our concept of reality is no more than a construct in language.

Similar to the previous chapter, "Chapter five," of *If on a Winter's Night a Traveller*, is an exemplary exposition of the notion of the "death of the author." We see, in this chapter, how the publishing house agent Mr. Cavedagna struggles to find the author of the novel that the reader intends to read. Jacques Derrida, in his epoch-making essay "Structure, Sign and Play in the Discourse of the Human Sciences," makes a study of myth in the book *The Raw and the Cooked* by the cultural anthropologist Claude Levi-Strauss and finally fails to find the "source," the "centre" and the "founding basis" of the book and concludes that the "absence of the centre is here the absence of a subject and the absence of an author" (97).

In a similar scenario, Cavedagna suffers a typical Derridean failure to locate the origin or the source or the centre or the founding basis of the book in the form of the author. Eventually, the letter of the translator Ermes Marana shown to the reader by Cavedagna in "Chapter five" puts an end to this ongoing beating around the bush in the complete depletion of the author from the text. In a tactful voice, Marana says: "What does the name of an author on the jacket matter?" (Calvino 101). Citing the instance of the anonymously authored Iranian epic Gilgamesh, Marana explains that after three thousand years, there will be some famous authorless books like Gilgamesh. On the reverse, there will be authors like Socrates none of whose works will survive whereas in another probable alternative, perhaps all surviving books will be attributed to a "single, mysterious author, like Homer" (Calvino 101). Effecting a disconnection between the author and the text, such descriptions by Marana confirm that the book is an authorless entity.

Cavedagna's understanding of the author's role in text in the same chapter is worth considering. The narrator's long speech about Cavedagna's understanding of the role of the contradictorily dubious and indeterminable positioning of the author is worth considering. He says:

> For many years Cavedagna has followed books as they are made, bit by bit, he sees books be born and died every day, and yet the true books for him remain others, those of the time when for him they were like messages from other worlds. And so it is with authors: he deals with them every day, he knows their fixations, indecisions, susceptibilities, ego-centricities, and yet the true authors remain those who for him were only a name on a jacket, a word that was part of the title, authors who had the same reality as their characters, as the places mentioned in the books, who existed and didn't exist at the same time, like those characters and those countries. The author was an invisible point from which the books came, a void travelled by ghosts, an underground tunnel that put other worlds in communion with the chicken coop of his boyhood. . . . (Calvino 101-103)

As evidently explained in the above passage, the author having their subjective emotions like ego or indecision or fixations are not the true authors whereas the true authors are only "a name on a jacket," a "part of the title" (Calvino 101), a mere linguistic element, an "invisible point from which the books came" and a "void travelled by ghosts" (Calvino 102). On the other hand, he exists and does not exist at the same time. Intriguingly, the authenticity and credibility of the author are thrown into an unviable and dubious limbo thereby destabilizing his very credible existence. In continuation of such a perception, the narrator of "Chapter seven" conceives of the author as an "alien voice" and a "silent nobody made of ink and typographical spacing" (Calvino 148). Eliciting a similar thinking, M. H. Abrams, in his influential essay "The Deconstructive Angel," reprises the Derridean emphasis on the disappearance of any sort of subjective agency once the play of language begins. He construes:

> Since the only givings are the already existing marks, 'deja ecrit,' we are denied recourse to a speaking or writing subject, or ego, or cogito, or consciousness, and so to any possible agency for the intention of meaning something ('vouloir dire'); all such agencies are relegated to the status of fictions generated by language, readily dissolved by deconstructive analysis (245).

Evidently, the subjectivity agency, being an effect of language, dissolves unassumingly in the sea of language form which it is produced. Adding a further dimension to the liberation of the text from the authorial ascendency, the reader Ludmilla in "Chapter five," asserts the textual autonomy by saying that the novel should have its "own growth, like a tree, an entangling, as if of branches and leaves" (Calvino 92). Through Ludmilla's voice, we hear a reiteration of Derrida's notion of the automation of writing, as exemplified in his epoch-making book *Writing and Difference,* through its extrication from the author. Writing is an automatic activity as it does not originate from the author; rather, the author becomes a mere diaphanous element in the automatic going forth of writing. The author, says Derrida, should leave writing then. He beautifully explains it as: "To leave writing is to be there only in order to provide its passageway, to be the diaphanous element of its going forth . . ." (70). Apart from "writing," Ludmilla also expects "reading" to be cleansed from the last reminiscences of any implicit authorial persuasion through "rediscovering a condition of natural reading, innocent, primitive" (Calvino 92).

It is not just the author who mingles unassuming to the realm of language; rather, it is the whole world that mingles unassumingly into the realm of language as "everything is language (tout est language)"[3] (Benjamin 82). The whole world is a construct in language or in other words, the whole world is a text, to use a Derridean paradigm of thought. This maverick conceptual framework through which the world is conceived as a written text finds true reflection in the words of the narrator in "Chapter three" as he says: "... this world dense with writing surrounds us on all sides ..." (Calvino 49). Such an altered premise of thought attributes supreme ascendancy to language which constructs the whole world in the form of a "unitary book" (Calvino 255) of which the individual books are mere constituent fragments. These fragmented parts of the single book act as mere corollaries or confutations or references to each other and finally merge into the unique single text of the world. Such a thinking is beautifully explicated in the following lines of the fourth reader in "Chapter eleven":

> Every new book I read comes to be a part of that overall and unitary boom that is the sum of my readings. This does not come about without some effort: to compose that general book, each individual book must be transformed, enter into a relationship with the books I have read previously, become their corollary or development or confutation or gloss or reference text. For years I have been coming to this library, and I explore it volume by volume, shelf by shelf, but I could not demonstrate to you that I have done nothing but continue the reading of a single book. (Calvino 255-256)

Latoria's adoption of a maverick method of reading a novel in "Chapter eight" poses another set back to the author's reign. Instead of reading the book in conformation to the authorial directionality, Latoria reads it electronically using a properly programmed computer that determines the meaning of the text from the order of the frequencies of its linguistic components like "articles," "pronouns," and "particles" (Calvino 186) etc. In addition, the Irish writer Silas Flannery is convinced, in this chapter, that "the whole responsibility of writing weigh on those isolated syllables" (Calvino 189), not on the author. He also continues by saying that it is not he who creates the book; rather the "avalanche of isolated words" (Calvino 189) could construct his book and could express a truth which he himself does not know.

Flannery's candid confessions are worth quoting: "Perhaps instead of a book I could write lists of words, in alphabetical order, an avalanche of isolated words which expresses that truth I still do not know, and from which the computer, reversing its program, could construct the book, my book" (Calvino 189). Eliciting a glaringly anti-humanist attitude, such an instance privileges language over the author in the detection of the textual meaning. Such an overturn of the pre-existing man-language relation echoes German philosopher Heidegger's voice in his book *Basic Writing*: "Man acts as though *he* were the shaper and master of language, while in fact *language* remains the master of man" (348). This change, believes Paul Sheehan, is part of a "linguistic turn" that is "quite explicitly antihumanist" (23).

"Chapter six" of *If on a Winter's Night a Traveller* offers revealing insights into the realization of unimportance of the author in a text. The translator Ermes Marana could convince the Irish author Silas Flannery that his unfinished novel can be completed easily by the appositely programmed computers with "the stylistic and conceptual models of the author" (Calvino 118) intact. We also learn in the same chapter that in the scenario of

Flannery's inability to finish his work, there is the emergence of "a team of ghost writers" who can finish such half-written works with the original "nuances and mannerisms" (121) of the author.

Chapter 8 entitled "From the diary of Silas Flannery" offers more fascinating instances in this direction. In this chapter, Flannery meets a person who informs him about an ongoing outrageous practice of the publication of unauthorized translations of his books and as an evidence, he shows him one copy written in Japanese. Intriguingly however, we learn that Flannery has no knowledge of Japanese and it finally turns out that he has never authored the book which is mysteriously attributed to him. In a startling revelation, it is finally learnt that a firm in Osaka has hacked the secret code or formula of Flannery's novels through which it is able to produce Japanese books in the name of Flannery even though he has never written them. In another act of "diabolical swindle" (Calvino 179), the above-mentioned Japanese book is also translated into English and circulated in the market with Flannery's name as its author. Most significantly, it is also learnt that these fake copies contain "a refined and arcane wisdom that true Flannerys lack completely" (Calvino 179), a shocking discovery that asserts the author's needlessness in a text.

The translator Ermes Marana's theorization of the author's role in a text is worth discussing here. In his atypical vision, the author of every book should be a "fictitious character" (Calvino 180) invented by the real author so that he can doubly distance himself from the text. Moreover, Marana is interested in the author Flannery because he can both fake and be faked thereby reducing the role of the author to either a faker or a faking material. Finally, he believes that the ideal author is he who is "dissolved in the cloud of fictions that covers the world with its thick sheath" and is capable of "identifying himself with the whole" (Calvino 180). This cloud of fiction covering the whole world is nothing but a construct in language and hence, the author merges anonymously into the labyrinth of language from which he is born. Finally, Flannery also gets influenced by the theory of Marana and tries to find another fake name to be the proxy-author for him. In a convincing voice, he declares: "I, too, would like to erase myself and find for each book another I, another voice, another name, to be reborn; but my aim is to capture in the book the illegible world, without centre, without ego, without I" (Calvino 180). He heartily realizes that his "true vocation" is to be like what is known as "a ghost writer" (Calvino 180-181) in America, a "professional of recognized usefulness even if not of great prestige" and finally, a mere "writing hand" that gives "words existences too busy existing" (Calvino 181).

Arguably, Flannery self-consciously re-presents himself as an "ego-less," "cogito-less," "centre-less" and "I-less" "writing hand" that places words in their proper places in the thoughtless, mechanical process of writing. We can also find a fragmentation of the "self" of the so-called author Flannery when he declares that he could have "multiplied . . . [his] I's" and assumed "other people's selves" (Calvino 181) through a process of continual authorial displacement and erasure of personality. Moreover, we find in "Chapter eight" that some pages from Flannery's manuscript are stolen by the shadow of a stranger whereas he again finds the lost pages intact after some days. In a dramatic turn of events, nonetheless, he is not able to recognize his own manuscript and finally, he is not able to recognize his own self. Moreover, we also find that the reader Ludmilla finds that the image of the author she forms of her reading of the book and the real author are not the same person.

The deliberate distortion of the identity of the author into hazy, ambiguous individuations is the oblique references to his figurative death. Moreover, the automatic production of the book through the author-shaman is expressed by the most appropriate allusion where the author writes "as a pumpkin vine produces pumpkins" (Calvino 189). Moreover, the author's act of writing is accurately expressed through similar epithets like "the wind that shapes the mountain, the wrack of the tides, [and] the annual circles in the bole of trees" (Calvino 189). Such epithets are adequately indicative of the fact that the author is not the creator of his writing, rather, is the ineffectual medium through which writing takes place.

In this process of the dethronement of the author, it is not just Flannery who becomes the casualty; the great Allah and his earthly incarnation Prophet Mohammed also are sacked from the authorial cathedra of the Holy Koran. Their authorship gets metonymically substituted by the scribe Abdullah who, nonetheless, fails to realize that he is also the meaning-maker of Koran through his "physicality of the act of writing[4]" (Calvino 190) through which he does the work of "organizing the sentence," of orchestrating the "internal coherence of the written language," of maintaining its "grammar and syntax" (Calvino 182). Finally, he loses faith. In Flannery's estimation, however, Abdullah was wrong because he "lacked faith in writing, and in himself as an agent of writing" (Calvino 182).

Abdullah conceives of Allah and Mohammed as the real authors of *Quran* with their diction and sermonizing and himself no more than a scribe. Flannery, nevertheless, is aware that without Abdullah's writing, the great Allah would have never been able to express himself in *Quran*. Mohammed knew this fully well and hence, allowed Abdullah to complete his unfinished sentence. In a sense, Abdullah becomes the author of the *Quran*, not Mohammed. Flannery describes such a situation very aptly as: "The scribe's collaboration was necessary to Allah, once he had decided to express himself in a written text. Mohammed knew this and allowed the scribe the privilege of concluding sentences; but Abdullah was unaware of the powers vested in him" (Calvino 182). What evolves here is the privilege of language (through writing) over the subjective presence of the author who is no more than an object of endless displacements that is suggestive of his figurative death.

Rendering writing an "impersonal form," Silas Flannery, in "Chapter eight," authenticates the depersonalized statement

"Today it writes" just like "Today it rains" (Calvino 176) simultaneously disregarding the authorial statement "Today I write." The possession of the depersonalized qualities of writing becomes explicitly evident as Flannery ascertains: "Only the ability to be read by a given individual proves that what is written shares in the power of writing, a power based on something that goes beyond the individual" (Calvino 176). Giving another blow to the authorial claims to originality, Flannery reveals that in his act of writing, he is merely copying from Dostoevsky's famous novel *Crime and Punishment*. He candidly admits that he almost "succumb[s] to the temptation to copy out all of *Crime and Punishment*" (Calvino 178) and seems to be thoroughly fascinated by the "inconceivable vocation . . . of the copyist" (Calvino 178). Hence, we see a clear regression on the part of the author from the respectable position of an all-important creator to the obnoxious status of an unscrupulous copier.

The narrator in the chapter "Looks down in the gathering shadow" gives another blow to the author's omnipotence. In a candid mode of confession, he finds his own narrative to be the intertextual imprint of so many other stories already written or told thereby undermining his own notion of originality. His writing outstrips his control as he sees his own narrative as "a forest that extends in all directions" where the reader finds this narrative forest "dispersed into so many trickles" (Calvino 109). In such a situation, the reader feels that he can move "in all directions, as in space" and the essential events of the present story are only the "last echoes and reverberations" (Calvino 109) of so many other stories intertwined with the present one. Roland Barthes very convincingly presents a similar idea in his essay "Death of the Author" as he demonstrates: "We know now that a text is not a line of words releasing a single 'theological' meaning (the 'message' of the Author-God) but a multidimensional space in which a variety of writings, none of them original, blend and clash. The text is a tissue of quotations drawn from the innumerable centres of culture" (149). This is precisely the reason why the reader of the story "may feel himself a bit cheated" (Calvino 109) for not being able to trace exactly the single author's story in the main narrative. The narrative, therefore, extends beyond the author and hence, the narrator self-consciously keeps his position "below the narrative possibilities at . . . [his] disposal" (Calvino 109).

Calvino's oblique hint at the "death of the author" can also be traced in "Chapter six" where a letter from the remote South American novel Cerro Negro provides a powerful evidence of the above-mentioned issue. The letter informs about the old Indian "Father of stories," a man of "immemorial age" with a timeless presence and a curious study material of anthropologists and parapsychologists. It is startlingly revealed that this old Indian had recited so many novels of famous novelists even before their novels appeared. The letter describes him with the epithets like "the universal source of narrative material" and "the primordial magma" from which develop the "individual manifestations" (Calvino 117) of other authors. It moreover describes him to be the timeless reincarnations of scores of other famous authors including Homer, the story teller of the *Arabian Nights,* the author of the *Popol Vuh,* Alexandre Dumas and James Joyce.

Manifestly, the books of these authors are no more their creations; rather are the plagiarized versions of the old Indian's recited stories. Such a thing is a frontal attack on the claims of originality of these texts by the above-mentioned authors thereby incurring their figurative death. Hans Robert Jauss expresses a similar opinion in his essay "Literary History as a Challenge to Literary Theory" in which he asserts that no literary work is completely new and original, rather, a reawakening of the memories of the texts that are already read. He construes: "A literary work, even when it appears to be new in an informational vacuum . . . It awakens memories of that which was already read . . ." (1554).

The reader Ludmilla puts another nail to the author's coffin in "Chapter seven" where she sees the author as a "ghost with a thousand faces and faceless" (Calvino 159). As a reader, she communicates not with the living author, but enters into "fickle, carefree relations" with multiple "incorporeal persons" (Calvino 159) who have contributed to the formation of the book. This, subsequently, defeats the "idea that behind each book there is someone who guarantees a truth" (Calvino 159). Echoing a similar tone, Ermes Marana dreams of "a literature made entirely of apocrypha, of false attributions, of imitations and counterfeits and pastiches" (Calvino 159) without any genuine link between the author and the text. Iterating Marana's ideas, Silas Flannery in "Chapter eight" intends to be the "author of apocrypha" (Calvino 193). The word "Apocrypha," having its etymological root in the Greek word "apokryphos," refers to texts "falsely attributed to a period or to an author" (Calvino 193). Effecting a typical postmodernist disconnection between the author and the text, Flannery, in partnership with Ermes Marana, desires to "flood the world with apocrypha" and "camouflage his falsifications" by arbitrarily assigning names of the "numerous and productive" novelists to the "flourishing production of genuine raw materials" (Calvino 193). The purposeful instauration of the concept of "apocrypha" by both Marana and Flannery is amply evocative of the fact that the very act of designating the author to the text is no more than a sham and falsification. Flannery finally declares his own death as a writer in the end by saying: "Something in me has gone: perhaps the ego, perhaps the content of the ego. . . . Isn't depersonalization what I was trying to achieve?" (Calvino 192).

In "Chapter ten," the Director General of the State Police Archives of Ircania, Arkadian Porphyrich refers to the attitude of the mysterious woman associated with the Cagliostro of counterfeits towards books, authors and finally, the very process of reading. In the words of Pophyrich:

> For this woman . . . reading means stripping herself of every purpose, every forgone conclusion, to be ready to catch a voice that makes itself heard when you least expect it, a voice that comes from an unknown source, from somewhere beyond the book, beyond the author, beyond the conventions of writing: from the unsaid . . . (Calvino 239)

What becomes pressingly expository here is that it is not just the author is depersonalized, the text and the act of reading also join the process of depersonalization. Reading, devoid of any compelling subjective intrusion into its realms, is stripped of "every purpose" and becomes a never-ending process thereby resisting closure or "every forgone conclusion" to the text. The written substance of the book flows not from the authorial voice, rather from an indeterminable voice that extends beyond the author, beyond the book as the Cagliostro claims that "behind the written page, [there] is a void" (Calvino 239).

The alterations of significances of the author and the reader is all the more evident in "Chapter eight" entitled "From the diary of Silas Flannery" where Flannery feels that the reader's "eye that sucks up the flow of . . . [his] sentences" and "leads the story in the directions that elude [Flannery]" (Calvino 170). Furthering the deterioration of the authorial value, Flannery says: "I feel a throng of readers looking over my shoulder and seizing the words as their set down on paper" (Calvino 170-171). Such feelings on the part of Flannery are overwhelming indications of the fact that the text takes shape not according to the author's plan of things, rather according to the reader's expectations to the extent that they suck up the flow of Flannery's sentences diverting them in the direction they want. In a sense, the "reading" of the readers concomitantly stimulates "writing" where the Manichean binary between the two is on the verge of destabilization. Both "reading" and "writing" mingle into one signifying practice of the creation of the text as Roland Barthes fittingly comments in his "From Work to Text": ". . . the Text requires that one try to abolish (or at the very least to diminish) the distance between writing and reading, in no way by intensifying the projection of the reader into the work but by joining them in a single signifying practice" (1474).

With the disappearance of the author, the meaning of the text also liberates itself from his clutches. It no more resides in the authorial intent, rather, remains in the language which constitutes the text. "Language," believes Saussure, "is a system of signs expressing ideas . . ." (8). The narrator of the chapter "Outside the town of Malbork" provides the most fitting example of the self-referentiality of language by citing the example of the food item "schoeblintsjja." The very word generates its own meaning "with its sound or only with its visual impression" thereby suggesting "an acidulous flavour" (Calvino 34) to the reader. The basic purpose of such a description is amply suggestive of the fact that language has the innate ability to generate its own meaning without a meaning thrust on it from outside. Now, it remains for the reader to decode the meaning generated by language itself. In such an altered premise, the authorial preeminence is jettisoned with the ensuing "birth of the reader" (Barthes 150) with a transference of the meaning-making onus to the reader. Such a retreating magnitude of the author with a resultant escalation of the reader's import explicitly noticeable in the Chapter 8 entitled "From the diary of Silas Flannery." Instead of being the controller of his own writing, he is rather crushed by it. He says: "This is why writing presents itself to me as an operation of such weight that I remain crushed by it" (Calvino 172). Now, he has "neither expressive energy nor something to express" (Calvino 190). In addition, he finds his own writing to be a stressfully unnatural process for him whereas on the reverse, he traces the firmest bond between "writing" and the reader as he finds the former to be the life-breath of the reader (Ludmilla in this case). He admits:

> . . . I say to myself that the result of the unnatural effort to which I subject myself, writing, must be the respiration of this reader,

> the operation of reading turned into a natural process, the current that brings the sentences to graze the filter of her attention, to stop for a moment before being absorbed by the circuits of her mind and disappearing, transformed into her interior ghosts, into what in her is most personal and incommunicable. (Calvino 169-170)

Validating such a conceptual transformation, Flannery asserts that "writing . . . will continue to have meaning only when it is read by a single person and passes through his mental circuits" (Calvino 176). The endless play of language is coded into the text in the form of signs inviting the reader to decode them and impart meaning to the text. Meaning, therefore, is not incarcerated in the author's motifs and intentions; rather, it becomes "a negotiable act of understanding between reader and text" (Clark 67). Different readers, however, belong to different "interpretive communities" (Fish 301) and hence, provide plural meanings to the text by decoding the above-mentioned textual code through manifold ways. Testifying the existence of the interpretive communities and unearthing the presence of an invisible bond between the two readers of an interpretive community, the narrator in "Chapter two" says: "There, you have said it. What is more natural than that a solidarity, a complicity, a bond should be established between Reader and Reader, thanks to the book?" (Calvino 32). Russian formalist Roman Jacobson talks about the nature and function of language in his famous essay "Linguistics and Poetics." Making his investigation in the special context of the verbal communication of language, Jacobson states that a message (constituted of language) contains a "CODE fully, or at least partially, common to the ... encoder and decoder of the message" (33). In case of writing, correspondingly, the different members of an "interpretive community" are telepathically connected through a similar secret textual code. The narrator in "Chapter seven" finds that Ludmilla and the "other reader" are connected through a similar textual "code between the two," a code that is "a means to exchange signals and recognize each other" (Calvino 148).

This code, nonetheless, can be subject to multiple decodings by various decoders who attribute the text a plurality of meanings. Meaning is essentially elusive in nature keeping in tune with the inherently slippery nature of language. Canvassing the polysemous nature of the language system, Mikhail Bakhtin, the pioneer of the concept of "heteroglossia,"[5] says: "Literary Language—both spoken and written— ... is itself ... heteroglot in its aspect as an expressive system, that is, in the forms that carry its meanings" (1211). Because of this, the text never achieves closure; rather, it is always a text in process. Regarding such a polysemous nature of a text, Jerome McGann fittingly comments: "... Instability is an essential feature of the text in progress" (517). Deleuze and Guattari, in their monumental treatise *A Thousand Plateaus*, talk about this instability of the text through a never-ending dialogic tension between territorialization and deterritorialization. The text achieves its semantic instability through these two opposing forces that prevent the text from becoming stable. Deleuze and Guattari explain such a scenario in the following terms: "In a book, as in all things, there are lines of articulation or segmentarity. Strata and territories; but also lines of flight, movements of deterritorialisation and destartification" (4).

We get another glimpse of the polysemous nature of language from the incident of Professor Uzzi-Tuzii's act of translation of the book *Leaning from the steep slope*. While translating, Professor Uzzi-Tuzii has to stop at every word to "illustrate its idiomatic usage and its connotations" that generate multiple meanings. This connotative nature of language makes the text contain more than "what the story is telling" (Calvino 68) or more than what the author is conveying. The text, believes Uzzi-Tuzii, contains "an inner afflatus" that gets dispersed in the air and contains the "echo of a vanished knowledge revealed in the penumbra and in tacit allusions" (Calvino 68). The basic purpose behind Uzzi-Tuzii's statement confirms that language contains the knowledge that extends beyond the capacity of the author through its infinite connotative suggestiveness. Expressing such an idea, Uzzi-Tuzii says: "All books continue in the beyond . . ." (Calvino 71). Silencing the voice of the author in such a scenario, it is language that speaks in the text. Language in the form of the "prose of the novel" gets better of "the uncertainties of the voice [of the author]" whereas the reader-interpreter-translator Uzzi-Tuzii swims "like a fish" (Calvino 69) in the ocean of language in search of the meaning of the text.

By rendering meaning to the text through their act of "reading," the reader, in a sense, becomes the "maker" of the text or the "self-imaging author" (239), as E.D. Hirsch Jr. would have it. The author-text nexus is substituted by that between the reader and the text. Providing a phenomenological approach to the reading process and establishing the unbreakable link between the reader and the text, Wolfgang Iser says: "The convergence of text and reader brings the literary work into existence" (189). "Chapter five" of *If on a Winter's Night a Traveller* offers a brilliant example of the reader being the maker. The narrator, initially feels that there is a "boundary line" between "those who make books" and "those who read them" to realize very soon, nonetheless, that: "The boundary line is tentative, it tends to get erased: the world of books who deal with books professionally is more and more crowded and tends to become one with the world of readers" (Calvino 93).

Roland Barthes, in his monumental work *S/Z*, reinforces the notion of the reader being the maker by introducing his concept of "Writerly Texts" where the reader, in a sense, is the writer of the text as Barthes feels "the writerly text is ourselves writing" (227). He moreover construes: " . . . the goal of literary work (of literature as work) is to make the reader no longer a consumer, but a producer of the text" (227). Evidently, the reader is elevated to the status of the "make" or the "creator" of the book in the continually shifting paradigm of the role of the author and that of the reader. "Chapter eleven" of the book offers revealing insights into the mechanism of the reader's act of "reading." In a prolonged conversation amongst different readers, one reader, while philosophizing on the act of reading, says that reading is a "discontinuous and fragmentary operation" where the object of reading (i. e. the text) is a "punctiform and pulviscular material" (Calvino 254).

Through this discontinuous and fragmentary operation, the reader breaks up these elementary components of language like words, phonemes and morphemes etc. and to decode their complex permutations and combinations through which they form the text. Meaning, therefore, lies in the language, not in the author's intentions. The reader in this chapter fittingly comments: "In the spreading expanse of writing, the reader's attention isolates some minimal segments, juxtapositions of words, metaphors, syntactic nexuses, logical passages, lexical peculiarities that prove to possess an extremely concentrated density of meaning" (Calvino 254). This act of reading or the decoding of meaning is an endless process giving rise to endless meanings of the text The reader therefore says: "This is why my reading has no end: I read and reread, each time seeking the confirmation of a new discovery among the folds of the sentences" (Calvino 255). Christopher Butler, in this context, thinks that by providing meaning to the text, the reader, in a sense, constructs the text and meaning becomes his property. He construes: "The text, as really constructed by the reader, ... [is] thereby liberated and democratized for the free play of imagination. Meanings ... [are] the property of the interpreter. Who ... [is] free to play deconstructively with them" (24).

The third reader, in the same chapter, feels that the process of reading is without an object where he considers "reading" as an object in itself. Making reading an endless and timeless process, this third reader robs reading of purpose, goal and objective. Neither the text nor the act of reading, in this process, is able to achieve closure. Every re-reading, feels the reader, is a new reading and every re-reading is a progression in time and space in a scenario where the text serves as only a pretext to the very act of reading. Continually progressive re-readings, therefore, surpass the single, confined boundary of meaning created by the author. His long speech is worth quoting here:

> I, too, feel the need to reread the books I have already read," a third reader says, "but at every rereading I seem to be reading a new book, for the first time. . . . is reading a construction that assumes form, assembling a great number of variables, and therefore something that cannot be repeated twice according to the same pattern? Every time I seek to relive the emotion of a previous reading, I experience different and unexpected impressions, and do not find again those of before. At some moments it seems to me that between one reading and the next there is a progression: in the sense, for example, penetrating further into the spirit of the text, or of increasing my critical detachment. At other moments, on the contrary, I seem to retain the memory of the readings of a single book one next to another, enthusiastic, or cold or hostile, scattered in time without a perspective, without a thread that ties them together. The conclusion that I have reached is that reading is an operation without object; or that its true object is itself. The book is an accessory aid, or even a pretext. (Calvino 255)

Reading, as explicitly made evident in the above passage, is a goalless construction with endless variables producing endless meanings. In this act of the creation of multiplicity of scopes for reading automatically leading to a multiplicity of endless interpretations, interpretations that go beyond the imaginings of the author thereby nullifying his role in the text.

In the final analysis, Calvino's *If on a Winter's Night a Traveller* offers a thorough understanding of the renewed Postmodern perceptions about the role of the author, the reader and the language in the text. Through a radical alterity of vision, Calvino topples the position of the author upside down reducing him from an individual existence to an invisible point easily mixable in the tangles of language. This novel convincingly arouses Calvino's conviction that it is not the author who speaks through the text; rather, it is language who does the talking and it is the reader who determines its meaning.

References

1. It was practised by poets like John Cage, Jackson MacLow and the L=A=N=G=U=A=G=E poets and a few prose writers of the OuLiPo group including Queneau, Calvino, Georges Perec, Harry Mathews and others.
2. Roland Barthes talks about the surrealist "automatic writing" in his essay "Death of the Author" where he says that "automatic writing" is achieved by "entrusting the hand with the task of writing as quickly as possible what the head itself is unaware of" (Barthes 148).
3. It is a reference to the famous structuralist principle that there is nothing outside the realm of language and our perception of the world is possible only through language.
4. Ludmilla in "Chapter eight" explains that "the truth of literature consists only in the physicality of the act of writing" (Calvino 190).
5. In linguistics, the term "heteroglossia" describes the coexistence of distinct varieties within a single linguistic code. The term translates the Russian *raznorechie* (literally "different-speech-ness"), which was first introduced by the Russian linguist Mikhail Bakhtin in his 1934 paper *Slovo v romane*, published in English as "Discourse in the Novel." Basically heteroglossia refers to the polysemous nature of language.

References

Abrams, M. H. "The Deconstructive Angel." *Modern Criticism and Theory: A Reader. Ed. David Lodge.* Delhi: Pearson Education, 1988. 242-253.

Bakhtin, Mikhail M. "From *Discourse in the Novel.*" *The Norton Anthology of Theory and Criticism.* Ed. Vincent B. Leitch. New York: W. W. Norton & Company, 2001. 1190-1220.

Barthes, Roland. "The Death of the Author." *Modern Criticism and Theory: A Reader. Ed. David Lodge.* Delhi: Pearson Education, 1988. 146-172.

______. "From Work to Text." *The Norton Anthology of Theory and Criticism.*Ed. Vincent B. Leitch. New York: W. W. Norton & Company, 2001. 1470-1475.

______. "From S/Z." Postmodernism and the Contemporary Novel. Ed. Bran Nicol. *Postmodernism and the Contemporary Novel: A Reader.* Edinburgh: Edinburgh University Press, 2002. 226-230.

Benjamin, Andrew. "Deconstruction." The Routledge Companion to Critical Theory." Eds. Simon Malpas & Paul Wake. London: Routledge, 2006. 81-90.

Bertens, Hans. Literary Theory: The Basics. London: Routledge, 2001.

Butler, Christopher. *Postmodernism: A Very Short Introduction*. Oxford: Oxford University Press, 2002.

Calvino, Italo. *If on a Winter's Night a Traveller*. Trans. William Weaver. London: Vintage, 1979.

Clark, Timothy. "Interpretation: Hermeneutics." *Literary Criticism and Theory*. Ed Patricia Waugh. New York: Oxford University Press, 2006.

Deleuze, Giles and Felix Guattari. *A Thousand Plateaus: Capitalism and Schizophrenia*. London: Continuum, 1987.

Derrida, Jacques. "Structure, Sign and Play in the Discourse of the Human Sciences." *Modern Criticism and Theory: A Reader. Ed. David Lodge*. Delhi: Pearson Education, 1988. 89-103.

______. *Writing and Difference*. Trans. Alan Bass. London: Routledge & Kegan Paul Ltd., 1978.

Foucault, Michel. "What is an Author?" *Modern Criticism and Theory: A Reader. Ed. David Lodge*. Delhi: Pearson Education, 1988. 174-187.

Fish, Stanley. "Interpreting the Variorum." *Modern Criticism and Theory: A Reader. Ed. David Lodge*. Delhi: Pearson Education, 1988. 288-306.

Heidegger, Martin. *Basic Writings*. Ed. David Farrell Krell. London: Routledge, 1978.

Hirsch Jr., E. D. "Faulty Perspectives." *Modern Criticism and Theory: A Reader. Ed. David Lodge*. Delhi: Pearson Education, 1988. 231-240.

Iser, Wolfgang. "The Reading Process: A Phenomenological Approach." *Criticism and Theory: A Reader. Ed. David Lodge*. Delhi: Pearson Education, 1988. 189-205.

Jacobson, Roman. Linguistics and Poetics." *Modern Criticism and Theory: A Reader. Ed. David Lodge*. Delhi: Pearson Education, 1988. 31-55.

Jauss, Hans Robert. "Literary History as a Challenge to Literary Theory." *The Norton Anthology of Theory and Criticism*. Ed. Vincent B. Leitch. New York: W. W. Norton & Company, 2001. 1550-1564.

Kristeva, Julia. "The Ethics of Linguistics." *Modern Criticism and Theory: A Reader*. Ed. David Lodge. Delhi: Pearson Education, 1988. 207-216.

McGann, Jerome. "The Textual Condition." *Modern Criticism and Theory: A Reader*. Ed. David Lodge. Delhi: Pearson Education, 1988. 513-520.

McHale, Brian. *Constructing Postmodernism*. London: Routledge, 1992.

Saussure, Ferdinand de. "The Object of Study." *Modern Criticism and Theory: A Reader*. Ed. David Lodge. Delhi: Pearson Education, 1988. 2-9.

Sheehan, Paul. "Postmodernism and Philosophy." *The Cambridge Companion to Postmodernism*. Ed. Steven Connor. Cambridge: Cambridge University Press, 2004.

3

Structural Legacies in Magical Reality: Borges as a Wandering Teller

Garima Kalita

Maybe it is a fact that Jorge Luis Borges is not strictly read as an author affiliating towards magical reality, but the ambience he creates in his fiction, the fantastical element that is introduced through the lines make it very much akin to it. It is our contention that he creates that aura through the terse form that he adopts, the suggestion that the simple or ordinary is led to a distance and defamiliarised, so that the conventionality disappears and a newness, a magical reality, replaces the authenticity of the real or the suprareal, and veracity and untruth. It is our contention that Borges is also a bricoleur who integrates diverse kinds of myth, legend, landscape, community, ritual, magic and psyche together, though he never accepts that his is a psychological study.

What is narrativity linked with magic realism? Or in a loosely asked question, how is the 'purpose' or objectivity fulfilled in a narrative by this extra realistic device that questions the plain and straight statements about the real and factual? These are characteristic seminal queries through which a narrative or a story reaches forward and in a conventional sense develops. Obviously the focus is now on a non-linear or circular mode of representation which ensures that the reader is confronted with an apparatus which structurally and also thematically enriches his imagination.

But after a while there is an inevitable pause that falters in more than two ways. First, the linearity of the fabula calls for a stern scrutiny and the resultant jumping or jarring episodes link themselves up not as an integrated whole, rather as autonomous identifying markers. One associated idea that is hundredth of times elaborated is the forked endings or multiple pathways through which the narrative is told, deciphered and registered or kept in abeyance.

Culler's assumption that in a narrative a double reading is almost always inadvertent, in itself seems to be crude generalizations because a few specifically specific cases by Freud or the reading of *Daniel Deronda* do not offer comprehensive peripherality. The distinction between Fabula and Sjuzhet in the first place seems to more preliminary than other serious issues at hand.[1] The narrative read solely on this trajectory of fabula/ sjuzhet dichotomy at moments offers a crude subscription of factoral[2] devices. But the question of linearity can best be overcome by the inclusion of an extraordinary device which in itself contains the subject object binary along with form content dialectic. The perspective or voice of the author is taken for granted in the sense that it remains in an altogether different plane. The constancy of the subject position, in fact to the benefit of the story, works by tilting the plane completely, whereby it changes the intensity of vision and equally the emotion.[3]

Once the term 'story' is uttered we tend to enter into the realm of a different identity, which is categorized or circumscribed by language – written or oral. So language becomes the autonomous tool which gives shape to the 'thing' or the essence of the story with a smalls.[4] But this is distinct from reality or the 'real', what is here we tend to visualize, fantasize or under delusion act and take for granted the erroneous, grafted, illusion for fact/ knowledge. This is actually acting upon reality or fact, the 'isness'. Culler in a winded manner called this skeletal essence which is preconceived as the 'story', that essential idea, which the telling or narration moulds within a specific structure. But what we contend here is that the story is the telling. Without the telling there is no story. This integrated whole of the story and the telling is better termed as narrative but it does not lose a substance if we identify one with the other.

The postmodernist emphasis on language or the structure and form essentially probes into the genealogy, a development and the culminatory form of story. For further clarification I'd like to draw a parallel between Borges and Marquez on one hand and Dickens and Defoe on the other. The reason why these authors are picked, actually highlights the nuances or the trajectory of story-telling, the space allotted to narrativity and ideas related to the narrative pattern.

Language as the perfect device does not merely convey, it forms a tradition, a culture (Lacan 82) which confers upon it the duality of being the means and the executor of the means, an autonomous doer. It works upon people, mode, psyche and also something called fate. The Heideggerian stress upon language, his distinction between the state of being and the state of becoming too, obliquely touches the essential conundrum of representation and fact. What he considers as the duplicity of states like "speaking of language" while actually "speaking about language" is rather highlighting that intrinsic quality of language. "We speak of language, but constantly seem to be speaking merely *about* language, while in fact we are already letting language, *from within* language, speak to us, in language, of itself, saying its nature" (Heidegger, 85). The complexity of matter is simplified by a lucid statement of the philosopher, when he deliberates, " This is why we must not prematurely break off the dialogue we have begun with the poetic experience ...." (Heidegger, 85). Of course the context Heidegger refers to is reading of a poem by Stefan George, which as he tries a subtle analysis of the nature of signification, becomes a statement about the word's reaching over to the "thing". But that fact does not deny us the use of a general statement founded upon the argument. Hence language is double faced (literally), and the concepts it carries too, in a rebounding manner pose questions, then offer answers themselves. The ambience of half truth and half reality created by magic realism is woven around the reader in such a replicated and overlapping manner that he who walks past it finds it magnificent and terrorizing. He cannot, as it were, shake it off; entrenched, he goes forward, and for the moment he forgets to draw a line between true and false, fact and fiction, illusion and reality. So it is a vacillating moment of acceptance, a state of duality but nevertheless a token of confirmation of life.

In the wandering tales of Jorge Luis Borges the state of perfection, the comprehensive world of unity manifest in "Aleph", also in "Funes –His Memories" and stories like "The Maker" and others, forms the crust and the essence. The universe is the enormous library[5] which fountainheads infinite number of tales, spins it rather as he says it or creates; in more precise terms constructs it from existing cues. The suspense of judgment which is achieved immediately makes for a smooth entrance of the state of dream or fantasy,

Borges develops language as sign, strictly on an arbitrary level, but another signifying sign of thing, *Map* standing for the land, does not profess that arbitrariness. For Korzybsky, the pioneer advocate for general semantics 'map is not the territory'[6] as everyone would tend to agree, but in Borges's satirical gestus the map is taken in its 'exactitude'. The story-teller tends to half mockingly suggest –Is science exact? Doesn't the exactitude of science lose some of its validity when an ancient map is produced ..." in that Empire, the art of cartography attained such perfection that the map of a single province occupied the *entirety of the city*..."? (p 325) The ingrained sarcasm of Borges does not profess bitter pungency; after all the elliptical pedantry of the lines suggest the futility of such vanities! In fact for the wise story-teller the part and the whole, 'the map and the territory,' the explanation of fact and fiction and in the utmost the signifier and the signified do not tantamount to surprised curiosity, rather an indifferent acceptance of life or fate.

Borges is a philosopher who attempts at probing into the light from the experience of darkness, the life from the experience of death.... ("A Prayer", 339, "His End and His Beginning" 340-341) or vice versa. Every narrative howsoever small contains the infinitisimal or the microscopic ingredient of life. "Borges and I" is an epigraphic self analysis or requiem at the death of a self in the light of a doppelganger, the Dostoevskian "Double". The stereotypical line " ...I live, I allow myself to live, so that Borges can spin out his literature and that literature is my justification" (324) curiously at the next instant strikes the reader with wondrous revelation that "Years ago I tried to free myself from him, and I moved on from the mythologies of the slums and outskirts of the city to games with time and infinity, but those games belong to Borges now, I shall have to think of other things." (324). The thin edge of mixing, fusion, becoming one with the other is the moment of epiphany in the discourse of the self and the other.[7] The subtlest of the subtle game is constantly being played by man with time and himself. The brilliant story of "The Garden of the Forking Paths" in syncopated rhythm narrates the coward/hero's dilation of time as the ultimate labyrinth which curiously absorbs himself. Time exposed here is almost like Fune's game at collective memory, which he can see through the individual bits but not anyway in general propositions. But in the 'Forking Paths' time's capacity at divergence and also convergence is tested. The fact that a man meets with diverse alternatives, and "chooses one and eliminates others" forms the crux of the narrative. But the character, the creator of the book of the labyrinth "chooses —simultaneously—all of them. *He creates*, there by, 'several futures', several *times*, which themselves proliferate and fork".

In the "Afterword", the line " few things have happened to me, though many things I have read", becomes a representative statement of Borges, as life is beyond the felt experiences, it is on par with the *Words.* It is like language, that has been read, that contains and, in a mysterious 'aleph'-like way reflects life, the essence of which is not perceived in living. The magnum opus is Life, the connectivity through signs and letters forms the tradition of language which is engrafted in infinity. In the 'Foreword' to *Brodie's Report*, the master narrator justifies as it were, his use of Ostrananie,[8] the device of defamiliarization. As he says, "I have set my stories at some distance in both time and space. Imagination has more freedom to work, that way"(347). This in fact serves as a preface to the magical realism that he portrays or realizes. Imagination is set free from the shackles of reality or nondescript facts, which forms the outer façade of his tales. The element of story, the conventional approach with which we probe into incidents or happenings, are treated by Borges without any discrimination, whether it is magical or mundane. He tells a tale as it is, howsoever apparent things are or howsoever contradictory. He refers to an anthology of narratives as "In Praise of Darkness" (1969) and the said book is said to be his 'fifth book of verse'. But curiously that statement regarding those tales like, "The Ethnographer", "Legend", "A Prayer" or "His End and His Beginning" does not seem to be a false statement. Lucid simplicity seems to be preeminent mark here. But with the same blatant cynicism and bemused aphorism he refuses to declare his aesthetics which to him is no more than "useless abstractions."

The story-teller at the beginning confirms his staunch belief, that of an impassive witness, the knower and the narrator, and then he speaks how something happened to him –the element of emotion and indifference, both are present curiously. That marvellous distancing of Borges makes him an isolated figure — a monk, an ascetic, a total recluse. He transmits that magical quality to his protagonists. But the most ironical moment arrives when the protagonist meets the 'other', his indivisible identity yet fully equipped with the sources of the self. As if the moment of identity constantly flickers yet remains at the same spatiotemporal situation. The ultimate dilemma and confusion are confronted and brought to the surface in the stories like, "The Other", "Borges and I", "His End and His Beginning" and also in "The Shape of the Sword".

Shklovsky's mature observation on defamiliarization[9] throws much light on Borges' is style of description, which is authenticated by close reading of the situation—minute splitting of observation and immediate shifting of thought towards a terse analysis of the given situation. As a result of this process of stressing, the hence-before unstressed, colouring the light or grey with stark crimson—ordinary with the sense of something special —make the narrative striking. Another striking feature one observes is the terseness of the lines, which not only condenses but also expands into thought. The reader reads the lines consciously, as riddles–(not to stress here, of course the strong poetic prose he uses) Borges crosses boundaries of terms and traverses limitations, geography for him becomes the familiar landscape. It contains something, as Lawrence calls it 'spirit of place'. Borges, as also his characters do, lives like a native pagan, pristine monk of some unnamed ritual of pronouncing words, inhabiting, sleering and dreaming the place, its spirit.

In Borges's magic realism a reverse ostrananie is at work, an act of defamiliarization giving extraordinariness to the mundane or day-to-day reflection or pain. At every line as it were there is a magical familiarity to the absurd, concocted reality made credible by the pithiest of arguments that are easily swallowed by the wondrous reader, the fellow traveller in the mystical journey undertaken towards meaning. On the interrelation between structural entity and hermeneutical semantics as Gerard Genette has pointed lucidly, it is not of "mechanical separation and exclusion, but of complementarity" (Genette, 71). Literary criticism to Genette is a metalanguage, "discourse upon a discourse" as said by Paul Valery. He even does not hesitate to call it a "metaliterature" (Genette, 63). Taking the same cue of narration within narration in Borges' fiction which obliquely tilts the usual plane of narrativity and switches between history, fact and fiction in a tantalizing manner, a linear yet curvature trajectory could be drawn. From this perspective Borges could also well be termed a bricoleur in Claude Levi Strauss's terminology.[10]

The way Borges integrates materials from myth, aphorism, legend, historical pieces, anecdotes, religion, parable and ties the broken pieces together, he deserve the efficacy of a ' maker' or an engineer bricoleur. In what seems to be a bemused acceptance or even denial, Borges speaks of the close yet remote relation of the reader and the writer. In the Baroque pieces of *A Universal History of Iniquity* (in the Preface) he describes the stories, "They are the irresponsible sport of a shy sort of man who could not bring himself to write stories, and so amused himself by changing and distorting (sometimes without aesthetic justification) the stories of other men" (*Collected Fictions 4*). This does not amount to the negation of one category as the admission of another in the sense that Borges must have been aware of the interdependence of texts upon one another—in other words, of intertextuality.

The arguments that Borges offers as justification of some events, decision, coincidences, and that set the line smooth or make the logic tenable also become sources of extraordinary and profound knowledge. They propel the magic imbibed therein to an easy glide and the tale finds its track forward. I am illustrating only a handful out of the infinite number of elliptical, profound maxims that dominate his world.

"Though blind to guilt, fate can be merciless with the slightest distractions." Or "Reality is partial to symmetries and slight anachronisms" ("The South" 174, 175)

"From learning to pity the misfortunes of the heroes of the novel, we wind up feeling too much pity for our own; but not Recabarren, who accepted his paralyais as he had earlier accepted the severity and the solitudes of the Americas. A man in the habit of living in the present, as animals do, he now looked up at the sky and reflected that the red ring around the moon was a sign of rain." ("The End" 169)

"Whatsoever one man does, it is as though all men did it. That is why it is not unfair that a single act of disobedience in a garden should contaminate all humanity; that is why it is not unfair that a single Jew's crucifixion should be enough to save it." ("The Shape of the Sword" 141)

Maybe it is a fact that Borges would have never liked himself to be associated with the genre called "magical realism", maybe he would have preferred a straighter version of it, but going back to the inherent structure of his fiction, that fantastical element that always gives it the spectacular feel of being typically Borgesian, makes it an integral part of story-telling (story + form) or narrative or narrativety itself.[11]

References

1. Jonathan Culler in his brilliant treatise "Story and Discourse in the Analysis of Narrative" excerpted in *The Pursuit of Signs*; Routledge, London(1981), 2005 on a general level distinguishes between the two main axes of analysis for a narrative or work of fiction said to be fabula and sjuzhet or story or plot.
2. In the same treatise Culler offers radical reading of Freud's case histories, especially *The Wolf Man* and *Oedipus Rex*. He also dictates a novel perspective of Goerge Eliot's novel *Daniel Deronda* on the same axes of Fabula sjuzhet dialectic advocated by the Structuralists and the Russian formalists.
3. The contention that I propose to raise here is not a denial of structural formulas of Culler which he rereads; here my reading is an extension of the structural axis pointing or tilting towards an openness which, to my mind, would accommodate Borges's careful strategy of form–content binary.
4. Jacques Lacan's contracted formula of the endless chain of signifiers over the real or signified symbolized by the small s stand thus; S/s, which problematises the subject object or word thing equation. Refer to "The Insistence of the Letter in the Unconscious" in David Lodge, *Modern Criticism and Theory* (London and New York, Longman, 1988).
5. Reference is to the parallelism used by Borges in "The Library of Babel" between the library and the universe. "The universe (which others call the Library) is composed of an indefinite, perhaps infinite number of hexagonal galleries." p. 112, also *The Library has existed ab aeternitate.* p. 113 (*Jorge Luis Borges Collected Fictions*, Trans. Andrew Hurley, Penguin, 1998).
6. Alfred Korzybsky in his book, *Science and Sanity: An Introduction to Non-Aristotelian* Systems (1933) introduced general semantics to the world.

In this discourse the author attempts at solving-general problems of either or logic of the great philosopher. The symbols are not essentially connected to the thing symbolized. It is analogous to "The word is not the thing" or "The map is not the territory" et cetera.

7. In his seminar on "Mirror stage as Formative of the function of the I" reveals the formation and function of the "ego" in a child of eighteen months when confronted with his own image in the mirror. This is the formation of the I and also curiously the other. Lacan calls this developmental stage as *Imaginary* as opposed to *Symbolic* and the *Real.* Refer to Lacan: *Ecrits: A Selection*, Trans. Alan Sheridan, London and New York, Routledge, 2001.
8. Ostranenie or defamiliarization is a term which once used by the Russian formalists became a key word for their critiquing the literariness of the language used in literature. Shklovsky in his seminal essay, "Art as Technique" stressed that the deformation of reality, 'making strange' was central to all art.
9. Shklovsky in the same essay also discerns, "The purpose of art is to impart the sensation of things as they are perceived and not as they are known. The technique of art is to make objects 'unfamiliar', to make forms difficult ...Art is a way of experiencing the artfulness of an object: the object is not important." (Lodge, *Modern Criticism and Theory*, Longman, p. 20)
10. The term bricoleur denotes a state of integrated engineering. Claude Levi Strauss uses the word for the literary critic who breaks down a structure into its elements. The parallelism is used mainly in order to point to the effective strategy undertaken by Borges the 'teller', of the bricolage, his narrative.
11. The preface to *The oxford Book of Latin American Short Stories* ; ed Roberto Gonzalez Echevarria, Oxford, New York,1999 discusses Borges as one affiliated towards the cause of his land, people and also culture.

Works Cited

All the lines from Borges' fiction, quoted here, are excerpted from his *Collected Fictions*; Trans Andrew Hurley, Penguin, 1998.

Genette Ge'rard: "Structuralism and Literary Criticism" in David Lodge, *Modern Criticism and Theory*, Longman, 1988.

Heidegger Martin: " The Nature of Language " in *On the Way to Language* (1959) Trans. Peter D Hertz (New York, Harper One, 1982).

Lacan Jacques: " The Insistence of the Letter in the Unconscious ", Lodge, *Modern Criticism and Theory, Longman.*

4

In-between Theories: Articulating Postcoloniality in Translation

Hemang Desai

A bird's-eye view over the history of translation in the West and to a certain extent even in the East is enough to reveal that the relationship of poetry and translation has been rather inverse at worst and strained at best. Extremist postulates like, poetry is something "which is lost in translation", best describes the worst while Fitzgerald's allegory of a live dog being better than a dead lion worst describes the best. Both these approaches are woefully reductionist and purblind to the finer points and subtler issues involved in the extremely complex and reticular act that translation professes to be. The early theoretical formulations in the realm of translation fanatically zeroed in on the concepts of pure and total(itarian) equivalence and a weird idea of interlingual synonymy. Much to the translator's chagrin, the ghost of equivalence still haunts him in the form of the self-styled poet-critic-theorists who naively liken the act of translation to an Indian woman matching the color of a blouse-piece with that of her newly-purchased sari.

If at all any theory has to depend on imagination and analogy, a metaphysical conceit of gene therapy should practically merit sizable theoretical attention to descsribe the act of translation which has always been embedded in contexts of socio-cultural politics and power. According to this radical metaphor, translator brings about an alteration in the genetic code of the poetic cell of the original and transmits it to the mutant offspring i.e. translation, thus ruling out the conception of the idea of equivalence by any wild and wayward stretch of imagination. For too long, translation has been viewed parochially and essentially as an aesthetic act obsessed with the quixotic ideas of establishing interlingual synonymy and/or a dialogue between cultures in flagrant disregard of ideological issues that it fundamentally involves. Postcolonial discourse has explicitly acknowledged the hugely political role that translation played at the site of colonial encounter to uphold and perpetuate superiority and consequent domination of one culture over another. "By employing certain modes of representing the other-which it thereby also brings into being-translation reinforces hegemonic versions of the colonized, helping them acquire the status of what Edward Said calls representations or objects without history" (Niranjana, 1995). This has further created a theoretical space for understanding asymmetrical power relations between languages and cultures foregrounded by the act of translation.

Formulations that set up the problem of translation as one of judging how faithful a translation has been to the original or how well it reads in the target language, divert attention from the fact that translation takes place where two, invariably unequal, worlds collide, and that there are always relationships of power involved when one world is represented for another in translation (Tharu *et al* 1993). In response to their ruthless orientalization, the empire also resorted to "assimilative" or "subversive" politics of translation as a way of manifesting its anti-imperial and anti-colonial stance. The notorious fatwa against Salman Rushdie for alleged (mis)representation of source culture in *The Satanic Verses* unequivocally manifests the coercive power of ideological valences that govern all intercultural transfers including translation. Translation is generally less heated affair at present but the process of translating texts from minority cultures can in fact become fraught for ideological reasons (Simms 1983) and the bloody history of *Bible* translation represents the flashpoints of future.

The metaphor of gene therapy might appear somewhat blasphemous in so far as it criminally desecrates Anton Popovik's idea of an "invariant core" that should ideally and thoroughly be transmigrated in the target text, it definitely facilitates contextual vantage points from which one can investigate, interrogate and relocate political strands undergirding the activity of literary translation. After the terms of seeing are altered thus, the question of whether the mutation is harmful or beneficial would not bother aesthetes more than what actually motivates and necessitates such alterations. In a nation – if I can use the qualification for India— with a comparatively long history of colonization, both sorts of mutations can be, have been and should be justifiably practised in an endeavour to revise and rarefy the skewed frames of reference through which historical, cultural and colonial interrelationships have been envisaged. This particularly facilitates the perspective shift from a putative idea of single, definitive and self-reliant translation to one which acknowledges the instability of the original text and historicity of translated text. The present analogy liberates translation activity from essentialist binary of original vs. copy and underscores its political underpinnings.

Busting the Binary: 'Rewriting' the Myth of Originality

A prevalent misconception about translation as being the accurate transcription of words from one language into another encourages us to forget the fact that "translation" carries with it the strong sense of changing, transforming, or altering one thing into another and that it is also intimately connected with the act of interpretation. Consequently, out of the five meanings isolated by *The Oxford English Dictionary* of translation, at least three underscore its explanatory, interpretive and transformative aspects. The asymmetrical statuses accorded to the original and translation in West are largely due to the emergence of printing which concomitantly bred the idea of an author as the sovereign 'owner' of his text which can be claimed by a translator only with a self-deprecating sense of personal ineptitude and inferiority. Alluding to the Christian myth of fall, exile and wandering, G.N. Devy (2000) has averred that in western metaphysics translation is a "perpetual exile", a fall from the origin. Perhaps western literary traditions evolving mostly from monolingual and monocultural conditions have always been apprehensive of the intrusion of 'other', a foreign culture entering their lives, through translation. The bloody history of Bible translations into different world languages bears a testimony to the western obsession with the question of authenticity as undergirding the act of translation.

Andre Lefevere (1988) designates such an essentialist understanding of literature as corpus approach to literature which is indebted to the romantic concepts of a writer as a quasi-divine 'creator' with peerless 'artistic genius', 'creativity' and 'originality' and a translator as a drudge, a proletariat indulging into 'second-hand', 'second-rate' activity of botching up the original. Such a *de facto* dichotomy between the original and translation is ascertained off and on by literate in terms as lopsided and sweeping as Matthew Arnold's (1960) who famously said, the way to gain "any sense of the power and charm" of the great masters is "not through [their] translations…but through the original poetry." The emergence and empowerment of heady idea of ownership surprisingly synchronized with the initial stages of European imperialistic project. Thus, the simulative identity of translation is due, more significantly, to the imperial project of colonial expansion and consequently to the politics of 'representation', whereby the Europe, with its logocentric underpinnings, assumed the status of the original regulating the identities of its inferior colonies which were obliged to be 'translated' in tandem with Eurocentric discourse. It should not, then, surprise one that Western theoretical perspectives on translation are woefully fixated on the glorification of the original and the valorization of notions of transparency, equivalence and fluency as positive attributes of translation.

In obsequious deference to such essentialist, simplistic and politically fraught theoretical conceptualization of translation, the activity of translation in East as much as in West, despite its exponential proliferation, has continued to be invisible and on that account undervalued.

However, recent work in translation theory has exhibited a propensity to emphasize the transformative, transgressive and interpretive elements in translation. No doubt, this avant-garde departure apparently draws on Walter Benjamin's seminal essay "The Task of the Translator", but it has its roots first in the "linguistic turn" translation theory took under the influence of deconstruction, and later the "cultural turn" it took in its assimilation of recent anthropological and cultural theory. Where conventional approaches to translation were "unified by a conceptual framework which assumes original presence and a representation of it in the receiving society" (Gentzler 1993), deconstruction shifted attention away from the interlinear to the transformational elements of translation by raising a series of questions about both presence and representation in translation. Derrida (1981) questioned the absolute position that a literary text occupied in the traditional critical discourse and argues that each new instance of reading text is a different occasion to experience the absence of its meaning. Deconstruction shifted the attention from identity to difference, from meaning as a reflection of the "real" to meaning as the product of a play of differences within a system with no fixed reference points outside it. Derrida thus imparted unprecedented primacy to translation bestowing upon it the status of literature since a translator, like a creative writer, signified meaning as independent presence.

In his famous explication of Walter Benjamin's essay, Paul de Man, first freezes the fluctuating and reciprocal relationship in translation between faithfulness and freedom and then radically fractures the problematic mutuality so as to undermine the role of loyalty in translation. He builds upon Benjamin's likening of translation and literary criticism to aver, "both criticism and translation are caught in the gesture which Benjamin calls ironic, a gesture which undoes the stability of the original . . . . The translation . . . shows in the original a mobility, an instability, which at first one did not notice" (de Man, 1986). He moves farther than Benjamin in comparing the act of translation with critical philosophy, literary theory, and history precisely because "they do not resemble that from which they derive . . . they disarticulate, they undo the original, they reveal that the original was always already disarticulated . . . . They kill the original . . . bring to light a dismembrance" (ibid. 84). Scholars advocating cultural approach to translation have added a consideration of forms of institutional and social power to the deconstructive location of translation into infinity.

If de Man attributes the impossibility in translation of loyalty to the original to the difference eternally inherent in language and the ironic disarticulation at the heart of critical commentary, philosophy and history, Susan Bassnett and André Lefevere (1990) look upon translation as a creative and constructive rewriting of the original. "Translation is . . . a rewriting of an original text. All rewritings, whatever their intention, reflect a certain ideology and a poetics and as such manipulate literature to function in a given society in a given way. Rewriting is manipulation, undertaken in the service of power, and in its positive aspect can help in the evolution of a literature and society. Rewritings can introduce new concepts, new genres, new devices, and the history of translation is the history also of literary innovation, of the shaping power of one culture upon another."

If the discourse of deconstruction and its theoretical architects, thus, established a literary text as no more than a copy, the polysystems theorists like Andre Lefevere, Gideon Toury, Theo Hermans and Itamar Evan-Zohar articulated a subversive contention according to which a translation is no less original than its source. Paul de Man's contention as to ironically circular relationship obtaining in original that lends translation into an arbitrary language game is set at a remove from a newer perspective focusing on the cultural and social function of translation conceived as a strategic and motivated rewriting of the original. Bassnett and Lefevere observe, "Translations are never produced in an airlock where they, and their originals, can be checked against the *tertium comparationis* in the purest possible lexical chamber, untainted by power, time, or even the vagaries of culture. Rather, translations are made to respond to the demands of a culture, and of various groups within that culture." (ibid, 1990)

Polysystems theorists viewed literature as a complex and dynamic system and further advocated an approach to literary translation which is descriptive, target-oriented, functional and systematic. They drew the problematic of translation away from the obsessive idea of finding equivalents to a systematic concern with the critical examination of "the norms and constraints that govern the production and reception of translations...in the place and role of translations both within a given literature and in the interaction between literatures" (Hermans 1985). If de Man envisages rewriting purely in linguistic terms as an "ironic gesture," a violent dismembering, they see it as a complex ideological and poetic attempt to manipulate the function of discourse in society, to exercise a "shaping" power with the potential to create new concepts, genres, and devices. The radical reconceptualization of translation they endorse—translation as "appropriation," as "mimicry," as "parody"—is right out of Derrida and de Man, but their stress is on the critical and even liberatory possibilities of translation as an undoing and displacement of dominant discourses and cultural forms (Jay 1997). They are interested more in describing the status, function and reception of a translated text in the target culture as well as the power of culture on the decisions that a translator makes than in explicating the process of translation.

In a radical formulation, Andre Lefevere (1984) posits that the quest for the meaning of / in a text is overambitious at best and futile at worst because meaning(s) is derived under a set of strict controls and definite regulations which, more often than not, seek to adapt a work of art to a specific ideology or to a certain poetics or to both. He extends this problematization of the process of arriving at meaning in a literary work to all those activities which are directly or indirectly involved in generating or imparting meanings like criticism, translation, anthologization, literary historiography etc and covers them under an umbrella term 'refractions'. Lefevere posited that primary texts do not stand in isolation but are always surrounded by different processing modes and mechanisms through which they are rewritten. The exercise of rewriting presupposes a process of interpretation which in turn exposes the ideological underbelly of all refractive undertakings. Refractions, to Lefevere, "are made to influence the way in which readers read a text; as such they are powerful instruments in ensuring the 'right' reading of works of literature and in perpetuating 'right readings'". In other words, refractions rewrite a text to validate, valorize or redefine the value structures of a canon. Such a stance invests the activity of translation which is "probably the most radical form of rewriting in a literature, or a culture" (Lefevere 1985), with the esteem and status formerly claimed only by source literary texts.

In its highly contentious and political role of exercising the shaping power of one language over another, translation has striking semblance with anthropology. Anthropology has been identified as "an art of translation" and the phenomenon of cultural translation is seen as uniting different ethnographic paradigms and different schools of anthropological thought. (Pálsson 1993) The metaphor of cultural translation implicates turning from the literal translation of one language into another to a figurative translation, one that has less to do with linguistic transcription than with explaining and interpreting a given set of social and cultural practices to an audience that does not understand them. This approach to translation is exemplified by the feminist critic, Barbara Godard, who insists that "the possibility of future feminist intervention requires an ironic manipulation of the semiotics of performance and production" in the act of translation (Godard 1990). Godard sees translation as a rewriting, "production, not reproduction . . . [a] playful repetition. . . . as performance".

A feminist theory of translation enlarges the idea of translation to accommodate imitation, adaptation, quotation, pastiche, parody—all different modes of rewriting: in short, all forms of interpenetration of works and discourses" (ibid. 1990). In a similar vein Talal Asad assumes a critical position against Benjamin's advice to mimic the form and genre of the original and advocates creative freedom in translation. "It could be argued that "translating" an alien form of life, another culture, is not always done best through the representational discourse of ethnography, that under certain conditions a dramatic performance, the execution of a dance, or the playing of a piece of music might be more apt. These would all be productions of the original, not authoritative textual representations of it." (Asad 1986)

It follows from the foregoing discussion that the theory of translation has experienced an elemental shift in the final quarter of the last century; the traditional value of fidelity has given way, first to a deconstructive critique that seemed to erase the difference between "original" and "translation," and secondly to a general reconceptualization of the phenomenon of translation, one that linked it to a range of cultural activities—interpretation, critical rewriting, performance, the manipulation of language with political purpose—and therefore revised our sense both of its purposes and its forms.

Post-colonial Translation: Radical vs Indian Theories

The unforgiving exposé of the history of translation sullied by colonial lust for power and the politics of (mis)representation has given birth to radical theories of translation in postscolonial countries through which the empire now assertively writes back. There is a general though somewhat grudging consensus amongst postcolonial writers and theorists that the empire can and should translate back only in an increasingly defamiliarized english if not in the hegemonic English of the colonial masters (Ashcroft et al., 1989). However, in Indian context, it remains to be seen whether the post-colonial assertion of self through English translation of native literatures is to be achieved by a sheepish recourse to Eurocentric theoretical models, however radical, or by turning to rich classical Indian tradition of translation.

In her seminal book *Siting Translation* (1995), Tejaswini Niranjana draws on Benjamin, Derrida, and de Man to identify the contexts of representation and power in intercultural transfer. She upholds, "In a post-colonial context the problematic of translation *becomes* a significant site for raising questions of representation, power, and historicity. The context is one of contesting and contested stories attempting to account for, to recount, the asymmetry and inequality of relations between peoples, races, languages." Niranjana's claim that the postcolonial theory and translation can "reinvent oppositional cultures in non-essentializing ways" is compatible with the poststructuralist call for the celebration of heterogeneity. Thus, she presses the postcolonial translator to conscientiously tune his translatorial efforts to paradigmatic rather than syntagmatic level, to privilege "literalness" over meaning so that an attack over homogenizing and continuous narratives can be constructed and a discursive space for the assertion of socio-cultural identities can be engineered. Critical of the communicative model of translation, Niranjana emphasizes that just as one can't aspire for accuracy in translation, a complete denial of historicity and referentiality is impossible.

Brazilian translator Haraldo de Campos likens translation to blood transfusion that nourishes the health of the translator. In his view, *Antropofagia*, the Brazilian-derived metaphor of anthropophagy, develops an avant-garde and radical poetics of translation. Disrupting dichotomous views of source and target, *Antropofagia* and its application to translation entails a double dialectical dimension with political ingredients; it unsettles the primacy of the origin, recast both as a donor and receiver of forms, and advances the role of the receiver as a giver in its own right, further pluralizing (in)fidelity (Vieira 2000). Haroldo de Campos coins neologisms for translation like 'verse-making', 'reinvention', 'translumination', 'transparadisation', 'transtextualization', 'transcreation', 'transluciferation' and so on to offer a radical poetics of translation as textual revitalization brought about not by blocking foreign influences but by absorbing and transforming them through the addition of autochthonous input. The translation of creative texts, de Campos argues, is always recreation or parallel creation, the opposite of literal translation, but always reciprocal; an operation in which it is not only the meaning that is translated but the sign itself in all its corporeality (sound properties, visual imagetics, all that makes up the iconicity of the aesthetic sign). (de Campos 1992)

While much of the post-structuralist discourse in monolingual west, as noted earlier, has subjected translation to a rigorous scrutiny and sited it as a remove from the antiquated notions of gradation, transparency and synonymy of late, in multilingual and multicultural India, translation has been nothing less than a way of life for centuries. Niranjana rocks the bottom out of the lachrymose West's laments over things lost in translation by foregrounding the postcolonial theoretical agenda focusing on the need to "make sense of 'subjects' already living 'in translation'". Bilingualism or multilingualism, that too devoid of the notions of mutual psychological animosity or cultural otherness, is invariably the hallmark of the linguistic competence of every Indian and many a time it obviates the need for translation felt by the monolinguals. Such polyglottism has brought about the development among Indians of "translating consciousness" which perhaps accounts for the progressive, non-essentialist and reader-empowering practice of translation in ancient and even modern India. In India, with its long history of oral composition and transmission and the dominant early phase of bhakti or devotional poetry in all its modern languages in which the poet surrendered to and sought to merge his individual identity with his divine subject, the distinction between an original writer and a translator was never half as wide as it has been in the West. (Bassnett *et al* 2000)

The territorial apprehensions implicit in the Western appellation 'translation' is significantly absent in its Indian counterpart 'anuvad' with distinct temporal underpinnings, which denotes repetition of vedic textual enjoining with different wording. The repetitive, explanatory, illustrative, corroborative and interpretative connotations of the term anuvad reveals that to Indian society steeped in oral literary traditions of *smriti* and *shruti*, differing versions were the norms rather than exceptions. (Choudhury, 2010) As against the western horror of the 'other', India's amazing capacity to assimilate alien cultures and her faith in syncretic Vedantic values has been instrumental in effecting a phenomenal erasure of the disparity between self and the other. Thus in pre-colonial India, liberal and liberating practice of translation has led to innumerable inventive reworkings of *Ramayana* and *Mahabharata*, the two great epics of the subcontinent, in Sankrit as well as in other bhashas, with appreciable thematic and ideological shifts ranging from convolutions in the storyline to swapped roles of the characters. It might sound sacrilegious to a European ear but every retelling of the great epics were / are heard, read and enjoyed by its audience with the same sense of appreciation, reverence and awe with which a western reader would approach an original.

Drawing on Indian metaphysics with its faith in the soul travelling from one body to another without losing its essential significance, Devy (2000) affirms that soul or significance, even literary significance is a historical in Indian view. To him, Indian literary traditions are essentially traditions of translation because they do not lay undue stress on originality but put the writer's capacity to transform, translate, restate and revitalize the original to test. Tulsi Das's Hindi reworking of *Ramayana* and

Jnaneshwara's free Marathi translation of *Bhagavad Gita* are the epitomes of the characteristic Indian tradition of translation marked unequivocally by ideological shifts and radical subversions. In what might have appeared a blasphemous move to Western translation theorists, Jnaneshwara extends the dialogic structure of original *Bhagavad Gita* from three levels to five, seamlessly incorporating discourses between his guru Nivrittinath and him at one level and between him and his disciple Satchidanand at the other. "In adding these levels" remarks Indranath Choudhury, "the poet endows legitimacy on the oral as a form of literature as valid as the written emphasizing thereby that the "Jnaneshwari Gita" is more a *suta* (to be sung in another language) than a mantra (Sanskrit verse) text." Similarly, Tulsi Das's creative retelling of Valmiki "*Ramayana*" was essentially a subversive act aiming to liberate the scripture from the monopolist control of Sanskrit scholars and priests. In fact the whole medieval Bhakti movement was consecrated to an enormous democratization of literary language, morphing the cultural forms of caste hegemony in favour of the artisans and peasants, put up a brave front against Brahminical domination and problematization of the gender construction of all dialogic relations (Ahmed 1992).

Needless to say that Tulsi Das, a brahmin by birth, had a taste of bitter pill from the fundamental forces in his community, but in the face of all enraging exigencies, he remained firmly attached to the way of life prescribed by his tradition and religion to him i.e. non-violence and vegetarianism. Bassnett and Trivedi (ibid). institute a clever metaphorical comparison between subversive translational acts enacted by Tulsi Das and Brazilian cannibals in order to spell out the theoretical subtleties of Indian translational perspective. To them, Tulsi Das's appropriation of *Ramayana*, "could thus hardly be called an instance of brazillian cannibalism; it marked rather a natural process of organic, ramifying, vegetative growth and renewal, comparable perhaps with the process by which an ancient bunyan tree sends down branches which then in turn take root all around it and comprise an intertwined family of trees." In other words, Indian translatorial sensibility always envisaged a symbiotic relationship between the mother tongue and the other tongue, the original and the translation, a mutually enriching collaboration based on affection and care for both the languages. Gayatri Chakravorty Spivak echoes the same sentiment in her famous essay *The Politics of Translation* (1993) when she says that a translator must practice total, unconditional 'surrender' to the rhetorical dimension of the original text, similar in intensity to that of a gopi for Lord Krishna, as translation is the most intimate act of reading.

The apparent predilection of the ancient Indian translator for adaptation or appropriation over what Tejaswini Niranjana calls literal translation or what Sanskrit scholars called "chhaya" (shadow) or verbatim translation, if absorbed by modern-day translator rendering Indian regional literature into English, should not be miscalculated as an obsequious rubbishing of postcolonial agenda of resistance and transformation. Though the medieval Indian view was primarily to produce a reader-friendly translation, it was never at the cost of what Popovic identifies as "the invariant core", i.e., stable, basic and constant semantic features of a text, as well as specific cultural and historical signifiers embedded in the source text because the fundamental motivation behind undertaking the translation was to be able to understand and enjoy the original rather than to efface it in the interest of an altogether new work.

Niranjana's radical aesthetic of postcolonial translation draws on Walter Benjamin and Derrida's theories of translation which were suitably and exclusively applicable to translation between connate European languages. Benjamin's view on the place and role of the reader in the process of translation borders on cynicism when he posits in *The Task of the Translator* (1969) a typically essentialist formulation along which he discredits the consideration of reader in the appreciation of a work of art as hopelessly unproductive and simplistic. Furthermore, more often than not, he observes that it is the original that houses "the laws governing the translation" and thus translatability of a given text does not so much depend on extra-textual factors like the nature of relationship between two languages, translator's bilingual skills and most importantly the interest and expectations of the readers from the translation as it does on some abstract code inherent in the text in the form of a "pure language". He argues, "A real translation is transparent; it does not cover the original, does not block its light, but allows the pure language, as though reinforced by its own medium, to shine upon the original all the more fully. This may be achieved, above all, by a literal rendering of syntax which proves words rather than sentences to be primary element of the translator. For if the sentence is the wall before the language of the original, literalness is the arcade."

A.K. Ramanujan, an eminent Indian English poet and a conscientious prolific translator, countered Benjamin's position by calling it wholly unsuitable to translation between Indian regional language like Tamil and English which are far-flung in terms of space and time. He held a unyielding conviction that though a translator unavoidably shares a relationship of subjectivity with the author of the original, a subjectivity that might oblige him to the Italian accusation *traditore, traduttore* (i.e. translator is a traitor), he might find a way out of this wild rumour by pledging conflicting, yet thorough, allegiance to the reader of the translation, the culture and historical context of the original. Being an ardent supporter of reader's response theory, Ramanujan firmly believed that the 'real' or 'imagined' reader of the translated text actively partakes in the process of translation heavily influencing the decisions made by the translator.

The reader's expectation from the translator, according to him, ranges from metaphrastic and formal loyalty to the source-text, accuracy in the representation of the language, culture, history and tradition of the original to finally translation's subjective claim to being a creative artifact in its own right. While the translator can satisfy the demands of verbal faithfulness and poetic pleasure when he or she negotiates the difficulties of metaphrase, the search for inner and outer forms, and the intrusion of poetic desire and subjectivity that create a tension between representation and appropriation, he or she can fulfil the norm of pedagogic utility only by stepping beyond the immediate constraints of textual transmission and invoking his or her allegiance to a phenomenon that stands outside the text and beyond its reader in translation (Dharwadkar 2000). The phenomenon resistant to the boundaries of textual narrative refers to the distinctive elements of culture in which a source text is embedded and which unmistakably intertwine with an existing web of intertextuality invoked metonymically by it. Understandably, all the intricate network of such metonymies, unable to be carried over in its entirety in the textual fabric of the target text, spills over in extra-textual sites in the form of introductions, glossaries, notes and footnotes, afterwords, and commentaries. This is what Ramanujan means by his strategy of translating non-native reader into a native one. He goes on to elaborate his position in considerable detail in *The Interior Landscape* (1967), "The translations and the afterword (which some readers may prefer to read first) are two parts of one effort. The effort is to try and make a non-Tamil reader experience in English something of what a native experiences when he reads a classical Tamil poem."

On a note of utmost caution, it is to be borne in mind that Ramanujan's translational aesthetics and ethics ought not to be confused with Nida's principle of equivalent effect as both perhaps represent the polar extremes of quality and beauty of the translation. Ramanujan's effort, when he rendered classical Tamil verse into English, was singularly focused on the optimum translocation of the rich native tradition and historical climate in which the verses were ensconced. In doing so with the help of translations and paratextual discourse surrounding them, a translator enters into a huge network of intertexuality covering expressions in diverse genres, media, and methods across a huge stretch of time and space. The goal of every painstaking translator should ideally be to accomplish a carryover of heterotopias of time and space in his translation and juxtapose it with creative metamorphosis of aesthetic and textual dimensions that he has brought about to impart a unique identity to his finished product. In a way, Ramanujan's ambitious theory of translation evolves out of tenets of the ancient Indian school of translation and a judicious negation of hyper-radicality inherent in certain post-colonial approaches.

Conclusion

In typical postcolonial and diasporic contexts, the relationship obtaining between two cultural poles in translation is complicated by the fluid and volatile concept of culture, which denies warranting coherent and well-bound 'national' and 'ethnic' realities. The discipline of Cultural Studies has effectively worked the concept of "hybridity" for quite some years now to draw critical attention to how colonized and border cultures developed by synthesizing themselves out of elements of multiple cultures. Cultural studies has highlighted the special or distinguished status of hybrid spaces vis-à-vis the supposedly monocultural nature of colonial societies that relied on purist notions of identity and belonging. This perhaps aptly explains Rushdie's conscious interspersing of Hindi and Urdu words and expressions in linguistic texture of his novels. In *Imaginary Homelands* (1991),

Rushdie makes a particularly poignant observation upon the negative reception of *The Satanic Verses*: "Those who oppose the novel most vociferously today are of the opinion that intermingling with a different culture will inevitably weaken and ruin their own."

I am of the opposite opinion. *The Satanic Verses* celebrates hybridity, impurity, intermingling, the transformation that comes of new and unexpected combinations of human beings, cultures, ideas, politics, movies, songs. It rejoices in mongrelization and fears "the absolutism of the Pure." Rushdie's observation invites the possibility of epistemological "third-space" where meaning is not governed by preexisting interpretative frameworks and where condition of aporia forces attention to other subaltern aspects of migrated, postcolonial subjectivities. In this regard, translation becomes an agent not of innocuous cultural interaction ("inter-cultural translation") but a subversive exercise in cultural production. To quote Sherry Simon, "Translation then is not simply a mode of linguistic transfer but a translingual practice, a writing across languages[,] which permits new kinds of conversations and new speaking positions" (28). The migrant writers located in these new spaces of enunciation draw on processes of abrogation, hybridization, and creolization to articulate complex translations that challenge the very notion of "authority" and "authenticity" of "original" sources.

Just as for a postcolonial writer the narrative device of bilingualism serves the dual purposes of overt authentication of authorial identity and foregrounding the reality of difference, for a post-colonial translator, the natural thickening and defamiliarization of standard English—not out of jingoistic zeal for preserving the sacredness of the source texts—should account for his commitment towards staging the fundamental fluidity and interstitial character of life and literature in India in particular and third world in general. The bilingual nature of translation would positively imply the valorization of subcultures and marginalized languages as well as authenticate multiple realities that a polyphonic nation feeds on. Such a challenge, Simon suggests, proposes "translation [as] a necessary means through which knowledge is tested, recontextualized, submitted to critical scrutiny" (ibid). At present in India, a host of plurilingual writers, creating literature in English or bhashas (regional languages), make wide-ranging use of upabhashas (dialects) in their works. These are nothing but the languages growing in interstices, expressing experiences of people negotiating these interstices and consequently require the formulation of a creative idiom which can translate in interstices.

To bring such a noble aspiration to fruition, archaic and essentialist models of translation have to be deconstructed in favour of ones that can do a classic balancing act between freethinking and interventionist approaches. Adoption of the early post-colonial policy of reverse otherization is passé now. And it's time, as well as the best way to wind up the present discussion, to temper the theoretical radicalism of the analogy of gene therapy with the analogy of recombinant DNA technology, corresponding to Bhabha's "third space", as describing the act of translation. Combination of diverse cultural, poetic, historical, and ethnic molecules inserted into a host textual organism would engender a new genetic combination useful to transnational and translational pedagogy.

Works Cited

Aijaz, Ahmad. "'Indian Literature': Notes towards the Definition of a Category" in *Theory: Classes, Nations, Literatures*. Verso, London, 1992, p. 243-85.

Arnold, Matthew. *Essays in Criticism* in S.R. Littlewood (ed.), Macmillan: London, 1960, pp.39-40.

Asad, Talal. "The Concept of Cultural Translation in British Social Anthropology." *Writing Culture*. Ed. James Clifford. University of California Press, Berkeley, 1986. 141-64.

Ashcroft, B., Griffiths, G. and Tiffin, H. *The Empire Writes back: Theory and Practice in Post-colonial Literatures*. Routledge, London, 1989, p.8.

Bassnett, Susan and André Lefevere. "Introduction". *Translation, History and Culture*. Ed. Susan Bassnett and André Lefevere. Pinter Publishers, London, 1990. pp. 1-13.

______ and Trivedi, Harish. (eds) *Post-colonial Translation*, Routledge: London and New York, 2000.

Bhabha, Homi. "The Third Space" in J. Rutherford (ed.) *Identity, Community, Culture, Difference*. London: Lawrence and Wishart, 1994, p.5.

Benjamin, Walter. "The Task of the Translator: An introduction to the Translation of Baudelaire's *Tableaux pariseins*" in H. Arendt (eds) his *Illuminations: essays and Reflections*, (trs) harry Zohn, Schocken Books, New York, 1969, p.79.

Choudhury, Indranath. "Towards an Indian theory of Translation", *Indian Literature* 259, 2010, pp.113-123.

Derrida, Jacques. *Positions*, (trns) by Alan Bass, Univeristy of Chicago Press, Chicago, 1981, p.33.

de Campos, H. "Translation as Creation and Criticism", *Metakinguagem e Qutras Metas: Ensaios de Teoria e Critica Literaria*, 4th rev, and enlarged edn, Perspectiva, Sao Paulo.

de Man, Paul. "'Conclusions': Walter Benjamin's 'The Task of the Translator.'" *The Resistance to Theory*. University of Minnesota Press, Minneapolis, 1986. pp. 73-105.

Devy, Ganesh. "Translation and Literary History: An Indian View" in Bassnett and Trivesi (eds) *Post-colonial Translation*, Routledge: London and New York, 2000. pp. 182-187.

Dharwadkar, Vinay. "A.K. Ramanujan's Theory and Practice of Translation" in Bassnett and Trivesi (eds) *Post-colonial Translation*, Routledge: London and New York, 2000, pp 114-140.

Gentzler, Edwin. *Contemporary Translation Theories*. Routledge, London, 1993. p.144.

Godard, Barbara. "Theorizing Feminist Discourse/Translation." in Susan Bassnett and André Lefevere (eds).*Translation, History and Culture*. Pinter Publishers, London, 1990. 87-96.

Hermans, Theo, "Translation Studies and a New Paradigm" in Hermans, Theo. (ed.). *The Manipulation of Literature: Studies in Literary Translation*. New York: St. Martin's Press, 1985. p.7.

Jay, Paul. "Translation, Invention, Resistance: Rewriting the Conquest in Carlos Fuentes's 'The Two Shores'" in *Modern Fiction Studies* 43:2, 1997, pp. 405-431.

Lefevere, Andre. "'Beyond Interpretation' or the Business of (Re) writing" in *Essays in Comparative Literature: A Systems Approach*. Calcutta: Papyrus, 1988, p.16.

______. "Why Waste Our Time on Rewrites? The Trouble with Interpretation and the Role of Rewriting in an Alternative Paradigm." in Hermans, Theo. (ed.). *The Manipulation of Literature: Studies in Literary Translation*. New York: St. Martin's Press, 1985, pp. 215-43.

Niranjana, Tejaswini. *Siting Translation: History, Post-Structuralism, and the Colonial Context*. Hyderabad: Orient Longman, 1995, p.3.

Pálsson, Gísli. "Introduction: beyond boundaries." in Gísli Pálsson (ed) *Beyond boundaries: Understanding, Translation and Anthropological Discourse*. Oxford: Berg, 1993. 1-40.

Ramanujan A.K. (trans). *The Interior Landscape: Love Poems from a Classical Tamil Anthology*. Indiana University Press, Bloomington, 1969.

Rushdie, Salman. *Imaginary Homelands*. Viking Press, New York 1991, p. 394.

Simms, N. "Three Types of 'touchy' translation" in N. Simms (ed.) *Nimrod's Sin, pacific Quarterly Moana* 8 (2) – special issue, 1983, p. 24.

Simon, Sherry and Paul St. Pierre (eds.). *Changing the Terms: Translating in the Postcolonial Era*. University of Ottawa Press, Ottawa, 2000. pp- 27-28.

Spivak, G.C. "The Politics of Translation" in her Outside the Teaching Machine, Routledge, New York, 1993.

Tharu and Lalita. *Women Writing in India*. Vol.2: The Twentieth Century. London: Pandora, 1993, p.xx.

Viera, P.R.E. "Liberating Calibans: readings of Antropofgia and haroldo de Capos' poetics of transcreation" in Bassnett and Trivedi (eds) *Post-colonial Translation*, Routledge: London and New York, 2000, pp.95-113.

5

Management of Face in Vikram Seth's *A Suitable Boy*: A Socio-semantic Study

Vijay Singh Thakur

There has been quite a lot of work in the studies of language in relation to society explaining how speakers are polite to one another in what they say and do, and how they try to mitigate impolite behaviour linguistically in order to uphold social cohesion. As literature, in many ways, reflects societies, the investigation of principles of politeness in literary discourse can tell us a lot about language, society, culture and thought, and thereby can uncover new meanings, implications, and insights into the nature of literary communication that are generally not explained through a strictly traditional analysis. Based on the premise of who speaks; to whom; when; where; how; and why in a variety of contexts, including social contexts, the present paper examines some supra- sentential stretches of dialogic discourse in diverse inter-personal relationships from Vikram Seth's magnum opus *A Suitable Boy* (ASB) in the light of Brown and Levinson's (1987) *Face Saving View of Politeness.*

Various issues concerning face management related to personal motives, solidarity principle, power principle, etc. that are opened up through the analysis of the conversational behaviours of characters and the governing force for their choices of one strategy over others within the framework of face-saving politeness can help us better account for the aspects concerning the construction and performance of various personalities and identities— particularly through the inferences generating about the changes in one's character in different inter-personal and socio-cultural contexts. Furthermore, the application of pragmatic interpretative strategies in the literary studies would also produce multi-level discussions and interpretations of literary texts which may help heighten literary appreciation.

Introduction

How do readers of novels get from the words in conversations to judgments concerning the 'personalities' of characters? Generally, the readers' judgement is based on anecdotal references in the story and hence it tends to become tentative. It is against this backdrop that the present paper attempts to show as to how the face-saving model of politeness, as proposed by Brown and Levinson (1987), could be used to uncover real meanings of character utterances through the marked culture-specific discourse features in conversational exchanges regulated by the characters' personal motives and their respective milieus. This may help the readers to form better judgements related to the development of different aspects of personalities of characters through the novel.

The fundamental assumptions of this face-saving view of Brown and Levinson are combined with Goffman's (1967; 1972) concept of 'face', i.e., an individual's publically manifest self-esteem. Face is something that is emotionally invested by every competent member of a society and that can be lost, maintained, or enhanced, and must be constantly attended to in an interaction. Such cooperation is based on mutual vulnerability of face. Put another way, normally, everyone's face depends on everyone else's being maintained. Since people can be expected to defend their faces if threatened, and in defending their own faces, also to threaten others' face. The notion of face reflects two related aspects:

a. *Negative Face*: It refers to the basic claim to territories, personal preserves, right to non-distraction, i.e. freedom of action and freedom from imposition.

b. *Positive Face*: It is related to the positive consistent self-image or personality claimed by interactants which certainly includes the desire that this self-image be appreciated, understood, ratified, approved of, liked or admired.

The two aspects of face can be treated as basic wants which every member knows and every member desires, and it is in the interest of every member to partially satisfy them. Negative face wants are related to the politeness of non-imposition whereas positive face wants are concerned with the reduction of person's self-image or personality directed towards the other person. Although the content of face will differ in different cultures, the mutual knowledge of members' public self-image or face and the social necessity to orient oneself to it in interaction are universal.

Normally, the respect for face is treated as norms or values but not as an unquestionable one. Face can be, and routinely is, ignored in cases of social breakdown or affrontery and also in situations of urgent cooperation and emergency. In any particular society one may expect the notion of face to be culturally highly elaborative. This core concept of 'face' is subject to cultural specifications of many sorts, e.g.: What kinds of acts threaten face? What sorts of person have special rights to face protection? What kinds of personal style (in terms of graciousness, ease of social relations, etc.)? are specially appreciated. On the other hand, notions of face naturally link up to some of the most fundamental cultural ideas about the nature of social persona, honour and virtue, shame and redemption and thus to religious concepts. But, despite all rich elaborations, the core ideas in the notion of face have a striking familiarity. Let us, before we actually get down to examining the management of face in ASB, look at the interface between politeness and the concept of face.

The Concept of Face and Politeness

Politeness, as House and Kasper (1981:157) remark, seems to be a social value that occurs in all civilized societies and the norms relating to what is polite and what is impolite behaviour may vary across cultures. Politeness phenomenon can be derived from the Goffman's (1967,1972:319-346) notion of face. Every person creates or builds a self- image in terms of the positive and negative sanctions of his society. Goffman (1972:319-346) argues that the self is a social construction or, more specifically, an interactive construction. One way of viewing the self as a public construction is through the notion of face, i.e. the positive social value a person effectively claims for himself by the line others assume he has taken during a particular contact. A verbal interaction thus becomes a cooperative endeavour or a common pursuit in the direction of maintaining inter-personal faces.

When politeness is self-centred, it has a defensive orientation towards saving one's own face and in being other-centred it holds a protective orientation towards saving the other's face. Both these defensive and protective functions are fulfilled by politeness. These two aspects are implied in politeness being seen as strategic conflict avoidance (Leech 1977:19) or as a device used in order to reduce friction in personal interaction (Lakoff 1975:64). In correspondence with Grice's Conversational Cooperativeness (1975), Lakoff (1973:298) proposes three rules of politeness in 'Don't impose', 'Give options', and 'Make hearer feel good, i.e. be friendly'. These rules agree with the parameters that Leech (1980:79-117) has set up for defining politeness in language using the cost and benefit scale in minimizing cost to other and benefit to self and vice versa, i.e. maximizing cost to self and benefit to other. Thus, politeness is essentially a matter of consideration for others. Communication of a message is not the sole purpose of human interaction. A major portion of one's verbal and non-verbal interaction is designed to avoid offence and establish camaraderie with one's fellow beings. Put simply, people constantly try to establish and maintain cordial relationships or minimize discord, if any, in their relationship with others.

Various views related to the theory of politeness are common in that the notion of politeness involves a description of how language is situated in particular circumstances of social life, and, how it reflects, and adds meaning and structure in those situations. The need for analysing politeness phenomena through the management of face in ASB is aimed at discovering the socio-cultural descriptions of the conversational behaviour of the interactants in the novel. Such an analysis will lead us into a search for explanations of human conduct and help us interpret various aspects in the novel in new ways entailing a broader perspective of characters' identities.

In this paper we shall examine the operation of the face-saving view of politeness in ASB. What concerns our discussion here is related to the examination of the characters' perception of each other's public self- image and the way they threaten it. Needless to say that characters' status, authority, occupation, ethnic identity, friendship, and situational factors will play a major role in dealing with the concept of face in their conversational behaviour. The insight thus emerging from the discussion would help us better understand the growth and development of characters in new ways.

It's time now to take up some pieces of dialogic discourse from the novel under study and examine as to how the characters handle the face work in certain communicative situations.

Example One

Mrs. Rupa Mehra:	No, (said Mrs. Rupa Mehra vehemently, shaking her needle for emphasis). My daughter is not going to act in any play. No. (She glared at Lata over the top of her reading glasses.) ... Boys and girls together–acting! ...

Lata: Like in Julius Caesar last year (ventured Lata).

Mrs. Rupa Mehra: You be quiet (snapped her mother). No one has asked you to speak. Have you ever heard of Savita wanting to act? To act on the stage with hundreds of people staring ? And going to those nightly gatherings with boys– (777-78)

Analysis: The speakers estimate the cost of a particular speech act in terms of its relative threat to speaker, hearer or both using their perceptions of the degree of social distance between speaker and hearer, the degree of dominance or affiliation, and the relative status of a particular type of act within a given culture. Then they choose the appropriate conversational style. Rejections of requests and proposals are on their own face-threatening but the degree of the involved face threat and face loss varies from culture to culture. In the present extract under investigation the face-threatening act of Mrs. Rupa Mehra's blunt rejection of her daughter Lata's proposed request to act in the annual day play of her college has been done directly and without any ameliorating efforts to cover the involved face threat and face loss. On the other hand the perlocutionary response of Lata in her submissive compliance doesn't seem to display any sad, serious or hurt feeling of losing face as a result of her negative face being challenged in her mother's attempts to control and curb her individual freedom and autonomy with snubbing and scolding. Conversely, in her very cooperative response, she is trying to preserve her mother's positive face in not contradicting and arguing against it in the ongoing conversation. Reasons are socio-cultural. Unlike Western cultures, Indian culture represents in a strong, solid, and unquestioned authority of parents even on their grown-up children to question and influence their personal matters and they are taught (as a part of their growing up) to avoid confrontation and arguments with parents and elders on views and opinions especially when they are at variance with commonly held beliefs. Indians, in general, believe that free mixing of young girls with boys and showing overly free attitude to life are something not to be displayed in public in order to maintain a clean public reputation and image. Thus, Indian culture does not seem to value individualism and personal autonomy and group solidarity is regarded more important than individual identity. The opposite is true for American or British culture where the same conversation between a mother and daughter is most likely to be taken to be extremely face-threatening which may amount to almost total loss of face resulting in a severe retaliatory perlocutionary response from the addressee. Such situations should be referred to as examples of, what Blum-Kulka and Olshtain (1984: 196) call, cross-cultural variation.

ExampleTwo

Ustad Majeed Khan:	Malti (said Ustad Majeed Khan), carry the tanpura with respect, with both hands. It isn't the offspring of a cat. What is the matter with you?
Malti:	(silence; no answer.) (1265)

Analysis: Ustad Majeed Khan's reprimand in his bitter remark for Malti goes against her positive face wants of individual desire to be ratified, understood, approved of, liked or admired.The speaker is doing his face-threatening act of criticizing in a bald manner, i.e. without any redressive action attached to it. He is scolding the addressee for carrying the tanpura (a musical instrument) with one hand in most direct and unambiguous words without caring about her feelings. Observing the social and cultural tradition of paying a very high degree of deference for one's guru (the traditional reverent concept of teacher in India), Malti maintains a submissive silence as a perlocutionary mark of her apology and deference for her music teacher (Ustad Majeed Khan). The guru's reaction against her student's carrying the tanpura with one hand is motivated by the age-old cultural tradition where music is treated as a spiritual art and the related musical instruments sacred and both are nearly worshipped. In carrying the tanpura carelessly (in a casual manner) like an unimportant routine item reflected that Malti was not paying due respect to the instrument which resented Ustad Majeed Khan. Ustad Majeed Khan's on-record face-threatening act of reprimanding his music student Malti, without any mitigating effort, may sound absurd or eccentric to the observers who are not in a position to share this socio-cultural factor of a special deference attached to the concept of the guru and the art of music and musical instruments in India. Such an understanding of the speech act, especially of the readers from other socio-cultural backgrounds, may lead to the area of what Flowerdew (1988:77) calls, a socio-pragmatic failure. This displays that the question of the appropriateness of realization of the two speech actions involved in the exchange is intricately related to the underlying social and cultural situation of the speech act in question.

Example Three

Rasheed's father: Anyway ... why don't you have a cup of tea now that you've made such an effort to come. I'll summon Rasheed's friend, and we will talk...

Football (Tiwariji): No, no– no tea, no tea.

Rasheed's father: But we will all be having it together, Tiwariji, it is not poisoned. Even Kapoor Sahib will join us.

Football (Tiwariji): He drinks tea with all of you?

Rasheed's father: Indeed. He eats with us too.

Football (Tiwariji): ... But I have just had tea, you know, with my breakfast– I've just had tea and also far too much to eat before I left my house. Look at me. I must be careful. Your hospitality knows no bounds.

	But–
Rasheed's father:	You aren't saying, by any chance, Tiwariji, are you, that what we are offering falls below your expectations? Why don't you like to eat with us? Do you think we will pollute you?
Football (Tiwariji):	Oh, no, no, no, it is just that an insect of the gutter like myself does not feel happy when offered the luxuries of a palace. Heh heh heh! ... (659)

Analysis: In this extract both the participants are doing face threatening act. In rejecting Rasheed's father's offer of tea, Tiwariji, in effect, is saying that he does not want what his speaker wants. This is a threat to the positive face of the speaker, i.e. to the desire that others want the same thing that self wants. Further, Rasheed's father's criticism of Tiwariji's rejection of his offer is a threat to the negative face of the addressee, i.e. to the desire that one's own needs and wants be unimpeded and unintruded upon.

The speaker meaning in both the cases is situated in the socio-cultural context of the ethnic identity of the participants. Tiwariji is a Brahmin and Rasheed's father is a Muslim. Both are friends. The caste rules of brahmins forbid Tiwariji to eat or drink anything with non-brahmins. Tiwariji could have expressed his refusal to drink tea, due to caste rules, in an on-record mode without redressal attempts but he was compelled to be evasive in it because of Rasheed's father's status of a friend and his social power of being a wealthy landlord. Motivated by his addressee's strong status Tiwariji had to soften the threat of his rejection by way of giving an elaborate mitigating account. Furthermore, his addressee- elevating and addresser-lowering language is an attempt to bridge the distance created between them as a result of declining the offer of tea on the basis of caste.

Tiwariji represents a divided social self caught between his caste rules (that forbid drinking tea with his host) and the personal authority of his host's friendship (which compels him to have tea with him). He tried to balance the situation in being both a public character (in not having the tea) and a private performer (in saving the face of his friend by a tactful mitigating account).

Using Strawson's (1971:51-54) interpretation we can term this speech act of offer as a conventional speech act for the reason that the successful performance of the act here depends on the extralinguistic convention of the addressee's caste rules. The ameliorated perlocutionary response of the addressee deserves some explanation. If we refer to the social roles and the relative authority of the interlocutors here, in the Indian social set-up of 1950s (the time frame of the story in the novel), the communicative situation tends to be an unequal encounter. Put simply, the relative social authority of a brahmin will be powerful over the non-brahmin. In such a context of social powers and the expected patterns of relative behaviour; the mitigating account of Tiwari, given to his non-brahmin and non-Hindu addresser, hints at the changing trend and caste rules going into the melting pot on the one hand and also approving of the relative social authority of the addresser as a friend and as a wealthy landlord on the other.

Example Four

Jha: I have seen the circular that has been distributed (said Jha).

Sandeep Lahiri: Circular?

Jha: About the fund-raising for Independence Day.

Sandeep Lahiri: Ah, yes (said Sandeep Lahiri).

Jha: I was wondering if I might ask for your help with that.

Sandeep Lahiri: If you, Sir, respected as you are, were to encourage people to contribute, it would have a considerable effect .... In fact, Sir, I am counting on your help.

Jha:	And I am counting on your help (said Jha with a broad smile).That is why I have called you.
Sandeep Lahiri:	My help? (said Sandeep, smiling helplessly and warily.)
Jha:	Yes, yes. You see, Congress also has plans for Independence Day, and we will take half the funds you collect, and use them for a separate display ...
Sandeep Lahiri:	(This was precisely what Sandeep had feared ...)
Jha:	So, then, I will expect half the funds. Good? ...
Sandeep:	Well– (said Sandeep, and threw up his hands in a gesture that implied that if matters were in his discretion, he would have been delighted to give the entire sum he collected to Jha ...)
Jha:	(Jha's face darkened.)
Sandeep:	You, see, Sir ... my hands are tied.
Jha:	(Jha continued to stare, then exploded.)What do you mean? (He almost shouted.) No hands are tied. Congress says that no hands are tied. Congress will untie your hands.
Sandeep:	Sir, it is like this– (began Sandeep Lahiri.)
Jha:	(But Jha did not let him continue.)You are a servant of the government (said Jha fiercely) and the Congress Party runs the government. You will do as we tell you.
Sandeep Lahiri:	Mmm (said Sandeep Lahiri in a noncommittal voice ...)To be fair, sir, we would have to give an equal amount to all these parties– to the Communist Party, to the Bharatiya Jana Sangh ...

Jha:	What! (burst out Jha.)What? (He swallowed.) What? You are comparing us to the Socialist Party? ...
Sandeep Lahiri:	Certainly, Sir, why not? The Congress is just one of many parties. In this respect they are all the same ...
Jha:	You equate us with the other parties? (he asked ...) In that case (continued Jha), I will show you. I will show you what the Congress means... (962-64)

Analysis: The face work in this dialogic discourse is based on specific role relationship and the network of distance, power, and ranking between the two conversants Jha and Sandeep Lahiri. As the role relationship goes, Jha, a 55-year-old senior Congress man is an important political figure in being a friend of the Chief Minister and the Chairman of the Upper House of the State Legislature. Juxtaposing him Sandeep Lahiri is an SDO (Sub Divisional Officer) in Rudhia District. As a contextual clue to the ongoing conversation there is an attitudinal contradiction between the style of working of the politician and the administrator. Jha was used to being consulted by the SDO on all important matters but Lahiri on the other hand saw no need to consult a party leader on matters of routine administration and he tried to keep local politicians at arm's length.

The extract under examination displays two different approaches that the participants adopt in maintaining each other's face. In the given situation Jha is, by all means, superior to Sandeep Lahiri in respect of power and ranking. Obviously, with his powerful status he is not worried about redressive actions for his addressee Sandeep Lahiri. But Lahiri, being an administrative subordinate to him, has to observe and maintain an official distance in his conversation with him. So, he needs to adopt deferential modes. The communicative situation is related to the issue of fund-raising for the Independence Day celebrations and there seems to be a difference of opinion between the two. Jha, in his utterances, is overtly threatening Sandeep Lahiri's negative face in challenging and interfering in his individual administrative freedom and autonomy without using any redressive device by referring to his own political status and giving orders and even issuing official threat. On the other hand Sandeep Lahiri is trying to protect Jha's negative face by mitigating his face-threatening act of contradicting and disobeying his order in avoiding confrontation and arguments with him adopting a hesitant and indirect deferential mode of expression. Lahiri is exploiting deferential modes to claim immunity from imposition and freedom of action and also to suggest to the speaker (Jha) that though he holds a powerful political status he is not powerful enough to coerce his compliance. Thus deference seems to be a two-sided phenomenon which manifests both in observing compliance and flouting it.

The aggressive conversational behaviour of Jha against a submissive and polite behaviour of Sandeep Lahiri in this extract displays a culture- specific feature related to the expression of disagreements and disapprovals. Indians often tend to see disagreements with another person as a personal matter. That is how Jha's behaviour grew aggressive and ended up in a threat. Frank criticism or expression of disapproval is not typically expressed, unlike Western cultures, in such situations as meetings and conferences, where people of different rank and status are interacting. Thus, a traditional Indian is often surprised, for example, when he sees Americans or British vigorously disagreeing or questioning each other's opinions in a class or conference and then cordially chatting or sharing a drink outside the meeting room. From an early age Western children, it seems, are encouraged to express their opinions, even when these are at variance, with those of their parents, siblings, teachers, and so forth. Disagreement is regarded as an essential element in situations, where information and attitudes are exchanged or discussed, such as meetings or conferences. Indians, motivated mainly by their solidarity- oriented cultural texture, are trained to do the opposite. Thus the tendency for Indians to downplay disagreement can be seen manifested particularly in international conferences, meetings, and seminars. Thus the speech act realizations of this illustration reflect Hudson's (1980:111) sociolinguistic stance which stresses the cultural aspects of speech acts and suggests that speech act categories are cultural concepts, hence are expected to vary from one society to another.

Example Five

Maan:	Nand Kishor! (he shouted.) What are you doing in this gang? Aren't you ashamed of yourself? You're supposed to be a teacher. (Nand Kishor, a middle-aged, bespectacled man, looked sullen.)
A young man:	Shut up– (said the young man to Maan viciously.) Just because you like circumcised cocks do you think we'll let the Mussalman go? (Again he prodded Firoz and drew another smear of blood down his sherwani.)
Maan:	(Maan ignored him and continued to address Nand Kishor. He knew that the time for dialogue was short. It was miraculous that they had been able to speak at all– that they were still alive.) You teach my nephew Bhaskar. He's part of Hanuman's army. Do you teach him to attack innocent people? Is this the kind of Ram Rajya you want to bring about? We're doing no one any harm. Let us go on our way. Come! (he said to Firoz, grabbing him by the shoulder.) Come. (He tried to shoulder his way past the mob.)
The young man:	Not so fast. You can go, you sister-fucking traitor– but you can't (said the young man).

Maan: (Maan turned on him and, ignoring his lathi, caught him by the throat in sudden fury.) You mother-fucker! (he said to him in a low growl that nevertheless carried to every man in the mob.) Do you know what day this is? This man is my brother, more than my brother, and today in our neighbourhood we were celebrating Bharat Milaap. If you harm one hair of my brother's head– if even one hair of his head is harmed– Lord Rama will seize your filthy soul and send it flaming into hell– and you'll be born in your next life as the filthy Krait you are. Go home and lick up your own blood, you sister-fucker, before I break your neck ... (1060-61)

Analysis: The conversational behaviour of the participants in the dialogic transaction under investigation is being directed by the powerful situational factor which is fierce and chaotic and leading to surface the worst in human beings. Due to religious conflict and confrontation between the two processions led by Hindus and Muslims on the occasion of Moharram and Dussehra, which coincided that year, a devastating riot broke out. Muslim mobs were roaming around the city setting fire to Hindu shops and murdering any Hindu they could find. Hindus, on the other hand, were doing the same to Muslims. In the event depicted in this transaction Maan and Firoz were caught by an angry Hindu mob which suspected Firoz to be a Muslim from his dress code and wanted to kill him. Maan is trying to save his Muslim friend from them. The conversation of the young man from the Hindu crowd with Maan is highly offensive causing maximum face costs to both the addressees. As it is a situation of social breakdown, affront, and quarrel the conversational behaviour of the speaker is aggressive, loud, angry, and bombastic. The addressees' face needs and feelings are totally ignored and neglected. To use Lachenicht's (1980:658) view, it's a negative aggravation of "coerce and impinge on hearer", the victims of which are being denied any kind of freedom of action and freedom from imposition and the social personality of the addressee is totally disapproved and shattered. In challenging the addressees in this case the speakers are trying to offend their sensibilities and negative face and are also trying to cause humiliation and physical harm to the hearers. As a defensive effort, in a subdued manner, Maan is also trying to offend the speakers' Hindu beliefs and sensibilities in explicitly challenging them in order to withstand their aggressive behaviour.

This face-destructing conversational behaviour of the participants should be seen as targeted against the community rather than an individual / individuals here. Then the factors of individual power, ranking, and distance become neutral in influencing the facethreatening acts involved in the verbal transaction. It is the situation of civil war that is taking over these factors in guiding the face-threatening activities in the conversational behaviour under consideration.

Conclusion: The present discussion of politeness principle in ASB is restricted to the face management in the inter-personal communication of the interactants. We have discussed here the operation of politeness principle in terms of face work in diverse socio-cultural communicative contexts of mother-daughter talk about the degree of public freedom to girls; of guru-disciple exchange on the issue of showing proper respect for musical instruments; a satirical conversation in an unequal host-guest situation; an official talk between a politician and his subordinate bureaucrat over a power play; and an exchange of arguments between attackers and attacked in a Hindu-Muslim riot situation. In these situations we saw as to how participants in the novel create, build, estimate the cost and benefit lines and maintain and threaten each other's public self-images or faces. The functional explanation of face-saving and face-threatening strategies, as employed by the characters in ASB, entails not only the structure and functions of these strategies but also various personal and socio-cultural factors that determine and influence their use in particular ways.

As has become apparent from this study the character utterances in the novel are sensitive to the social and cultural contexts and the values and the subjective experience of the participants. The whole gamut of inter- personal communication is mainly influenced by these factors. Thus the real significance of the Indian English Fiction under study or any other fiction for that matter cannot be studied, discussed, and appreciated without the correct understanding of the socio-cultural issues involved in the story. Then the most pivotal conclusion takes the form of a pedagogically important recommendation of an urgent need to inculcate and develop the right kind of cultural, textual, and linguistic competence in the students of literature in order to enable them to study and appreciate the discourse patterns in the novel in right perspectives. In order to avoid the pragmatic errors of interpretation that the students may make while studying various aspects of growth and development of characters in the novel, it is most important to include the pragmatic aspects of language use in the courses on literature teaching. To use House and Kasper's (1981:184) argument it seems also important to keep in mind that pragmatic considerations of communication, for example the markers of politeness, are an integral part of the foreign cultural system and should neither be used nor interpreted by reference to one's own native system. Thus, more effective teaching of the behavioural component may minimize native cultural interference and prevent impolite, ineffective, or inappropriate interpretation of the character utterances in the novel.

As for a statement on the limitations of this study, the kind of analysis which has been undertaken here is based on a relatively precise methodology and that a plural approach to conversation analysis of literary texts involving many different sociolinguistic frameworks / models is necessary if one is to capture the richness of character(s).

Works Cited

Blum-kulka, S. and Olshtain, E. (1984). Requests and apologies: A cross-cultural study of speech act realization patterns (CCSSARP). In *Applied Linguistics,*Vol.5, No. 3, 196-213.

Brown, P. and Levinson, S. C. (1987). *Politeness: Some universals in language usage. Cambridge*: CUP.

Flowerdew, J. (1988). Speech acts and language teaching. In *Language Teaching.* (Formerly LTLA), Vol. 21(2), CUP, 69-82.

Goffman, E. (1967). *Interaction ritual: Essays on face-to-face behaviour.* New York: Garden City.

______. (1972). On face-work: An analysis of ritual elements in social interaction. In J. Laver and S. Hutcheson (eds.) *Communication in Face-to-Face Interaction.* Harmondsworth: Penguin, 319: 346.

Grice, H. P. (1975). Logic and conversation. In P. Cole and J.L. Morgan (eds.) *Syntax and Semantics,*Vol. 3, Speech Acts. NewYork: Academic Press, 41-58.

House, J. and Kasper, G. (1981). Politeness markers in English and German. In F. Coulmus (ed.) *Conversational Routine,*Vol. 2, The Hague, The Netherlands: Mouton Publishers, 157-185.

Hudson, R. A. (1980). *Sociolinguistics.* Cambridge: CUP.

Lachenicht, L. G. (1980). Aggravating language: A study of abusive and insulting language. In *Papers in Linguistics: International Journal of Human Communication,* Vol. 13, 607-88.

Lakoff, R. T. (1973). The logic of politeness; or minding your P's and Q's. In *Papers from the Ninth Regional Meeting of the Chicago Linguistic Society,* 292-305.

______. (1975). Language and woman's place. NewYork: Harper & Row.

Leech, G. N. (1977). *Language and tact.* Linguistic Agency, University of Trier, Series A, Paper 46.

______. (1980). Language and tact. In Leech (1980), 79-117. (originally Linguistic Agency, University of Trier,Series A, Paper 46, 1977.)

Seth, V. (1993; rep. 2001). *A Suitable Boy.* New Delhi: Penguin Books.

Strawson, P. F. (1971). *Logico-linguistic papers.* London and NewYork: Methuen.

6

A Study of Patrick White's *Voss* and Its Cultural Elements

A. Sathikulameen

This paper aims to analyse Patrick White's *Voss* and its cultural elements, and its importance which closely linked to the historical past of Australia. There are various themes which are portrayed vividly in the novel which are multifaceted that detach from our humanity constantly: consciously, and through the very processes of living. These themes are of prominence in this novel and of significance for the broader human text. The pure idea of this novel is that, knowledge and change come not from maps but from death by torture in the country of the mind is not simply a personal theme, but the themes connect with the ideas about Australian history, and about history itself, that penetrate throughout the novel.

The novel sets in the nineteenth century Australia, in the period of Ludwing Leichhardt's actual expeditions. Voss is a protagonist, who is a realistic explorer, is the leader of an expedition set up in 1845 to explore the Australian bush, sponsored among other by a wealthy merchant, Mr Bonner. Despite his painful eccentricities and idiosyncrasies, he is similar in many ways to Ludwig Leichhardt, whose company disappeared without trace on his attempt to explore Australian bush in 1848, when they cross Australia from East to West. The writer presents us with the detailed pictures of journey inland from Newcastle to Rhine Towers, from Jildra into the desert, which are impressive and reveal his historical imagination of the time of the colonial Sydney setting. Before the expedition, Voss meets Mr. Bonner's niece, Laura Trevelyan, four times. There is some strange understanding exists between Laura and himself. They are the soul mates, realizing only after he has finally set off that they belong to each other. She is always imaginatively presented both in Sydney and with him as he dies ultimately.

The novel focuses on the mystery of Australia. Voss says that the expedition leads to the perfect understanding of the place which he plans really to explore and develop knowledge:

> Knowledge was never a matter of geography. Quite the reverse, it overflows all maps that exist. Perhaps true knowledge only comes of death by torture in the country of the mind. (White 446)

Voss leaves his expedition, accompanied by Palfreyman, an ornithologist and a rather tortured Christian Le Mesurier, an intense Youngman searching for a purpose in life Harry Robarts, a simple English boy and Turner, a drunken waste. Judd, an ex-convict, and Ralph Angus, a young landowner, joins the expedition later. Each character embodies a different aspect of Christ: Judd has been "tempered in hell". (White 137)

Voss stays initially at Rhine Towers with the Sanderson family and then at Jildra with Boyle. When he stays here, at this particular stage, he writes to Laura proposing marriage, and receives a letter of acceptance. They exchange their pleasantries by the letters. He inspires faith as a leader of his expedition. Both Voss and Judd are tested by the expedition. Judd is assailed by physical longing for his wife and sons, and because he is "wedded to earthly things" (White 243), his dignity is diminished in comparison with Voss's spiritual communication with Laura. The author states that "the desert of mysticism and the transfiguration of Christ are not the fate of the common man". (White 345)

In the midst of the novel, the Bonner's household in Sydney is disrupted by the pregnancy of a maid, Rose Portion. Her character is really mysterious throughout this novel and Laura supports and insists her that the baby should be born at home. As a time progress Rose gives birth to a girl, whom she names Mercy. Laura is very much affectionate towards the baby. Meanwhile, in the midst of Voss's expedition, he has been killed by an Aborigine Jackie who beheads Voss with the knife which was given to Jackie by him. Laura comes to know about Voss and his party by Colonel Hebden. He tells her that Dugald is dead, but that Jackie comes to Jildra sometimes, and that some aborigines had enacted a massacre of horses at Jildra.

Colonel Hebden sets off again to search for Voss and narrowly misses seeing Jackie, who has become possessed by the spirits of the dead Whiteman. Hebden turns back, passing close to the bodies of Angus and Turner, who died of exposure in the desert. Jackie is dying in a swamp on the day, Hebden sets off for home. He is totally confused and he fails to explain the circumstances of his journey. But he says to Laura that he saw Voss dead with a spear in his side, and he also states that Voss was a Christian. In the concluding chapter, Laura concludes her conversation with Ludlow about the history and future of Australia and she says that Australia is talked of as a country with a future, but Ludlow asks when the future becomes the present for Australia. Laura replies with sensational words, "Now.... Every moment that we live and breadth, and love, and suffer, and did"(White 448). She ultimately says that Voss is not dead, but a living legend.

The author seems to sympathize more with Laura, than the character of Voss. But Voss's legend is written down as it is given a kind of immortality by being inscribed in the narrative text. It is the novelist who has been troubled by it and who explores, heroically and ironically, the fundamental ambiguity in Voss:

> Was he god or devil? Success or Failure? Because the narrative is ironic and open-ended it is particularly important not to impose a facile Christian interpretation on his quest, not to interpret it as an exemplification of the simple idea that enters Laura's hallucinated mind about the three stages Of God into Man. Man. And Man returns to God. (White 386)

The last sentence of this novel preserves and gives us the ironic tone of this novel: "By which time she had grown hoarse, and fell to wondering aloud whether she had brought her lozenges"(White 448). The voice of prophecy does not normally report to throat lozenges. Thus, Voss is revealed as the prisoner of his own selfhood who finds only partial release through his heroic encounter with the Australian landscape and through his reluctant and grudging initiation into the selfless world of love through Laura Trevelyan.

The novel represents credible human beings and their experiences on new cultures, and it never hardens into the abstract over simplifications of pure allegory. The implications of this story are very short and specific as well as general. He portrays the human condition as a whole. But he is also very much concerned with the particular problems of his own country. His picture of colonial society in the nineteenth century Sydney is affectionate and at times nostalgia to him. He describes, exactly the trace of the perfect world of colonial gentility, strangely surrounded by mysterious gardens full of feathery bamboos, camellia bushes and scurfy native paper barks and the settings of colonial Sydney is portrayed with the sense of emitting cultural essence.

The people are as convincing as the setting and their character portrayals are splendid. The characters of the Bonners are presented with the strongly physical presence. Massed in the middle is of the Bonners family, the complacent husband, his comfortable wife, their creamy daughter and her rubicund young officer. The author is always able to keep within the limit of what are strictly necessary to his plot, content and design. He loves the pure creative play or flourish. The dowdy town and the easy country around it, against which the harshness of the desert will be measured, are clearly in the reader's mind: the decent average of the population against which the ferociously extreme nature of *Voss* can be tested has been established the relationship of Voss and Laura has been initiated, a relationship which, since they never meet again, is carried on in the imagination of each and opened up to the reader by their correspondence. The members of the group accompanying Voss have been delineated with just that right degree of definition to mark them off as separate persons and yet to loop them, they united in a single party. However, all the preliminary work on the gigantic figure of Voss is carried firmly through.

His narrative form weaves several novelistic forms together. He combines the different forms to create a perfect web, several cultural strains are recognizable: an English strain, a German strain, an aboriginal strain. When he combines all these yarns together, he achieves a multiple cultural identity. He says that he writes taking different forms according to the historical situation in which the fictional action takes place. His manner of presentation is perfect and unmistakable. He starts without preliminary beginning, the intense seriousness of attitude and the effort to describe experience in such a way that the account partaker itself in what it is referring to.

The readers see the dislocation of syntax, the naturally figured narrative, and the employment of modes one tends to think of as more at home in poetry. The language itself is an instrument which establishes in a palpable, solid way, both the character and meaning of Voss, a man who is to be above all outside and beyond the ordinary run of humanity.

The novel also interweaves the different threads of spirituality, while at the same time integrating the Australian land into his textual web. He integrates the discovery of an aboriginal form of spirituality that is the religious beliefs belonging to another culture:

> As (Jackie) placed his hands together, in the shape of a pointed seed, against his own breast, and opened them skyward with a great whooshing of explanation, so that the silky, white soul did actually escape, and lose itself in the whirling circles of the blue sky, his smile was radiant. (White 243)

The author's view of the human being and his world is basically religious. His heroes are often search for the true permanence structure under the illusory change, he says that the true freedom which is valid even beyond physical death. The novel concludes quietly in the third section in a mulled repetition and reminiscence of the positive vision. It is never too firmly or abstractly formulated, but instead generated by the pure substance of the novel. As a religious man, he has not found an answer to his spiritual quest, describing himself as a "lapsed Australian egoist agnostic pantheist occultist existentialist would be failed Christian" (Walsh 117). This is the same as Wilson Harris's "man's dual role is an attribute of being inability, a definite season of time and an infinite exclusion of certain human attributes" (Ibid. 120).

When Patrick White started writing this novel he said that he tried to write on the two planes; the immediate, detailed one and the universal. It is also as expression of his thoughts and ideas, he also so panic at what he saw as the Australian exaltation of the average:

> In all directions stretched the great Australian emptiness in which the mind is the least of possessions in which the rich man is the important man, in which the school master and the journalist rule what intellectual roots there is and the march of material ugliness does not raise aquiver from the average nerves (Walsh 41).

In this novel, he represents the collapse of the imported English cultural model he introduces a plurality of non-English languages, which leads him to raise the question of language and verbal communication and he further weaves the web that integrates several cultures, and anchors it in the geography of the land, its sands, deserts, scrubs, rocks and dead trees, and in the lives of the different inhabitants of the land: aboriginal ethnic groups and convicts. *Voss* is purely a historical novel in the western tradition, showing a process through which a country achieves political independence. At the beginning, Sydney is a part of a colony, which is ruled by a British governor, and at the end, there is a New South Wales Prime Minister. The historical line of evolution goes together with cultural change and a topic to which he shall revert.

The novel begins with an image of pure colonial Sydney, which it builds up over the first half of the novel. Sydney is portrayed with a small town, with only two streets, the countryside not being far off. A concentrated image of colonial Englishness appears on the occasion of the farewell ceremony with Colonel Featherstoodhaugh deputising for the governor at the leave talking:

> Colonel Featherstonehaugh did say many other things. Indeed, when a space had been cleared, he made a speech, about God, and soil, and flag, and our Young Illustrious Queen, as had been prepared for him. The numerous grave and appreciative persons who were surrounding the Colonel lent weight to his appropriate words. There were, for instance, at least three members of the Legislative Council, a Bishop, a Judge, officers in the Army, besides patrons of the expedition, and citizens whose wealth had begun to make them acceptable, in spite of their unfortunate past and persistent clumsiness with knife and fork. Important heads were bared; stiff necks were bent into attitudes that suggested humble attention. It was a brave sight, and suddenly also moving. For all those figures of cloth and linen, of worthy flesh and alone, and the souls tied to them, temporarily, like tentative balloons, by the precious grace of life, might, of that sudden, have been cardboard or little wooden things, as their importance in the scene receded, and there predominated the great tongue of blue water, the brooding, indigenous trees, and sky clutching at all. (White 113)

There are many scenes which offer us a brief glimpse of the social structure of the colony, in which it is possible to become acceptable, which is not the same as respectable, and it's

Englishness, which is overemphasised, also appears to have become threatened even by the natural surroundings. Laura says herself at the end of a novel that it is powerfully charged with the experience, the colour and the significance of Australia itself:

> I am uncomfortably aware of the very little I have seen and experienced of things in general, and of our country in particular. Quite the reverse, it overflows all maps that exist. Perhaps true knowledge only comes of death by torture in the country of the mind. (Walsh: 51)

The main core of the social structure includes the English merchants, prominent among them Mr Bonner, English draper, seen in one place jingling his money and keys and showing off his wealth very desperately. He is leading the life with a considerable bank account and a large house, a wealth, respectable and respected member of the colony. It also includes the Graziers, who form the landowning class, with the suggestion, made in the case of Angus who is a member of the explorers' party, that the so called landowners were originally land grabbers.

The society which is represented in *Voss* is still definitely English in its outlook: it regards England as Home, the old country many have the sense of not belonging in New South Wales they display a traditionally English attitude towards foreigners, in particular towards the German Johann Ullrich Voss, which somehow recalls that of Mr Podsnap's behaviour in Dickens's *Our Mutual Friend.* Yet this colonial society is seen moving away from its Englishness, in particular through their flawed manners: at parties, men may ignore women while talking about sheep, which is their main field of interest during a ball; the guests are seen bursting into the supper-room like hungry animals. It is disgraceful, "laughed Mrs Bonner, that a gathering of individuals from genteel homes should behave like cattle,". (White 326)

This invisible seed-shaped soul which is seen here soaring skywards refers to the souls of all the dead whose, countless multitude inhabits the outback and whose invisible presences float among the aborigines and the explorers. So that, at his death, Voss's soul goes to join the other souls, and becomes part of this community of spirits that hover between sky and land in the heart of the Australian continent. In the cave where Voss discovers, painted on the walls, the main figures of the aboriginal mythology, as wells as "an assembly of tortuous skeletons, bundles and blowing feathers". (White 274) Jackie once again makes the gesture which describes the way the route takes its flights after death and to the image of the soaring seed, Voss associates another image, that of the kites of his childhood, which he watched soaring skywards and sometimes breaking their strings:

> Voss remembered how, as a boy, he had flown kites with message attached to their tails. Sometimes the string would break, and the released kite, if it did not disintegrate in the air, must have carried its message into far places.... So that the walls of the caves were twanging with the whispers of the tangled kites. The souls of the men were only waiting to come out. (White 274-275)

The author had chosen two styles to convey the differences of intention and circumstances of Sydney society on the one hand, and of the members of the expedition on the other: the first less poetic, less self-revealing and more apt for irónic deception the second a language packed with metaphor and projecting the obsessed and fanatic nature of Voss. His achievement is not important in terms of the exploration of Australia, but he confronts the aborigines while exploring Australia. Laura's character gives us the importance of her own perceptions about Australia and in the novel she says that she understands her country:

> Do you know that a country does not develop through the prosperity of a few landowners and merchants, but out of the

> suffering of the humble? I could now lay my head on the ugliest rock in the land and feel at rest (White 239)

Each member of the party obeys the logic of his own nature and responds to the sufferings of the journey in his own way. McAuley sees *Voss* as a story organized around the contrast between the urban society of Sydney and the unexplored Bush: provincial gentility, commercialism, conventional piety, on the one side; on the other, the world of extremes in which concealment and compromises are torn away. Not that Voss relies on this too-simple contrast. It is a novel about "a journey to hell an' back". (White 43)

The novel is also purely about Australia and its national identity and out of a cultural diversity, and his novels often shares a national identity, in a way that recalls the function of the classical epoch, which in the case of Homer, asserts a national Greek identity out of a plurality of City states. The novel is not only contained within the Victorian period, but it also represents a middle class society, its social structures, its manners, in an often comic tone that continues Jane Austen and George Eliot.

The novel is profoundly presented the world of Sydney, for example, is the Bush, 'the country of the mind' (White 475) for Laura. The Bush pictures as inner world that the urban man may enter also "if he has the courage and metaphysical depth to explore his selfhood and his relation to God" (McAuley 36). The conquest of the continent is the outward aspect of Voss's inward expedition "what Voss is dedicated to is the self-deification of man to be achieved in his own person, through boundless will and pride and daring" (Ibid. 38). To be self subsistent, self- sufficient, God requires one to abhor humility and to need no one.

The Aborigines are the one form of humanity which evades the absoluteness of Voss' control. Their existence is surely a passage from moment to moment, hardly directed at all by the conscious will. They drift as easily as smoke and are as responsive to the play of the physical life about them. They cannot in fact be positively separated from it, they never take on sufficient antagonist force for Voss to meet and overcome. Voss is ultimately considered to be the ultimate perception of Australian experience.

In the concluding part of this novel, the readers feel that they see Voss moving from the present into the historical and then into myth. Voss, and a central truth about, or experience of Australia itself has become one. Australia is almost another character in the novel, certainly an impressive and influential force, the complex presence of which affects the organization and the feeling of the novel at many points. Australia is the sold opponent worthy of Voss's will. In reality, for Voss the expedition was a personal wrestling with the continent, the only opponent his pride would acknowledge as adequate. "Deserts prefer to resist history and develop along their own lines"(White 67) they have, that is, a natural hostility to submitting to the will of man and they are, therefore, a proper target for Voss's colossal pride.

The will to know Australia is the initiating impulse of the novel. It is Australia which appears in Laura's letters to Voss as the necessary and mysterious context and passion of Voss himself and he requires to experience the land. To experience here means not only, or not just, external or physical acquaintance. Rather, it is the mode of knowledge possessed by Jackie, the Aborigine who becomes a legend among the ethnic groups: He became a legend amongst the ethnic groups:

> He became a legend amongst the tribes. Of the great country through which he travelled constantly, he was the shifting and troubled mind. His voice would issue out of his lungs, and wrestle with the rocks, until it was thrown back at him. He was always speaking with the souls of those who had died in the land, and was ready to translate their wishes in to dialect (White 448)

The writer bolsters his conceptions that the novel remarkably communicates the human significance of the Australian continent and if the expedition is an apt metaphor for the stresses of human life, then Voss himself becomes a lucent symbol of man and his struggle, because the country and the landscape are evoked with precision and solidity. Voss's complex, flawed and stricken humanity are rendered with marvellous actuality and fullness. White never consumes the vital force in pursuit of utter clarity. But, as soon as one has said this, his skills with kinds of idioms have also to be noted, for example in the third part of the novel where it is most appropriate, where he uses speech remarkable for its elegance and urbanity.

Thus, we can conclude that, various themes of this novel have been explored, such as, the quintessential of everyday: food and hunger, body and soul, the landscape, gender, home-coming, and constructions of the spiritual. These are facets of our humanity that shift over constantly: consciously, and through the very processes of living. They are the themes of prominence in these novels and of significance for the broader human text. The pure idea of this novel is that, knowledge and change come not from maps but from death by torture in the country of the mind is not simply a personal theme, but the themes connect with the ideas about Australian history, and about history itself, that penetrate throughout the novel.

Works Cited

McAuley, James. *Gothic Splendors.* Ed. G.A. Wilkes. Sydney: Allen & Unwin, 1970.

Nikos, Kazantzakis, in a letter to Börje Knös, December 12th 1949, Helen Kazantzakis 1968: 485.

Walsh, William. *Patrick White's Fiction.* London: Allen & Unwin, 1977.

White, Patrick. *Voss.* London: Eyre & Spottiswoode, 1957.

7

Foucault's *Caring for Self*, Korzybski's *Time Binding Force* and the Failure of Aravind Adiga's *The White Tiger*

Sudhir K. Arora

"For what is ethics, if not the practice of freedom, the conscious practice of freedom (284)?" are Foucault's words that truly present the nature of ethics to a great extent. The word 'conscious' before 'practice of freedom' makes a human being feel the value of freedom. Freedom, if enjoyed without feel, takes a man to the kingdom of animals. But, when it is felt within, it directs his conduct that leads to the way of human kingdom. In this paper, Alfred Korzybski's time-binding force is interwoven with Michel Foucault's caring of self for caring others for the true realization of freedom that makes a man a useful being who with his time binding force binds time.

"Man has the capacity of time-biding—he binds time", says Alfred Korzybski. A man who cares for himself and remains confined only to himself without passing the output to others is no better than an animal. To be a human being is not simply to be a human being from outside but from within. If he comes to know his inner being and feels within, he can enjoy freedom in true sense. Such a man will not be a slave of his longings and belongings. But, if he is a slave, no doubt, he can enjoy the pleasures physically but always remains restless from within. Michel Foucault is right when he states: "Taking care of oneself requires knowing oneself. Care of the self is, of course, knowledge of the self—this is the Socratic-Platonic aspect—but also knowledge of a number of rules of acceptable conduct or of principles that are both truths and prescriptions. To take care of the self is to equip oneself with these truths: this is where ethics is linked to the game of truth" (285).

Caring for 'Self' is a prior condition to care for others. How can one care for others until or unless he cares for his own Self. If he takes care of himself properly, to use Michael Foucault, "he will, by the same token, be able to conduct himself properly in relation to others and for others" (287). Such a man is well aware of what others feel. He puts himself in their place and then acts—such act when applied to him may not harm. Using powers over others makes a man significant but how to use them properly qualifies him for being a true human being. Here, "power over oneself" helps in regulating "one's powers over others" (Michel Foucault 288). As a man is gifted with time binding capacity, he believes in "idealization" and never judges human beings with the space-binding force of animals. He knows that "survival in space" leads to "fighting and other brutal forms of struggle" while "survival in time" leads to "intellectual or spiritual competition, struggle for excellence, for making the best survive" (Korzybski 147).

Aravind Adiga in *The White Tiger* has employed the theory of "survival of the fittest" not as time binding force but as space binding force. He does not communicate, rather, barks. Korzybski's words "Those who speak of the "survival of the fittest" as in the Darwinian Theory of animals bark an animal language" (139) applies in Adiga's case. He makes his characters animals that do nothing except binding the space for the sake of their greed, exploitations and animal-like pleasures. Korzybski believes that "there is a vicious implication in using the name of an animal to denote a purely human product" (150). Adiga uses and judges man with the animals' standards. He is a total failure from the viewpoints of Korzybski's theory that propounds: "Animals units and standards are to be applied to animals, human standards to man, "Divine" standards to "God." (151).

Aravind Adiga's *The White Tiger*, as the title suggests, is a tiger of rare species in the form of Barlram Halwai, a man only in name but an animal in his deeds. It is he who believes in survival of the fittest not in time-binding sense but in space-binding sense. Though he seems to propagate the philosophy: "Let animals live like animals; let humans live like humans", he suggests one murder to be a man. How can animals live like animals and humans like humans when humans become animals? He does not understand why "Free people don't understand the value of freedom" (*The White Tiger* 117). What does freedom mean? Does freedom come only after committing murder? He is the only one who understands the value of freedom and so murders his master to be free. He goes to Bangalore where, for him, "the men of this city, frankly speaking are animals" (*The White Tiger* 298). When he gets him settled well, he plans to sell everything to begin an English language school where he will turn children into white tigers that will not learn ethics or religion but only science and technology. What will be the future of such a school and the students that he wishes to produce? For him, relationship is meaningless. What will happen? Is he not leading the state into anarchy where there will be the rule of 'might is right'? Murder a man to become a man. What a philosophy!

He treats his employees as animals, not as human beings. When the work is done, he kicks them out of the office. "no chitchat, no cup of coffee. A White Tiger keeps no friends" (*The White Tiger* 302). He does not call his employees servants because he speaks little. What his tongue cannot do is performed by his leg that kicks the employees as soon as the work is over? What will happen if the drivers follow his example? Is there any guarantee if an ambitious driver may murder Balram Halwai and become the master—the driver of driver's? 'Circumstances make man' gives place to 'man makes circumstances' for an ambitious man. What Balram speaks today will be spoken tomorrow by more powerful white tiger. "Once I was a driver to a master, but now I am a master of drivers" (*The White Tiger* 302). The story of murder will continue.

The school inspector calls Balram the white tiger and, this tiger, with the passage of time, crosses the village jungle to enter the city where he is called "the country mouse" by other drivers. The four landowners who present the view of feudalistic society prevalent at an early stage are Buffalo, Stork, Wild Boar and Raven. Adiga has not called them by their names but by the name of animals because of their animal appetite. The stork's sons Mr Mukesh and Mr Ashok are 'the mongoose' and 'the lamb' respectively. When the white tiger Balram kills the lamb Mr Ashok, he does not feel sorry or shame at the later stage rather he realizes that he "should have cut the Mongoose's neck" (*The White Tiger* 317). Even the whisky is also named after animals like 'Black Dog', 'Royal Stag', 'Wild Horse' etc. Not to talk of wine, even language does not escape from his space-binding force. He uses derogatory words for Urdu: "Some books were in Urdu, the language of the Muslims – which is all just scratches and dots, as if some crow dipped its feet in black ink and pressed them to the page" (*The White Tiger* 253). Is Urdu merely scratches and dots? Is it crow that writes it with its feet in black ink? The crow is nowhere; it is in the mind of Adiga who makes it write such.

As Adiga is ethically bankrupt, he enjoys playing with the religious sentiments. He may be a Marxist or any. He has full freedom to propagate what he wishes but he has no right to do it at the cost of defaming or hurting others' religious feelings. *The White Tiger* is a text that mocks everything—be it religion, politics or social system or human beings. The white tiger is a tiger—an animal in the form of a man but inwardly he is not a human being from any angle.

Gods are not gods for him; rather they seem to be 'arses' for kissing. Touching feet or kissing them is not in his culture. Adiga may be an atheist or a staunch believer in the principles of communism but he has no right to call gods 'arses'. For him, there are 36,000,000 Hindu gods, one Muslim god and three Christian gods making the total of 36,000,004 divine arses, among which he has to choose one. Later, he adds one more name to the list—Buddha when he answers to the question of the inspector about Buddha saying first that he was 'An enlightened man', then, 'An enlightened *god*.' What Adiga writes in bracket is worth-noticing. (Oops! Thirty-six million and five—!) (*The White Tiger* 34). He adds one more name—Buddha—to the list that now has the total of thirty-six million and five. But, what is worth-noticing is the hyphen after the word five. Is he afraid of the Chinese Premier or China where the followers of Buddhism reside? Has he no courage to fill the gap with the word 'arses'. He is a sadist who takes pleasure in hurting others. He is not satisfied with this and, so, makes Balram Halwai ridicule the Muslim bookseller.

He shook his head, but I kept flattering him, telling him how fine his beard was, how fair his skin was (ha!), how it was obvious from his nose and forehead that he wasn't some pigherd who has converted but a true-blue Muslim who had flown here on a magic carpet all the way from Mecca, and he grunted with satisfaction. (*The White Tiger* 253)

What is noticeable here is the way he flatters. He praises him for his beard and fair skin while the reality is that his beard is white and skin is black. Earlier, he describes his face as "a pitch-black face that was bedewed with sweat" (*The White Tiger* 253). The word 'ha' within bracket makes his intention clear that it is not his praise rather it is hatred that he has for the Muslims. To call him that he is a true Muslim who has directly come from Mecca is nothing except the emotional blackmailing. The use of the word 'pigherd' needs no explanation as it reveals the inner pattern of his mind. He commits, to quote Korzybski, "the same kind of blundering as when we intermix phenomena—meaning

"God" by human standards, or human beings by animal standards" (150). Gods are not gods, rather they are politicians who "seem to do awfully little work" and "keep winning re-election to their golden thrones in heaven, year after year" (*The White Tiger* 8).

Do Indians think of beak, arse, boobs, women's begging for dipping beak? or Is it Adiga's brain that gets erected and begin to work? The beak is in the brain. This is his beak that makes him see arses of 36,000,004 gods. When will the White Tiger kiss gods' feet in place of arses? He has his ready-made suggestion for curing any disease whether of body or mind through dipping the beak into a virgin? His sex market has earned a high profit. He has changed the previously script developing the body of culture into the culture of the body. Thanks to the boom of consumerism that has turned the world into postmodernism where everything is for sale. One day, when the tiger becomes old, he will be forced to think because of his approaching death that the beak is only a means of releasing lust that turns a man into an animal. What counts is man. Certainly, in old age, the beak of white tiger will become weak to the extent that it will not be able to colour the forbidden landscape. Then, "the beak into anything" will become "the beak into nothing" and out of this nothing, he will take out something which will give him a meaning to his life.

Adiga's *The White Tiger* is a total failure from the animal ethics. None but animal will like to feel such pleasure out of sheer selfishness that does not take others' selves into consideration. He has applied animal standard to human standard and the result is an atmosphere that creates greed, war, struggle and class differences. "Applying animal standard to time-binding beings", for Korzybski, is "like applying inches to measuring weight" (147). This is what Adiga has done in *The White Tiger* that justifies animal logic which ultimately results in "animal ethics and animal economics" (148). That's why the cunning white tiger keeps on fattening on "the living of the fruit of the dead" (148). The fruit in red bag containing cash makes him enjoy the pleasures that he wished to enjoy. But, there is no guarantee that the pleasures that he enjoys may remain with him as some other strong tiger may kill or snatch what he has gained out of selfishness. His freedom is short-lived because it is not according to the "ethos of freedom" which makes "a way of caring for others" (Michel Foucault 287). He abuses power and misuses his freedom in order to impose his own "fantasies, appetites, and desires on others" (Michel Foucault 288). This tiger longs for mastering over others without mastering over himself and hence fails to feel freedom in real sense though he enjoys freedom without inner satisfaction. If the white tiger, Balram had not taken care of himself properly, he would have never exercised his dominating power over others.

"Korzybski believes:" The fittest in time—those who make the best survive—are those who do the most in producing values for all mankind including posterity" (148). But, the white tiger has done nothing that may make him known to the mankind. He takes freedom as a license while the truth is that freedom is neither "license" nor "licentiousness". "Freedom", to quote Korzybski, "consists in lawful living —in living in accord with the laws of human nature—in accord with the natural laws of Man. (154).

Adiga has used "survival of the fittest" in Darwinian way that leads to the animal world that believes in space binding. His protagonist is not time-binder as he kills his master to encroach space. "I was blind. I was free" (*The White Tiger* 286). He is blind to time but quite awake to space where he enjoys his unlawful living. He is blind to ethics which approves the lawful living. The Darwinian specs make him see "the fittest" as "the strongest." When will the white tiger know that "survival of the fittest" means "best in science and art and wisdom" which is "a natural law for mankind, the time-binding class of life" (Korzybski 154)? Who will make him understand that the true freedom lies in being the master of self that cares for others and true pleasure is within which can be felt only when one knows himself properly. Who will tell him that true happiness is not in encroaching others' happiness but in giving happiness? When will he translate Foucault's 'Caring for Self' and Korzybski's 'Time Binding Force' in reality? Who will make him learn the new mantra: "Know what your true self is; come out of your space that binds you to selfishness; bind time with your rightful acts and then you will feel light of freedom that makes you radiant to the extent that others may enjoy what you feel"? He chants "murder and be a man", the only mantra that tempts him to bind space for caring his own self at the cost of others. He is merely a white tiger and will remain so. Hence, Aravind Adiga's *The White Tiger* proves to be a total failure when Korzybski's time-binding force and Foucault's caring for self are applied to it as touchstones.

Works Cited

Adiga, Aravind. *The White Tiger*. New Delhi: HarperCollins, 2008. Print.

Korzybski, Alfred. "Survival of the Fittest." *Manhood of Humanity: The Science of Engineering*. New York: E. P. Dutton and Company, 1921: 139-154. Print.

"The Ethics of the Concern of the Self a Practice of Freedom." *Michel Foucault: Ethics Subjectivity and Truth (Essential Works of Foucault 1954-1984 Volume I)*. Ed. Paul Rabinow. The New Press, 1994: 281-301. Print. (This interview was conducted by H. Becker, R. Fornet-Betancourt, and A. Gomez-Muller on January 20, 1984.)

8

Contextualising Aravind Adiga's *The White Tiger* in Postcolonial Paradigm

Bhagabat Nayak

Arvind Adiga's *The White Tiger* is an excoriating portrayal of the postcolonial realities of India. It is a moral biography of his protagonist who makes a long journey from a remote village in Bihar to the city of Bangalore. This presents how the proletarian yahoos are exploited by the capitalist houyhnhnms in postcolonial capitalist India.

The novelist projects India as a divided nation into 'Rich India' and 'Poor India', and attacks her economic miracle and rise as a global power. In the self of a sociologist, psyche of an economist, and spirit of a humanist he focuses the crude realities of India's socio-economic growth. Focusing on the realities of shining India he attacks her failure to establish democratic socialism. The capitalist mission of the rich helps them to exploit the poor that makes India a faltering nation.

The novelist is serious about the condition of the poor due to India's rise as a global power. India's alround progress without eradicating poverty is the authorial concern that disturbs the sociologists, politicians, economists and policy makers. He believes that this is a kind of internal colonialism in which his protagonist desperately fights for his existence. The rise of the rich and capitalist class in metropolitan cities and progress in industrial and IT sectors do not define the real progress of India.

The protagonist's movement from his native village to Delhi and Bangalore is a soul searching mission in an emancipatory zeal. While the protagonist murders his master it sounds like the story of crime and punishment but the nemesis reveals that the subaltern protests only to end his subalternity. A postcolonial reading of the novel reveals the difference between common man's imagination of India during freedom movement and her growth as a global power in the recent times.

Analysing a text critically in a theoretical context is often called textual politics in postcolonial theory. One can not avoid this politics while reading a text as it is necessary for the 'worldliness' of text. Postcolonialism / Post-colonialism does not mean only where the story of colonialism ends rather where the ruled and colonised self revolts and colludes with the imperialist self in the status of 'other' or in voicelessness. Aravind Adiga's *The White Tiger* (2008), the Man Booker Winner of the year, has drawn rave reviews better than his first book *Between the Assassinations* can be read as a postcolonial text from different perspectives. Focusing on the realities of two Indias —the India imagined during the freedom movement; and India, the growing global power for her economic miracle Adiga expresses his concern for the attitude of the rich towards the poor that makes India a faltering nation. He believes that class system is a major obstacle for the establishment of democratic socialism as it promotes inequality and divides Indian society on economic line. With India's independence Western colonialism has come to an end historically but internal colonialism of the rich in the form of economic exploitation has a spurt. There is no constitutional and conscientious support for this but the rich in their capitalist mission exploit the poor for their selfish desire.

Adiga's novel is a counter to the optimistic tales of India's roaring economy. It presents his anger against India's class system that creates a vast underbelly. Narrating India's class system that divides the Indian society he presents how the rich promote a colonial type oppression in their hegemony. The rich and poor are in an economic and emotional 'contact zone' that establishes 'Lordship and Bondage' relationship. In India's civilisational plenitude the poor are still treated as Calibans in George Lamming's paradigm. Narrating some fundamental problems of the backward classes in an epistolary form of the novel Adiga presents some 'unremitting realism' in his attempt to relocate India in colonial past and postcolonial context. The novel is a work of cynicism from certain angles for its less orientalist views and "lampooning the middle class who are, regardless of the tired accusations about "writing for the foreign market" (Overdorf 64). Narrating the moral biography of his protagonist, Balram Halwai he presents this "tedius, unfunny slog" and his "schoolboyish sneering" (Manjula Padmanabhan's expressions) in an excoriating manner. In spite of its uncomfortable reception at home the novel draws the attention of our policy makers who lacks constructive outlook to improve the condition of India's vast underbelly and underclass. Adiga not only presents them through the suffering of his protagonist but also expresses their simmering anger though him. The poor in India are still a colonised lot, their life and sacrifice is never canonised in nation's politics. Their socio-economic set up is such that this does not decolonise their mind rather it keeps them in a "spiritual subjugation" (Thiong'O 9).

In his letters to the Chinese Premier, Wen Jiabao on his visit to Bangalore, Balram Halwai presents his 'secular criticism' about India's class division that generates colonial oppression and promotes a social disparity on the basis of economy. The irony is that when India was colonised Indian mind was decolonised but when their body is decolonised mind is colonised in Hegelian phenomenology of master-servant relationship. Adiga is not a Marxist, nor a Naxalite nor he likes the Facist attitude of his protagonist but as a realist he projects the claustrophobic effect of poverty in human life. Presenting the facts about India he holds "a mirror to realities" (Deshpande 1) which we refuse to accept. Balram's letters to Jiabao appear to be Adiga's "secret, uncensored articles" (*Outlook* 64). The poor in India are presented as the

Fanonian 'wretched of the earth' for its class and caste structures. The rich have an amnesia for India's colonial past and the poor are not in a "will to forget' their traditional loyalty to their landlords and rich masters for their economic dependence that creates a "dreadful secondariness" (Said 207) in them. Focusing on the socia-economic and political condition of Bihar in the metaphor of 'Darkness' he gives an oblique reference to pan-Indian situation. In his reportorial narration his "characters at the colourful extremities of society are Dickensian grotesques ... adrift in a country that is lurching rapidly towards bland middleclass normality" (Suri 63).

In his fictional presentation Adiga expresses his concern for the colonial bent of mind of the rich and the psychic inferiority of the poor in their loyality to them. Poverty makes his protagonist a neurotic sort in an inferiority complex. Adiga is not happy to see India's slowness in eradicating poverty, malnutrition and common diseases that makes the life of the poor miserable. He presents how the poor live in subjugated and often in 'deterritorialised' condition. The poor as internal diasporas migrate to different cities in search of work and the rich as a ruling class become corrupt, venal and make the ruled class desperate and 'brazenly cannibalistic' in their imperialist attitude.

The novel appears to be a tourist's account on two Indias —the India that 'shines' and the India that 'unlits'. The India that shines in her corporate and industrial world is countered with her poverty and filth in villages and city slums where his protagonist Balram Halwai, the son of a rickshaw-puller grooms his career first as a chauffeur in Delhi and then an entrepreneur of driving technology in Bangalore. Vijay Nair rightly remarks:

> *The White Tiger* traverses the familiar territory of class and caste divide, poverty and exploitation and the triumph of the human spirit that one expects in a book that unfolds from a place called "Darkness" in Bihar and draws its protagonist from an impoverished family of rickshaw pullers who were in the business of making sweets before fate intervened (2).

Balram's life story is "The Autobiography of a Half-baked Indian" (10). He is a man from the Darkness where poor struggle in their life as rickshaw-pullers, taxi-drivers, coal miners. slum dwellers, pimps, ragpickers, vendors and beggers in different cities and metropolitan centres. He is proud of his native village Laxmangarh in the heart of darkness in Bihar where Ganga flows and Buddha had his birth and enlightenment. In Adiga's view the Ganga is not a fabled river which is decolonised from the Ganges to Ganga by T.S. Eliot but in his protagonist's view it is a living inspiration to Indian mind, psyche and belief. In existential reality and spatial suffering Balram's life story becomes a divine tragedy with the murder of his conscience. In the horrors of poverty Balram enjoys its debasing effect. His jorney from his village Laxmangarh to Dhanbad to Delhi to Bangalore does not bring any respite rather it presents the bleak realities of life in his working class status. The growing inequality between the rich and poor matters much for the social disharmony. In ambition and impatience the poor often gain some worldly wisdom. As millions migrate from their villages to Dhanbad, Gaya, Calcutta and Delhi Balram begins his picaresque journey from Laxmangarh and ends it in Bangalore. Adiga expresses his concern for the suffering of the poor, servants, drivers, gardners, cooks and people of lower ranks who obey their employers as the "way dogs understand their masters"(112).

Poverty is the worst kind of evil that mocks at postcolonial India's "marvels of democrary" (103). When India's policy makers boast of her economic success in corporate world and outsourcing of knowledge millions still remain poor, illiterate and live as slum dwellers. Balram's life and career, ambition, despair, loyalty, faithfulness and radical thinking not only present the fate of the exploited masses in the Darkness but also the schemy, corrupt and selfish nature of the rich. In Manichean allegory while the poor remain loyal to the rich in their economic dependency the rich confront the poor in their political and economic imperatives. The poor in the Darkness live below the povertyline, suffer from typhoid, cholera and many common diseases. They do not have sufficient schools for education, hospitals for treatment and roads for communication. Narrating the political scenario during election in the Darkness Adiga presents how the poor villagers fall victim to crafty and schemy politicians. These villagers fail to understand the political manifestoes of the politicians and discuss about their political ambition "like eunuchs discussing *Kama Sutra*"(98). The crafty politicians attract the young minds with their encouraging words, "We need more boys to come back and build India into a superpower" (104). The landlords also form a party, the All India Social Progressive Front and promise the people good roads, clean water, good hospitals etc. As a whole the politicians do not follow the philosophy of India's great leaders nor believe in India's great political tradition. Instead of doing populist politics they demonstrate public support for them by bringing truck loads of people from different places to their meetings for a political milage. They talk about Gandhian idealogy and their Nehruvian dreams but in reality they camouflage their selfish motives and work without ethics.

The novel is a mordant critique of "India Rising". It presents the brutal reality of a political and economic system that allows a small minority to prosper at the expense of a silent majority. In an investigative way the novelist presents India's economic miracle that helps the rich to lead a luxurious and comfortable life, and makes the poor cynical about their fate. The ever widening gap between the rich and poor exposes the rot in the three pillars of modern Indian democracy, enterprise and justice. Balram Halwai is called the White Tiger from his childhood for his right answer to the school inspector's question_"What is the rarest of animals —the creature that comes along only once in a generation?"(55) in any jungle. In the human jungle of Darkness Balram really appears as a White Tiger and tries to fulfil his father's ambition by learning reading and writing. He remembers his father who had a desire not to see him as "a human beast of burden"(27) and live on adulterated items for which children fail to maintain UN standard nutrition and grow with oversized heads. In the Darkness the future of the villagers is in the hands of the landlords and Naxals who are in eternal rivalry. He observes the acute economic disparity between the rich and poor that divides India. Balram is shocked to realise that "The story of a poorman's life is written on his body, in a sharp pen"(27). His shifting of career from his family occupation and father's profession to be a driver is just for a better life without any motive hunting malignity. He knows that ambition makes the postcolonial Indians dreamy with their "new ways of living and thinking" (Lyotand 90) but the millions of poor in their economic dependence fail to dream and feel life dull and dreary. His observation of class division at village teashop where the rich and high castes are offered plastic chairs; and low castes, rickshaw pullers and daily wage earners sit on the ground in squatting position terribly shocks him. Balram realises that poverty is the sole cause of their 'inferior rank' and this revolts his conscience. He is determined to fight against this inequality as the last man of Darkness.

Caste-based occupation still plays a great role in Indian society. In India's socio-political dynamics, cultural hybridity and globalised economy caste is not totally a forgotten concept. In rural economy it decides a person's fate and future. Equality irrespective of caste, creed and religion often sounds a misnomer due to India's traditional caste system. Balram's caste and occupation make him a subaltern. He can not make himself free from the caste prejudices of the rich whose caste based economy and landlordship help them to assert their economic and political hegemony. The landlords whom the villagers call Buffalo, Stork, Wild Boar, Mongoose and Raven, all in animal names refer to their real nature. Balram thinks that these landlords believe in Benthamite philosophy without having Kantian maturity to think good, be good and do good in universal ways. They can neither be the saviours of the poor nor they can do any miracle for them like the messianic harbingers. While the rich treat the poor in a 'hostile delirium', the poor enjoy the debilitating effect of poverty in silence. The rich rule them for their subordination because they have the full control over economy.

Narrating the neo-colonial scene in Bihar Adiga reminds us about India's colonial past when imperial control over economy was making the nation a slave. Partha Chatterjee rightly remaks "Postcolonial study implies to the structure of power. Its politics impel it to open up that framework of knowledge that presumes to dominate it, to displace that framework, to subvert its authority, to challenge its morality" (42). For Balram, "If postcolonility is to be reminded of its origins in colonial oppression, it must also theoretically urged to recollect the compelling seductions of colonial power" (Gandhi 4). He makes his journey from the land of Darkness to the cities of dazzles with an emancipatory zeal. But to his disillusionment he finds everywhere:

> Power is employed and exercised through a net like organisation. And not anly do individuals circulate between its threads ; they are always in the position of simultaneously undergoing or exercising their power. They are not only its inert or consenting target ; they are also the elements of its articultion. In other words, individuals are like vehicles of power, not its points of application (Foucault 98).

After his coming to Dhanbad and Delhi Balram fails to liberate him from his rich master Ashok and his wife Pinky Madam. In Delhi's metropolitan life he finds how the rich set 'Rooster Coops' for the poor drivers, cooks, gardners, ragpickers, slumdwellers and wage earners in which they can neither revolt nor can escape from it. He remains loyal, faithful and obedient to his master and his American wife and drives them in a Honda City to different public places, five star hotels, shopping malls and then back to their Gurgaon apartment. Sitting idle at the parkings he observes the fate of his fellow drivers who call him a 'village idiot' and a 'country mouse' in their seniority of living in the city. Balram shares his shock with them in the status of 'other' and enjoys life like them in the apartment dormitories and waits to attend his master.

In Delhi's civilisational plenitude and depravity Balram becomes a polemical critic of the rich and resists the hegemony of his master. He marks the differences of life when the rich live in Delhi's expensive flats, ride air conditioned cars, visit five star hotels and shoppings malls; and the poor mostly the beggars, vendors, slum dwellers live under overbridges, on the pavements and in the slums. The same difference he had found in his village where the rustics "go out to the fields with blackened sickles, begging one landlord or the other for some work" (27). In Delhi he observes the condition of drivers who wait for their master at the parking zones in churning stomachs or denied entry into the shopping malls for wearing sandals. In Delhi's entrepreneurial world he finds poverty and inequality in acute form. He interrogates the makers of modern India's glorious parliamentary democracy in their postcolonial success. This does not mean that Balram has no love for his country, countrymen and her success. He expresses his unhappiness over India's poverty, inequality; and futility of honesty and loyalty in life.

Balram writes to Jiabao that the Indians have a rare quality of entrepreneurship which the Chinese do not have but he appreciates China as a freedom loving nation. In a note of appreciation he writes, "(You) Chinese are great lovers of freedom and individual liberty. The British tried to make you their servants but you never let them do it"(5). After his reading of *Exciting Tales of the Exotic East* he has come to know that the other freedom loving nations are Abyssinia and Afghanistan which have never let themselves to be ruled by the forigners. He is unhappy that India has a failed past record to defend the exploiters for which millions like him are being toiled in slavery in their postcolonial status. His poverty promotes his faithfulness and faithfulness leads him to slavery in the tradition of an honest servant. Like servant-god Hanuman in Indian myth he expresses his loyalty to his master and carries him and his wife like Rama and Sita. The irony is that Lord Rama allowed Hanuman to be loved by his followers and worshipped by his devotees but his master Ashok falsely implicated him in a murder case which Pinky had caused in a road accident. His master compels him for a 'forced confession' of his crime on a legal paper. Now Balram apprehends that he will be sent to Tihar Jail for no fault and his family will toil in poverty for ever.

Balram knows that rich in Delhi are "citified fellow of debauchery, depravity and wickness" (197). He never believes that his master will be such a hypocrite to fleece him for his interest. In a pessimistic outlook he imagines that "The greatest thing to come out of this country in ten thousand years of its history is the Rooster Coop" (173) in which he waits for his fate. Mapping the metropolitan sociology and psyche of the rich and poor the novelist makes his protagonist a "human spider" (52). Faithlessness in the mutuality of master-servant relationship turns Balram into an intimate enemy of his master. In a combat mood he interrogates his colonial authority who conducts his power within multiple social relationship. He desires to liberate his colonised self in ethical inadequacy and escape from the 'Rooster Coop', "The capital of this glorious nation. The seat of Parliament of the president of all ministers and prime ministers. The pride of our civil planning. The showcase of the republic" (118). In Delhi's dazzles he finds roads are good, people are bad, police are rotten, drivers are worst and becomes cynical about Indian politics and politicians for their double-speak nature. He dislikes their craving for power without any ideological transparency. Balram develops a kind of disenchantment for Delhi. For him Delhi is no more a crazy city. Like Balram the poor have a "pessimistic perspective about India" (White 237). In Delhi's cultural hybridity, entrepreneurial economy and corrupt politics Balram finds the withering of basic human values in life.

Balram is a caste and class subaltern. His dependence on his master for his poverty does not allow him to speak against the injustice done to him. He thinks that the British have left India for good giving the charge of "Men with Small Bellies" to the "Men with Big Bellies" (64). The rich exploit the poor establishing a political and economic imperialism in the 'sign' of power. In Darkness the rich have a number of criminal cases in their names. Even they are convicted for murder, rape, grand larceny, gun smuggling and pimping yet they continue to be the ministers and claim to be the great socialists. During election the politicians in the Darkness organise special pujas, distribute mutton biryani infront of temples and seek public blessings for votes. As the leaders lack essential anxiety of Indianness in their values, tradition and culture the common men drift away from the mainstream of nationlism. This gives rise to separatist elements who get attracted for new political isms, smuggle Chinese bombs and plan to raise a civil war. The fate of judiciary often becomes miserable. Narrating the fate of judiciary in Ghaziabad court Balram writes to Jiabao :

> The judge gave an order that the lawyers didn't like, and they simply refused to accept his order. They went mad—they dragged the judge down and beat him, in his court. The matter was not reported in the press ... If people start beating the judges—in their own courtrooms— that what is the future for our country? (215).

If the rich and power-charged people become dishonest, immoral and selfish how long the poor can serve them as their servants. The poor cannot remain silent. Balram in his emancipatory zeal and ethical disenchantment slits his master's throat. His ungratefulness may have cathartic effect but it is a pragmatic necessity in his frustrated psyche. He has asserted his Spivakian claim for right. Murdering his master he liberates him from slavery. The novelist sanctions him a relief in postcolonial belief, "If the subaltern can speak then, thank God, the subaltern is not a subaltern any more" (Spivak 158).

Balram's murder of his master and running away with his bag of money brings an ending to the story of internal colonialism. In the deconstruction of his postcolonial status Balram realises that unless he ends his ethical and philosophical obligation to his master in an emancipatory zeal and 'triumpant utopianism' he cannot end his suffering. He realises that his poverty causes self-subalternisation and faithfulness has no use as this does not improve his life. He indigenises his inherited and acquired ethical gospels in a disenchantment to decolonise his mind. In postcolonial / postnational ethics he realises that the moral doctrines one learns from his family, tradition and subjugated life can help a person to be a divine being but it is not for his well-being. Ashok's attempt to implicate him in the crime of murder changed Balram's concept of loyalty, faithfulness and obligation. He likes no more to be a historical subject in the model of a loyal servant but in implacable enmity with his master he liberates his subaltern self.

> Decolonisation is the meeting of two forces, opposed to each other by their very nature .... Decolonisation is the veritable creation of new men ... the primary Manicheism which governed colonial society is preserved intact during the period of decolonisation; that is to say, the settler never ceases to be the enemy, the opponent, the foe that must be overthrown .... The immobility to which the native is condemned can only be called into question if the native decides to put an end to the history of colonisation—the history of pillage—and to bring into existence the history of the nation - the history of decolonisation, (Fanon30, 40-41).

Theorising nation as an identity Balram continues his struggle with India's caste, class and religious conflicts. The role of the ruling class, the privileged category and the politicians is so dubious that they demean India. He writes to Jiabao with regret that "The people of this country had a chance to put an efficient ruling party back in power, and instead they have voted in the most outrageous bunch of thugs" (280).

Bangalore is the technology paradise that prepares India for twentyfirst century. Balaram prefers this city to start his career as an entrepreneur with his late mater's money. In India's Silicon

Valley he invests his master's money which he had saved to bribe the politicians for evading tax. He invests that money in driving technology and ends his claustrophobic career. He desires liberation in a painful introspection that ends his master's bandit-mode for ever. His entrepreneurship in driving technology is an attempt to decolonise his mind. In a revolting conscience he believes if power is the means of conquest for his master he has the right to resist it psychologically. He renounces his traditional virtues and resists Ashok's capitalist rapacity. He becomes less emotional but more objective about his future. In Hegelian 'mutuality, master-servant relationship' is a philosophical elaboration but it does not allude him to be a rational being. His desire to be an entrepreneur in Bangalore with his master's money expresses his ingratitude in a weak-willed decision. As a subaltern he can not speak but revolt in silence. He believes if power asserts hegemony his ingratitude assures his emancipation. In existential reality a slave cannot live in non-aligned condition with his master because of his economic and other methods of dominance in capitalist psyche and political hegemony. He is motivated to raise a war against these civilised savages for whom millions like him toil in subordination. While his ethics makes him loyal to his master conscience makes him seductive to have a therapeutic retrieval from his 'dreadful secondariness'. Balram's psycological tenacity is a pathological outcome in his postcolonial thinking and his murder to his master is an attempt to end his master's imperialist hegemony.

Balram, the member of a Halwai family is supposed to make gulab *jamuns* and sweet pastries becomes an entrepreneur in India's Silicon Valley. He had gone to Delhi to make his fortune. As he found nothing good about his country and about his life he moves next to Bangalore. In Delhi he was fed up with human nature, character and selfishness. He believes that one's destiny is not delivered but deserved. In the neo-colonial policy of the rich, the poor cannot rise in their economic 'weightlessness' but in political disenchantment they have to search for an alternative.

In an expectation and confrontational psyche Balram Halwai can't get rid of the blood stains on his conscience. His personal guilt of realizing his ambition through murder—turns political and morally bankrupt man confesses to Chinese premier Wen Jiabao, telling the story of his rise from the swamp of Silicon Valley. But it becomes the story of the darkness that is India, ..." where the new economy means shiny call-centre workers still in air conditioned towers overlooking filthy shanties, and where an entrepreneur can survive the slime and grime of bureaucracy only by greasing palms" (Saxena 12).

In Bangalore he practises yoga to make his fugitive self stress-free. He finds Bangalore, the city of outsourcing famous for "doing things in India for Americans over the phone. Everything flowed from it—real estate, wealth, power, sex ... one way or the other" (298). He finds here how the highly qualified persons have become slaves to a rich country and become victims to its neo-colonial policy. The Bangaloreans live like the animals in a forest do. They "Sleep in the day and then work all night ... because their masters are on the other side of the world in America" (298).

Bangalore provides a new identity to Balram. After murdering his master he has snatched away his name. He is known as Ashok Sharma instead of Balram Halwai in Bangalore's entrepreneurial world. This may be an attempt to keep himself away from the police net but it expresses his victory over his coloniser and colonised self. Balram establishes his driving technology in the name of his late master and manages his driving business with drivers, vehicles, garages, mechanics and a silver Macintosh laptop. His late master's entrepreneurial strength is a no match to Balram's survival instinct. One can think him of becoming neurotic but in reality Balram becomes heuristic to liberate himself. If the master was Hegelian in the self-realisation of good Balram becomes Nietzchean, good with power now in his personal imperatives. Expressing a rational outlook for his crime he philosophises the history of Alexander the Great, Abraham Lincoln of America, and Mao of China who liberated themselves by killing their masters. Balram wanted to rise in his career graph. In a radical ideology and rationalist philosophy he thinks that Gandian protest has emotional advantage but it will not help the poor to rise at par with the rich in India's postcolonial space.

With the information on All India Radio Balram comes to know about Jiabao's visit to Bangalore next week. He prepares himself to project "moral and saintly India" (4) and her secular fabric before Jiabao where the Hindus believe in 36,000,000 gods, Muslims worship one and Christians worship three. Many like him are not educated enough but think wisely like great poets Rumi, Iqbal, Mirza and Ghalib. Viewing Balram's concept of religion, belief and practice Adiga narrates about the economy and political hegemony which plays an important role in the tolerant and secular view of the Indians in their postcolonial reality. In his view India is a funny country where people like Buddha and Gandhi are born, parliamentary democracy is popular, entrepreneurs take "technology like ducks to water" (12) and invent "hard-boiled eggs to space-ships" (173) on the internet; landlords who bear animal names of Buffalo, Stork, Wild Boar, Mongoose and Raven exploit the people; and millions like Balram serve their masters with loyalty or in impatience slit their masters' throats.

When India shines with the prospects of her globalised economy, the reality affects her dazzles for its defective economic planning that promotes a great social divide enabling one section to rise with exploitation, corruption and wickedness; and the other to be the victims of it. Adiga is not hopeful enough with 'India Rising' and questions in his narrative device how long Indian economy will exist on the outsourcing of knowledge. In negative capability he believes that loyalty, faithfulness and gratitude may be virtues in human life but in postcolonial world money and power demean them. One can not achieve his freedom from slavery with these traditional virtues.

Although the novel is written in non-fictional prose it is a worthwhile discourse on postcolonial theory in which man's eternal struggle for existence and quest for liberation is expressed in a realistic way. Adiga's White Tiger (Balram Halwai) though poor and lives in capitalist's 'Rooster Coop' he has an eternal desire to escape from it. Munna alias Balram alias Ashok Sharma thinks that "There's no end to things in India" (320). He sacrifices his virtues, and escapes from the 'Rooster Coop' for new possibilities in life. His escape deals with the sensitive effects of the history of colonisation. His slitting of his master's throat is the beginning of the decolonising process of mind of the poor. He is happy with India's great leaders like Gandhi who made India free from colonial chains but unhappy with his successors today who promote exploitation through an internal colonisation. In self-willed amnesia for the past and 'triumphant utopianism' for the future he transcends the boundary of 'contact zone' between him and his master and escapes in a psychological recovery and "conscious unified revolutionary self" (Parry 1987:30). Avoiding police and hangman's noose he dreams to become an entrepreneur, marry, have children, and groom his future. He translates his future plans in his letter to Jiabao:

> After three or four years in real estate, I think I might sell everything, take the money, and start a school —an English language school —for poor children in Bangalore. A school where you won't be allowed to corrupt anyone's head with prayers and stories about God or Gandhi—nothing but the facts of life for these kids. A school full of White Tigers, unleashed on Bangalore! We'd have this city at our knees ... I could become the Boss of Bangalore (319-320).

The revolt of his incorruptible self and murder of his master is an attempt to dismantle the science of imperialism in postcolonial discourses. This gives a clarion call to India's politicians, policy makers, sociologists and reformers for the ending of a jungle law and establishing a civil society for the promotion of democratic socialism.

Adiga cautions that the capitalist imperialism in India will frustrate the poor and these proletarian yahoos can liberate themselves from the capitalist houyhnhnms for their rights. Inequality never provides liberty but liberty is necessary for an egalitarian society. He criticizes the politicians and policy makers of India who think in Orwellian sense, "all animals are equal, but some animals are more equal than others". Adiga's excoriating portrayal of postcolonial India presents some aspects of realism in Orwell's *Animal Farm* not in fabular way but in Fabian way. If the rich favour capitalism in imperialistic way and the poor in sheer animalism believe—"Remove man (the capitalist master) from the scene, and the root cause of hunger and overwork is abolished for ever" (Orwell 11)—then instability will make India a faltering nation.

Postcolonialism had its emotional beginning before India's independence, historical beginning after independence and theoretical beginning in late 1970's. All the postcolonial Booker winning Indian novelists have expressed this 'underclass anger' in their novels. While Salman Rushdie's *Midnight's Children* (1981) presents the 'growth of pangs' with India's birth as a new nation with her social and political upheavals ; Arundhati Roy's *The God of Small Things* (1997) unveils India's regressive 'caste chains': Kiran Desai's *The Inheritance of Loss* (2006) presents the world of exploiter and the exploited in a turbulent socio-political movements; Aravind Adiga's *The White Tiger* exposes real India with her rich and poor divide. Adiga is neither cynical nor pessimistic in his vision. In his fictional presentation he not only highlights India's glory but also castigates her vices which foster caste and class system. The novel as an "emancipatory narrative" (Parry 2004 :7) deconstructs India in her post-nation theory. Lack of a strong plot and the narrative style in the manner of a political essay do not obstruct its artistic beauty. Reading the text of the novel is like an apolitical re-reading of postcolonial theory in protagonist's existential reality.

Works Cited

Adiga, Aravind. *The White Tiger*. New Delhi: Harper Collins Publishers, 2008. (All textual references are from this edition).

Chatterjee, Partha. *Nationalist Thought and the Colonial World: A Derivative Discourse?* London : Zed Books, 1986.

Deshpande, Shashi. "Debating Spaces". *The Hindu Literary Review*. 132:5 February 1, 2009.

Fanon, Frantz. "Concerning Violence". *The Wretched of the Earth* (1961). (Trans) Constance Farrington. London: Macgibbon and Kee, 1965.

Foucault, M. *Power/Knowledge : Selected Interviews and Other writings 1972-1977*. Ed. Colin Gordon. Hertfordshire: Harvester Press, 1980.

Nair, Vijay. *The Hindu Literary Review*. 132:1, January 4, 2009.

Orwell, George. *Animal Farm: A Fairy Story* (1945). Harmondsworth: Penguin Books, (rpt) 1981.

Overdorf, Jason. "The Alleged Booker Prize". *Outlook* : 48:43 October 27, 2008.

Parry, Benita. "Problems in Current Theories of Colonial Discourse". *Oxford Literary Review* 9: 1-2. 1987: 27-58.

______. *Postcolonial Studies: A Materialist Critique*. London and New York: Routledge, 2004.

Said, E"Representing the Colonized: Anthropology's Interlocutors". *Critical Inquiry*. 15:2, 1989.

Saxena, Shobhan. "Fact not Fiction". *Sunday Times of India*. October 19, 2008.

Spivak, Gayatri Chakravorty. *Post-colonial Critic : Interview, Strategies, Dialogues*. Ed. Sarah Harasym. New York : Routledge, 1990.

Suri, Sanjay *Outlook* 48:43, October 27, 2008.

Thiong'O, Nugi wa *Decolonizing the Mind*. Londan: James Currey, 1986.

White, J., ed. *Recasting the world : Writing After Colonialism*. Baltimore: The Johns Hopkins University Press, Maryland; 1993.

9

Naipaul-Complex: Naipaul's Love/Hate Relationship with India in *An Area of Darkness*

Jamsheed Ahmad

The paper attempts to trace the outcome of V.S. Naipaul's first face-to-face encounter with India focusing the negative aspects as depicted in his travelogue *An Area of Darkness,* one of his least touched books. Further the paper shall try to make the image of India so created by Naipaul more transparent with an oblique acceptance of most of Naipaul's observations about it. The paper accepts his anger as an unconscious attachment to India. The phrase 'Naipaul-complex' in the title has been used in a particular sense.

V.S. Naipaul (Vidiadhar Surajparshad Naipaul), Vidia to friends and Vido to family, born in Chaguanas, Trinidad on August 17, 1932 is a descendant of indentured labourers shipped from eastern part of Uttar Pradesh, India in 1880's. He has to his credit the authorship of about 15 novels and an equal number of non-fictional works. He got the Nobel Prize in 2001 and the Booker Prize in 1971 but surely no figure in contemporary literature has been as reviled as he. Over the years he has courted the wrath and hatched job of many of his contemporaries like Salman Rushdie, Edward Said, George Lamming etc. mainly due to his explicit and controversial writings. He has been in hot waters for his refusal to avoid unwelcome topics related to The Third World, racism, misogyny, disregard for Islam and his condescending comments about his contemporaries. He claims that he has never read Salman Rushdie (Suroor).

Naipaul spent most of his childhood and adolescence in the capital Port of Spain that impressed and coloured his sensitive imagination. His writings are merged with his personal experiences and no study on him can be conducted without taking into account the formative forces behind his literary talent. One such major force was the Hindu culture of the Caribbean in which he was born and brought up. His grandfather's house provided the first link with his Hindu self and with the India of his ancestors. Naipaul grew up with a highly eulogized idea of India and an image of an extremely extolled India got created in his mind. Although he could never understand much about the Hindu rules and rituals in his grandmother's house, there was always something sacred in his very idea of India. "Chaguanas, where Naipaul's grandfather had built his house was a place which kept its Indianness to its core. Amidst the 'Hindu rigours' of religion and caste, life was symbolically peasant Indian ..." (Zafir 262). His next introduction to India was his father's stories which epitomized for him the unity of the old world. As he grew up, he observed a chasm between the two worlds that he inhabited-one was the colonial world of Trinidad and the other was the old Hindu world of India. The paper attempts to trace the outcome of his first face to face encounter with India focusing the negative aspects as depicted in his travelogue *An Area of Darkness,* one of his least touched books. Further the paper shall try to make the image of India so created by Naipaul more transparent with an oblique acceptance of most of Naipaul's observations about it.

An Area of Darkness which is a child of Naipaul's pigeonholed memory with an incredible exactitude and flow of pure spirit of comedy published in 1964 records the dirge of his first visit to India. For him, "India had in a special way been the background of my childhood. It was a country from which my grandfather came, a country never physically described and therefore never real ..." (Naipaul 27). When Naipaul was asked about the reason behind his interest in India, the answer was quite unexpected. He replied, "Well I was interested in India because, and I still am, because of my concern, I hate distress, I hate poverty, and I wish to see it alleviated, it can't disappear unfortunately, but I wish to see it alleviated, that's what I go back to look for, I look for signs of that" (Kohn). At another place, Farrukh Dhondy writes, Naipaul lashes out at some of his contemporaries; about Forster: "...someone who didn't know Indian people", Narayan: "...his India is a ruin", Soyinka: "...a marvellously Establishment figure actually" and Joyce: "...he is not interested in the world".

For Naipaul, darkness has a double meaning. First, it symbolizes his ignorance about his ancestry, his native village and the country which has been described by colonial writers like Rudyard Kipling and E. M. Forster. That is why Naipaul came to India to dispel that darkness in his mind. Secondly, darkness refers to Naipaul's disillusionment with the mimicry society of contemporary India which is mired with filth, corruption, and communalism; a land which has not fulfilled the high expectations of its people after independence. He writes, "I have travelled lucidly over that area which was to me the area of darkness, something of darkness remains, in those attitudes, those ways of thinking and seeing which are no longer mine" (Naipaul 30).

The book starts with the "Traveller's Prelude: A Little Paperwork" where Naipaul in an ironic manner describes his plight when he is trapped in the outdated permit system of Indian 'babudom'. His liquor bottles are confiscated and he has to run from pillar to post to obtain a permit since Bombay was 'dry'. The red tape involved in the process is so long that his companion faints from exhaustion. This incident sets the key note of his first visit to India since it begins with disgust and anger at official apathy. He describes his early experiences and comments on the sloth and naivety of Indians, their colonial mindset, class prejudices, corruption, filth and hypocrisies of Indian society. He is critical of Indians' mimicking their colonial masters when he sees the dirt, poverty, disease, illiteracy and the corruption of our society. Naipaul perceives India as a "country suspended in time", a land of mimics; and the mimicry, he says, is present in every sphere of existence (Zafir 280). On his arrival, he finds an entirely different country from the one whose image had been in his mind for years. He feels bitterly angry because his idealized India looks far inferior to the West. He harshly satirizes the upper class illiterate Hindus who have an obsession for everything which is associated with foreign. He writes, "mimicry .... It is the special mimicry of an old country which had learned to make room for outsiders, but only at the top ... yesterday the mimicry was Mongol; tomorrow, it might be Russian or American; today it is English" (Naipaul 56). This anger is further given vent in a later novel titled *The Mimic Men* although the approach there is more mature and scholarly. However Naipaul's observation somewhere depicts his rigid stance and lacking in understanding and warmth as he is insensitive to the natural repercussions of such a long colonization of India in the hands of the British.

Quite contrary in *India: A Wounded Civilisation* Naipaul gives an impression that the British contribution to India's development was benign and it was they who introduced Indians to the modern institutions. A more mature stand would have been to find some explanation to this act of mimicry on the part of the Indians who had been under an alien rule for almost two hundred years. However this argument never means being on the side of the Indian mimics and no doubt can be raised about his mastery with which he places a mirror to our face and shows us the reality we live in.

Naipaul finds the middle class Indians irritating, who take pride in nicknames which are westernized so that Anand becomes Andy and Brijesh becomes Bunny. The Indian army is also laughed at by Naipaul for its overtly Western mindset; the Indian army officer "manages to look English; his gait and bearing are

English, his mannerism, his tastes in drinks are English, his slang is English. In Indian setting this Indian English mimicry is like fantasy" (Naipaul 57). Naipaul dislikes the Indian habit of fanaticizing and myth making which makes them escapists and impractical in day to day affairs. He is equally critical of Indian movies which add to this by creating an atmosphere of unreal characters and stories and which tend to make people romantic and sluggish. In the same vein, he makes fun of the Indian tendency to deify leaders like Gandhi about whom he says, "India undid him. He became a mahatma. He was to be reverenced for what he was; his message was irrelevant ... He failed to communicate to Indian his way of direct looking ..." (Naipaul 81-82). Quite cleverly and may be in order to avoid the wrath of Gandhians, he retreats by giving the impression that by treating Gandhi like a God, his sacred message is diluted and lost. However at many places he is somewhat critical of Gandhi and says, "... he moved out of his own historical blindness to great passion" (Kohn). He writes, "nothing remains of Gandhi in India but this, his name and the worship of his image: the seminars about non-violence, as though this was all he taught" (Naipaul 81).

Naipaul's visit to the Indian paradise, Kashmir finds a special mention in the book. He also makes reference to Jammu, where he stopped for lunch. Regarding Jammu he writes, "In Jammu city you will see them collecting filth from the streets with their bare hands. This is the degradation the society requires of them, and to this they willingly submit. They are dirt; they wish to appear as dirt" (Naipaul 75). His critical comments on the unhygienic conditions in India reflects something of Swift's microscopic scrutiny and recoil:

> Indians defecate everywhere; they defecate, mostly beside the railway tracks ... defecate on beaches; they defecate on the hills; they defecate on the river banks, they defecate on the streets, they never look for cover (Naipaul 70).

The holy Shankaracharya hill in Srinagar is also used as an open latrine by the Indian tourists. In Madras the bus station near the high court is one of the most popular latrines. And in Goa defecating is a social activity, when a young Muslim boy defended this habit by saying, "Indians were a poetic people ... And nothing was as poetic as squatting on a river bank at dawn" (Naipaul 70). Quite humorously, Naipaul becomes speechless as he could find no answer to such an expression. He somehow could not come to terms with the human degradation and suffering on a scale that simply defied any easy explanation or remedy. In an interview he says, regarding his ancestry,

> I think we all knew that we had come from a very poor country and that we had migrated there, because of the wretchedness of conditions in India in the 1880s when there were famines. I don't know why there should have been famines in India in the 1880s, or why it was so specially wretched... (Kohn).

In the same interview he blames the Muslim rulers in India whom he holds responsible for the poverty and utter wretchedness where people had no faith in institutions and had no one to appeal to. In Bombay he describes the gays, sweepers and filth as symbols of India's ever increasing degrees of degradation. He hints that the poverty in India is due to the blind faith of the people who believe in the idea of holy poverty. It is deducible from his writings that Indians live with a sense of defeat and do not want to come out of it. He says Indians are "unimportant, cynical ... a dot on the map" ("Naipaul's Anger"). If urban India disappoints Naipaul with its bureaucratic obsession, rural India leaves him more disillusioned:

> The narrow broken lanes with shine in the gutters, the choked back to back mud houses, the jumble of faith and food and animals and people, the baby in the dust, swollen believed, black with flies, but wearing its good-luck amulet" (Naipaul 45).

Commenting on the Indian communal living, Naipaul feels that Indians belong to a particular family or area and are never comfortable outside their community. His focus on family and customs contrasts sharply with the western concept of individualism. He observes that the cloistered and sectarian approach of Hindus and Muslims towards religion create barriers amongst the people and prevents the creation of a secular state. Regarding Muslims he writes: "at an early age I understand that Muslims were somewhat more different than others. They were not to be trusted, they would always do you down" (Naipaul 31). During the visit Naipaul meets a variety of Indians from various social classes. Jivan and Vasant represent the villagers who are lured by the material temptation of the big city. Malik and Bunty Boxwallah are the new brahmins whose love of lucre drives them to envy the foreign returned Indians like Malhotra. They reject the traditional values of caste and symbolize a new class whose motto is money. Naipaul tells Kohn that a very few people can come out of the caste system. "The caste system, that friendly society which provides people with every kind of cushion, in bad times, will be around for most people in India" (Kohn). At another place he says about *An Area of Darkness*, "What it says about caste is influenced by ideas I had picked up here, British ideas. I think differently about caste now. I understand the clan feeling, the necessity of that in a big country" (Dhondy).

Naipaul dislikes the Indian habit of not respecting other person's privacy and wherever he goes, same question is asked again and again, "Where do you come from? I had been answering it five times a day" (Naipaul 94). He feels Indians dislike physical effort and labour of any sort unlike the Europeans who are physically agile and values dignity of work:

> In India however the top bunk has the added advantage of being free of dust, the lower bunk is preferred, not because it is easier to spread one's bedding on it-there are porters and servants to do that, but because climbing to the top bunk involves physical effort, and physical effort is to be avoided as degradation (Naipaul 72).

Naipaul feels that service is not an Indian concept and that Indians join civil services only for prestige. In the chapter titled

"Emergency", with a typical western orientalist view, Naipaul is critical of the impractical approach of the Indian government to the Chinese aggression. Prime Minister Nehru, Defence Minister Krishnan Menon and the Army Chief General K. M. Cariappa are found short of tune by Naipaul with the enormity of the problem. They made no attempt to explore the psyche of nation jolted out of its first independence euphoria, bordering on a sense of invincibility. It explains why, when China invaded, the administration in Assam collapsed. Only plans were made with no real intention for the well being of the people. His disgust at this lack of service and stagnant atmosphere in government offices is sharply satirical:

> I was shouting now almost as soon as I entered government offices. At times the sight of rows of young man sitting at long tables, buried among sheaves of paper ... all Indian's human futility was more than I could bear. Don't complain to me. Make your complaint through proper channel .... Don't complain to me. (Naipaul 92)

This attitude bred delay and corruption which is the hallmark of the Indian system. Naipaul refers to one such incident of corruption. He writes, "It is estimated that in Kashmir, as in rest of India, one third of development funds drain away in corruption and the exchanging of gifts ... it was the only system that could work" (Naipaul 135). He has no respect for Indian politicians who are considered above the law. Ministers are not required to stop at the traffic signal. In order to get elected a man had 17 people murdered and still remains free and unpunished. Naipaul is severely critical of the Indian spiritual godmen and gurus who peddle to the western taste for instant salvation and have turned spirituality into a big business. In one such instance in the book Naipaul gives an example of the luxurious attitude of a holy man who fears that the journey from Delhi will strain him and he decides to follow by viscount aeroplane.

The book on the whole conveys Naipaul's keen perception and sense of comedy and there can be no denial to this fact. He describes the places, people and incidents and manages to convey the meaning which lies behind them. With his profound vision and linguistic simplicity, he gives the reader a deep insight into India. Yet the contradictions and the writer's subjective mind exist simultaneously. Although he has written two others books on India namely *India: A Wounded Civilisation* and *India: The Million Mutinies*, yet his stand on the country is paradoxical; at one place he says he wants "to settle down in Bombay and rediscover (his) identity by losing (himself) in the millions of India" (Gupta), yet at another, he contradicts, "I do not write for the Indians, who in any case do not read. My work is only possible in a liberal, civilized western country. It is not possible in primitive societies" (Hardwick). With such a stand he has earned the offence of most of the Indians across the length and breadth of the country. However Naipaul, whom Peter Webb calls the "Delphic Oracle" (qtd. in Zafir 15) of the post modern literary era, has proved himself to be a universal writer with his disliking of being associated with any particular country. Naipaul loathes the idea of being called an Indian writer. He says, "To be an Indian from Trinidad is to be unlikely. It is, in addition to everything else, to be the embodiment of an old verbal ambiguity. For this word 'Indian' has been abused as no other word in the language; almost every time it is used it has to be qualified" (qtd. in Garebian 29).

Many of his contemporaries have criticized Naipaul for his partial view of India: the principal accusation being that he has presented India from an occidental point of view and thus contributed to the Orientalist view of India. Many critics say that he is at his snobbish best in the books on India and still others blame him of writing polemics rather than travel accounts. Although he loves to be called an independent writer, his detractors term him as a reactionary, a man who attempts to dress up his thinly disguised prejudice in the grab of a courageous love for veracity (Iyer 86). C.D. Narasimhaiah argues that his views are 'obtrusively personal'; there are some critics also who hold an extreme view that the books are more about Naipaul's perception of his Indian sensibility than the India that he visited (Zafir 278). At another place noted critic Edward Said denounces him as a "native informer" (Wheatcroft). George Woodcock, while discussing the first two books on India writes:

> As one reads through these two very uncharacteristic books, it becomes evident that Naipaul is writing less about India than about himself. In fact, on none of his journeys did he travel widely in the Indian hinterland, with its extraordinarily in cities founded by the British, like Bombay and Delhi and Calcutta, and in the old resorts of the raj like Kashmir and Simla. (8-9)

Iyer writes, "Naipaul's narrative is abstracted from reality, it is an exposition of Naipaul's own mind, a long essay of observation. It moves from travelogue to reminiscences and reflection" (88). A between the lines reading of *An Area of Darkness* creates a doubt in the minds of common readers that the impression given in the book is ill conceived and based on his impression rather than his experience. In this context, "what he saw or chose to see was not what he had expected to see, and he became sullen, he felt disillusioned ... The things he saw and recorded with a tiresome peculiarity were certainly there, but there were other things too which his observant eye shouldn't have missed" (Nandakumar 267). His non-commitment to India along with his macabre tirade and private responses against it may be attributed to his disinheritance from all the traditions and his rootlessness; the roots for which he visited India but found them sterile and gnarled. Although a few things in India like the majestic Himalayas, the fantasy of his childhood, does appeal to him but quite cynically he somehow manages to attach it to the Indian symbol of loss. Yet on the other hand, a sensible Indian cannot deny all the observations made by Naipaul particularly the ones regarding red tape, poverty, unhygienic conditions and corruption, keeping in view the slow development in all these areas and the recently unearthed scams in our country. In this context Anna Hazare's recent hunger strike with a mass following substantiates the concept of a corruption ridden India.

Conclusion: The Indian society is marked by gross lack of sanitation, nationalism, religion, history, economic and social development. The lack of governance and dishonesty on the part of politicians inhibit the development of modern progressive society. Naipaul is contemptuous of Indianness which pervades throughout and bears a negative influence on the aspects that make up our national identity and impedes Indian's progress and development. India, the country remains a complex abyss to Naipaul. He sees it as a puzzle which cannot be completed because the pieces of the puzzle keep it apart. He wanted to illuminate what was in his mind a sphere of darkness; he wanted to find himself in India, not the India of Kipling or Forster. However he returned disappointed.

Although Naipaul dislikes to be labelled as an Indian writer but his observations about India in the book give ample proof of his unconscious attachment to India. Unlike Naipaul who feels angry, a typical Western writer would have described India quite objectively. Naipaul's anger gives a proof of his being an insider. Besides, Orientalist writers find an exotic charm in the elements like snake charmers and sadhus in this country which is missing in Naipaul and is again an indication of his uncanny Indianness. *An Area of Darkness* is the median encounter of diasporic writer—though not diasporic in the strict sense of the word—with the place of his ancestry. He came to India with high expectations, but found that reality didn't match the romantic image he had harbored in his mind for so long. He ends at neither being an Indian nor English or Caribbean but a talent who knows no nationality.

Works Cited

Dhondy, Farrukh. "Indian Writers don't Know Why their Country is in a Mess." *Ontology.buffalo.edu.*13 Aug. 2001. Web. 22 Nov. 2010.

Garebian, Keith. V. S. Naipaul's Negative Sense of Place." *Journal of Commonwealth Literature,* 10.1 (1975): 23-35. Print.

Gupta, Shyam Ratan. "Interview with V. S. Naipaul." *The Hindustan Times Weekly,* 31 May 1981. Print.

Hardwick, Elizabeth. "Meeting V. S. Naipaul." *New York Times,* 13 May 1979. Web.

Iyer, N. Sharada. "Naipaul's India – An Area of Darkness." *V. S. Naipaul Critical Essays.* Ed. Mohit K. Ray. New Delhi: Atlantic Publishers. 2002. Print.

Kohn, Rachael. "India Through V. S. Naipaul's Eyes." *Satyameva-jayate.org.* 15 July 2006. Web. 18 Nov. 2010.

"Naipaul's Anger at Indian Writers." *News. Bbc.co.uk.* 22 Feb. 1999. Web. 24 Nov. 2010.

Naipaul V. S. "*An Area of Darkness.*" London: Penguin, 1968. Print.

Nandakumar, Prema. *The Glory and the Good.* London: Asia Publishing House, 1966. Print.

Purdue OWL. "MLA Formatting and Style Guide." *The Purdue OWL.* Purdue U Writing Lab, 10 May 2008. Web. 15 Nov. 2009.

Suroor, Hasan. "Naipaul Says it's all over for him." *The Hindu,* 22 Nov. 2010. Print.

Wheatcroft, Geoffrey. *Newsstatesman.com,* 2 Feb. 2004. Web. 24 Nov. 2010.

Woodcock, George. "Two Great Commonwealth Novelists: R. K. Narayan and V. S. Naipaul." *The Sewanee Review* 87.1 (1979): 8-9. *Jstor.* Web. 23 Nov. 2010.

Zafir, Kishwar. "Expatriate Concerns in the Works of V. S. Naipaul." PhD thesis. Aligarh Muslim University, 2006. Print.

10

Recognizable Images of 'Dark India': Orientalism and Adiga's *The White Tiger*

Arindam Ghosh

Aravind Adiga's *The White Tiger* (2008), while exploring the poverty and hardships, inequality and caste discrimination, crime and corruption rooted in the marrow of Indian society, has reaffirmed the exoticist image of India. It makes poverty a profitable brand; and invests spirituality and mystery within the context of a prosperous journey of a lower-class to a business tycoon. The Eurocentric perspective of the conventional East is manifest in his attempt to portray an almost homogeneous standard of rural Indian life. In contrast to the elitist lifestyle of the city of Bangalore is present the superstitious illiterate villagers of the Laxmangarh which adds to the spiritual mysticism to the image of India. The recurring theme of servitude reminds us of our colonial past. The effort to treat common people as anonymous and without any individuality overtly shows the influence of the Western cosmopolitan model of writing. With the presentation of the narrator's obsession with the distinction of skin colours, the reverberation of the word 'Darkness', the depiction of the hellish and primitive almost animal-like standard of living assert that the author in his attempt to create a counter-hegemonic culture for the third world ends up in capturing the 'imaginative' or psychological 'geography' of the orientalist thought.

Edward Said's 'Orientalism' (simply put, the word suggests an academic discipline focusing on the study of oriental culture and language) centres around a Eurocentric discourse that reaffirmed the age-old notion of the orient as inferior and 'the other'. This is a non-coercive form of Western colonialism based on the assumption of the preeminence of everything 'occidental'. The 'East' exists in the Western psyche as 'fascinating', 'exotic', 'mystical' and the 'seductive'. Its people, assumed as homogeneous masses ('Collective Self-consistency') are defined not by conscious individuality but by 'instinctive emotions' and reactions. In Said's words Orintalism was "a Western style for dominating, restructuring and having authority over the orient".[1] The well-known myths about Eastern laziness, sensuality and deceit are actually the projection of the hidden desires of a Western mind, concealed under the garments of rationality. Orientalism was challenged for its generalizing and universalizing trends. However, since the 1980s Saidian ideas were supplemented by Marxist theory of 'Ideology', Derrida's 'Deconstruction' and also by 'Cultural Materialism'.

The 2009 Oscar for the film 'Slumdog Millionaire' as well as the recent advertisement for the 'incredible India', featuring the 'Mystic Maroon' (red-clad worshippers) reflect the old Western preoccupation with India: making poverty a saleable brand; and investing spirituality and mystery to add to the commercial value of India. The winning of the Booker Prize by Aravind Adiga's *The White Tiger* has reaffirmed that the exoticist image of 'Dark' India; and the book 're-orientalizes' (Lisa Lau's term, meaning 'the perpetration and development of orientalsim by the orientals)[2] the representation while deconstructing the fairy tale myth about world's spiritual capital. Its appraisal in the Western reception on the one hand confirms the jargons about 'the Other' India, and consequently it raises the issue of the encounter between the Orientalized East and the so-called cultural East with all its renovative forms and modes of theoretical insights.

The novel *The White Tiger* ironically explores the poverty and hardships, inequality and caste discrimination, and crime and corruption, rooted somewhat exaggeratedly in the marrow of Indian society and thus debunks the myth of the idyllic India. The theme of the novel is 'entrepreneurship' (actually a sudden rise in social and economic order) in which the process itself is highlighted than the means through which it is achieved in the context of a Third World country. The novel in epistolary form unfolds the prosperous journey (through crime though) from lower-class to a business tycoon of Balram Halwai through a series of letters to the Chinese Premier Wen Jibao. The central persona Balram who is penning the letters, descends from a poverty-stricken family in the northern Indian village of Laxmangarh. He thoroughly depicts his family background, his short-lived school life, his fear of the lizards, the suppression of the proletariat by the rich zamindars, his own ambitious nature, his plight for becoming a driver, social and economic relationship between the master and the servant; and all these are mired in a juxtaposition of corruption, exploitation and crime. And the narrator's (who reminds us of the unnamed narrator of Ralph Ellison's *Invisible Man*) presentation brilliantly touches all the issues from crime and punishment to servility and resistance.

The Eurocentric perspective of the conventional East has been discussed in a range of different texts dealing with cultural analysis and the issue of identity politics. Vidhu Verma's *Non-discrimination and Equality in India: Contesting Boundaries of Social Justice* assesses the concept of social justice from the period of colonialism to the present. In *The Culturalization of Caste in India: Identity and Inequality in a Multicultural Age* by Balmurli Natarajan analyzes the survival of the caste system even in front of a dominant Western culture and thus addresses the issues of ethnicity and multiculturalism. Often prejudiced interpretations of the Eastern culture and its people are derived from the review of certain novels like Anita Desai's *Fasting, Feasting* ('unhappy Indian families are unhappy in their own ways'); Rohinton

Mistry's *Family Matters,* set in an over-crowded and politically corrupt Bombay; or Martel's *Life of Pi,* a small, slim man with an Indian complexion.[3] *The White Tiger* seems to satisfy this essentializing Western view about the 'Exotic' east.

Adiga provides a near pejorative view of the almost homogeneous standard of lowly Indian life. And thus he falls into the same old trap of Eurocentric attitude. Assumptions, stereotypes and prejudices get confirmed when the central persona attempts to describe his nation at the very beginning: "... it has no drinking water, electricity, sewage system, public transportation, sense of hygiene, discipline, courtesy or punctuality ..." (Adiga 4); and this is precisely what reigns in the Western psyche as the economic and social reality of the East. Again sometimes later the categorization of India as 'India of Light' and 'India of Darkness' only displays the functioning of a dominative high Western culture. Deplorable and underdeveloped rural villages are equated to the 'Dark India' with its 'black river'. On the other hand, enlightened India is only the sea-side half-westernized cities boasting of technology and progress; sea ('Ocean') itself metonymically stand here as the 'well off' Western civilization.

At the outset the book is a thorough assessment of the social reality of India: a study of Contrast between India rising as a powerful global economy and the emaciating and pervasive poverty it has to face. But in doing so knowlingly or unknowingly the narrator creates an aura of 'illusion' around India which in turn satisfies the concept of the fictional and imaginative India. In spite of the assertion that "the future of the world lies with the yellow man and the brown man" (Adiga 5) and the setting of Bangalore and Delhi with their sophisticated, elitist lifestyle a certain sense of mystery (Mystery/Muddle in A Passage to India) about the enigmatic new India raises its head time and time again. There are various subtle and overt references to religion and rituals and superstitions. Indeed, religion has had a major role to play in this part of the world. But in the novel it has ended up by being a chain of superstitious customs and symbolic actions: for instance, a film begins by showing the image of Goddess Lakshmi or the magic number 786; praying to a higher power is treated in such a manner that it has fallen to a level of mere paganism and nature worship: the symbolic presence of 'the faded mural of Lord Buddha'; Balram decorating the car with 'the small statue of Goddess Lakshmi', images of mother-goddess Kali and a small fluffy ogre with a red tongue; or the comparison of Balram's speech to Mr. Ashok with that of Lord Krishna's in the *Bhagavad Gita*; the 'bored driver's Asana'; or the corrupt police officers working under the image of God and Gandhi all these are anything but normal in the Western gaze. Certain religious rituals and myths are depicted in such a way that their abnormality and 'difference' is firmly established than the belief and sincerity that run behind them.

Through the past ages the river has always been the provider for the Indian civilization. The value of this mythic river has been undermined by a diametrically opposed standard of culture and hence it has been associated with flood, poisonous reptiles and the bounty of scattered gold. Ultimately this 'Black river', 'River of death' in a nutshell comes to objectify the true facts of living (living under pollution, corruption and superstition) in this part of the world. The narrator further aggravates the mythic situation by evoking myth of 'Mother Ganga': 'Daughter of the Vedas', 'river of illumination', 'protector of us all, breaker of the chain of birth and rebirth'. "Everywhere this river flows that area is the darkness" (Adiga 15). The description of the village temple although managed realistically, is an effort to fit it in the conventional ideological framework of a powerful cultural institution: "...a tall, whitewashed, cone like tower with black intertwining snakes painted on all its sides" (Adiga 19). The central deity of the temple – a 'Saffron-coloured creature' Hanuman, 'half man half monkey' is mocinkly presented in order to heighten the meek, servile manner of the Indian people; faithfulness in servitude becomes the goal to achieve. Again some conscious efforts have been invested to romanticize and to mystify the presence of 'the Black Fort'. The fort on the crest of the hill, built centuries ago is now abandoned and its obscurity tantalizes and frightens the local village people. Latter on it becomes the symbol of the throne of India (occupied by monkeys); in Balram's imagination 'an enormous lizard' lived there; myth and gossipy stories are merged with the association of the monkeys and the 'reincarnated souls'. However, the 'Black fort' turns into a concrete symbol at Balram's first visit there: it seemed to have provoked his hidden desires. All these are to invest awe inspiring features to quench the western thirst for mysterious India. Ritual and superstition are combined in the elaborate description of the last rites of Munna's mother. Covering the corpse with 'a saffron silk cloth' and with chanting 'Shiva's name' the gaudy procession came to the burning ghat. Now, burning the dead body is the Eastern idea of purification, sanctification and renunciation. But the depiction is made to appear in such a way that the process of salvation of the soul becomes antique.

As *The White Tiger* happens to be a tale set in a colonized country the theme of servitude recurs in this novel throughout. China, Abghanisthan and Abyssinia resisted service under any country. From the European point of view this is resisting the fruits of civilization; hence, 'Exciting Tales of the Exotic East' mostly deals with the pirates and gold in Hong Kong. The case is different with India and its people: willingly or unwillingly they first served under the Mughals and then under the British. So is the case with the protagonist Balram: "I was a servant once". Even the suggestion is that the Indians prey to hanuman who faithfully served his master Lord Rama for he set an example of 'how to serve his master'. Again Iqbal's poetry is associated with the theme of slavery: slaves cannot appreciate the beauty of the world. However, Balram's fate was 'not to stay a slave'. Balram directly compares himself with the servant God Hanuman while driving Mr. Ashok and Pinky madam. Again displacing Ramprasad, Balram becomes the 'servant number one'; this points to the struggle among the servants for a comparatively better place. 'The fake servant grin' is only a sign of understanding his master like a dog does. The existence of the servant's quarter speaks of the parasitical nature of aristocratic existence; servants, looking like monkeys in uniform are merely 'Alsatian dogs'. Balram's unhygienic habits and red, blackened, rotting teethes symbolically become the features of a whole half-civilized nation. The social hierarchy is working in order to keep most of the people of this country 'to exist in perpetual servitude'. In the first world countries there are many rich people but they have to perform their own private works of their own, but here in India: millions of poor servants "... get off at their master's posh houses – and then clean the floors, wash the dishes, weed the garden, feed their children, press their feet – all for a pittance" (Adiga 176). Servitude in India, as the narrator implies, is not one's social condition, it is rather there in our blood and instinct: "Once a servant, always a servant: the instinct is always there..." (Adiga 299). Even at the later stage of the story servitude has become Balram's nightmare. At the culmination of the story Balram voices the cry of all colonized people and defends all his heinous adventures just as his extreme urge to know: 'what it means not to be a servant.'

Now, the dominating Western perception comes into play whenever the people of India are addressed or described: 'Thousands and thousands of them' become so much like the faceless workers of Conrad's *Heart of Darkness.* The small brown men of India with their 'popped out eyes and stubby moustache' (39) are again and again categorically put throughout the novel, as: "could be half the men in India; 'thin bodies, filthy faces ... the animal-like way they live" (Adiga 120). The police poster presenting an effeminate and weak Balram ('Blakish', 'Thin', 'Small') is just one instance of the many undervalued depiction of the people of India. In Balram's rural household the buffalo is fed before human beings partly displaying religious belief and partly an effort to show the insignificance of human life in this

Indian context. The tendency to homogenize Indian people abounds in the novel: "the road is full of them – thin, sticklike men." In Bangalore the passerby identifies himself with fugitive Balram's poster and the narrator significantly comments: "...it could be the face of half the men in India"; they are like 'mound of indistinguishable bodies' without individuality or any personal identity. Sometimes human beings are interpreted through animal images and actions: for instance, each of the landlords of Laxmangarh is given animal names according to their behaviour. The rickshaw pullers are simply 'beasts of burden'. And using this refrain the whole Indian village society is compared with a jungle, full of ignorant beasts lurching in darkness. After that in its prosperous time India 'was like a zoo. A clean, well-kept, orderly zoo'; but after its independence from the British rule "... the cages has been let open; and the animals had attacked and ripped each other apart" (Adiga 64). Here the implication is that the British Govt. was quite successful in its noble mission of enlightening the native people. Thus the idea of the 'White man's burden' resurfaces. The narrator's mode of presentation allows the 'conventional' constructed view of India to intervene with facts which reaches its climax when in a soliloquy Balram repents his past life (brought up in 'filth' 'to live like an animal?).

The obsession and the tendency to categorize human beings regarding their skin colour vehemently persist in the novel. One might be reminded here of Said's concept that the superiority of the skin colour (white) was one mode of inducing slavery to the natives for black was made to appear naturally inferior. Our narrator seems to have gladly accepted the distinction as he goes on to label the Chinese as 'Yellow men', the Indian as 'Brown men' while the colonial rulers are 'White skinned'. The reference to the 'skin-whitener' cream seems to be a vein effort to catch the Western standard of existence: so that, 'Indian men can look white as westerners'. The case reaches vulgarity when we find that in a red light area some girls are dressed as 'American' to tantalize the customers; this is a case of skin fetishism (however, Balram prefers the 'light-skinned' Nepalies). A person whose whole body has been discoloured due to disease, at first glance draws respect and attention of other fellows as 'An American'. Apart from these 'the mascot of the gym – an American with enormous white muscles' fascinates all; Balram keeps as memento the 'strand of golden hair' of the Russian whore. The most obviously overt statement regarding skin colour comes with: 'White skin has to be respected' (Adiga 228); the essence of orientalism is inculcated through this scathing statement. Along with this precondition of skin colour it must be noted that the reference to 'Darkness' or 'Blackness' reverberates throughout this novel. The narrator begins by praying to God 'to shine light' on his 'dark story'. The sophisticated city of Bangalore is the harbinger of light but the average rural India is mired in 'Darkness'. Coal pits, black money and grim corruption have been deftly associated to emphasize the pervasive darkness overcast everywhere. Balram and other drivers are easily recognized as persons from 'darkness' and his journey from Dhanbad to Delhi is seen as a journey from darkness to light. Industrial pollution has made small rivers literally 'black'.

Adiga is quite successful in creating a realistic Indian ambience with subtle touches and minute details: be it the turban of the sikh driver, or the smoking of hookah, or chewing of beetle leaves or even the pecking of teeth with neem sticks. Amid this a subterraneous Marxist conflict between different social and economic groups in a politically sensitive atmosphere is incorporated into the body of the narrative. But while presenting the pictures of social mobility and extremes of poverty his views get stifled under the provocative influence of a dominating western culture. Thus his efforts to re-establish the image of Indian socio-cultural life end up becoming biased and exaggerated. Conventional Eurocentric perspective and reality mingles through the artistic lucidity of the narrator's voice. When the narrator was ruminating about his own childhood we encounter the complexity of attaining individual distinction through names for here in the rural villages there is no formal way to name a baby: 'Munna' is Munna because his parents 'forget to name their child(ren)'. Then the inadequacy of the education system has been pointed out by the narrator when he considers himself as 'half-baked' Indian: for he and millions like him 'were never allowed to complete their schooling'. The result is equally pathetic: the system leaves us with 'half-cooked' and 'half-formed' ideas. In order to convey the true nature of the exploitation he imagines himself 'caught in the Rooster Coop'. Almost everyone is working for the convenience of a lucky few who happen to be comfortably placed at the top of the social and economic ladder. The same is evident with the portrayal of the people of the semi-feudal world of Laxmangarh: they are trapped, subdued and totally shunned of opportunities and facilities. The inhuman condition of the village hospital, the harsh indifference towards the working class sentimentality, the coercive-rigging in the name of election and democracy, and bribing the political leaders under broad daylight coupled with disrespect for duty and ideals of loyalty and oppressive social norms which ignore the basic humanity take us back to a country of a pre-enlightenment era, and it dismantles the identity of India as a developing economy. The country with an ultra-modern city like Bangalore and all its entrepreneurs is submerged under the shadow of a third world country which is both 'constructed' and 'recognizable' by an omnipresent Western ideology. And if go by Fredric Jameson, in the Third World "the telling of the individual story or experience is the laborious telling of the experience of the collective self" (Nayar 130), the narrator's individual encounters in life becomes the reality for a whole nation.

Throughout I have tried to show that Adiga's *The White Tiger* on various occasions captures the 'imaginative Geography' of the Orientalist thought. Thus India's postcolonial achievements are undervalued; and the indigenous culture and tradition are forced to bow under a colonial tendency to legitimatize the stereotypical image of India. To consider the nation's history as a whole, to question the assumptions of white discourse and to move away from 'nativism' are the means suggested by E. Said in *Culture and Imperialism* to counter the dominating culture and to replace them with a newly integrated narrative style. But *The White Tiger* does not show any inclination to decolonize the narrative structure. Balram's adoption of a distinct social life and his learning of the fragments of English language (colonizer's language: obviously reminds of Caliban's case in *The Tempest)* suggests the possibility of a new paradigm (more than mere 'Civil-savages) for the working class. But the situation couldn't be balanced properly. The author could not resist the conceptual and superior intellectual framework. So he meekly grabbed the Eurocentric model of dominating discourse and thus reinforced the discrimination and stereotypes instead of deconstructing them.

References

1. As quoted in P. Waugh. *Literary Theory and Criticism.* London: Oxford U P, 2006.Print.
2. L. Lau & A.C. Mendes (eds.). *Re-Orientalism and the South Asian Identity Politics: the Oriental Other Within.* London: Routledge, 2011. Print.
3. M. Chowdhury & C. Jain in *Sad, Bad and the Mysterious Indian: Exploring the Image of the Indian* have made an elaborate attempt on these novels.

Works Cited

Adiga, Aravind. *The White Tiger.* New Delhi: HarperCollins Pub., 2008. Print.

Desai, Anita. 2000. *Fasting Feasting.*, London: Vintage. Print.

Lau, Lisa & A.C. Mendes (eds.). *Re-Orientalism and the South Asian Identity Politics: the Oriental Other Within.* London: Routledge, 2011. Print.

Mistry, Rohinton. 2002. *Family Matters*, London: Faber and Faber Ltd. Print.

Nayar, Pramod K. *Literary Theory Today.* New Delhi: Prestige, 2002. Print.

Said, Edward W. *Cuture and Imperialism.* New York: Vintage, 1993. Print.

______. *Orientalism.* New York: Vintage, 1979. Print.

Want, Lily. "The Poetics and Politics of Cultural Studies in Aravind Adiga's *The White Tiger*". *Asiatic.* 5.1: 2011. Print.

Waugh, Patricia. *Literary Theory and Criticism.* London: Oxford U P, 2006. Print

11

Embedding History: A Perspective of Sam Selvon's *The Housing Lark*

M. Rosary Royar

> History moves forward to gather in the future as well as looking backward to gather up the past.
>
> —Bill Ashcroft

Sam Selvon interfuses the history of the Empire and reconstructs the Caribbean history. The Caribbeans move towards nationhood in spite of their differences and the Mother Country's hostile attitude. Histories get embedded and interrogated. Postcolonial writing, setting a different trend, tends to cross over borders. Literary text carries within itself several functions and coheres varying disciplines that a reader can decode the text from multiple points. Representation and misrepresentation in a text conjure and build worlds of illusoriness and reality, which can in turn be a tactic to impose and unravel certain specific truths and factualities of happenings. A literary text making an inscape of historical happening testifies to the reality of the time/period.

Bill Ashcroft claims "History, indeed temporality itself, is a construction of language and of culture, and, ultimately, the site of a struggle for control which post-colonial writing is in a particularly strategic position to engage" (83). At the same time, he is conscious of the fact that "post-colonial interpolation of history occurs in ways that refuse to leave it intact" and also positions "the problematizing of the boundary between literature and history" (99). Such is the intermixing of genres in the hybridized world to express resistance. Resistance enables to interrogate, to disprove, and to redefine the imposed identity.

Edouard Glissant perceiving the acute consequences of the Western history for such societies as the Caribbean comments, "History is highly functional fantasy of the West, originating at precisely the time when it alone made the history of the World". If Hegel relegated African peoples to the ahistorical, Amerindian peoples to the prehistorical, in order to reserve history for European people exclusively, it appears that it is not because these African or American peoples 'have entered history' that we can conclude today that such a hierarchical conception of 'the march of history' is no longer relevant'. His rejection of Western history which has held the status of the master narrative, the imperial history that recognised none other country's history, paves way for interrogation. In fact, he assures that "History [with a capital H] ends where the histories of those people once reputed to be without history come together" (qtd in Bill Ashcroft 98-100). Histories of different societies from a postcolonial perspective invade the centre to reallocate centre-margin positions. Transforming history has begun with the writers inhabiting the third space and reclaiming representation, which has been denied to the other. And Bill Ashcroft points out the remedy lies not in re-insertion of a nation's history into the Empire history but re-vision of history from a differing stance.

Sam Selvon, a Trinidadian, in his novel *The Housing Lark* (1965) interfuses the history of the Empire with that of the Caribbean and India. Michel Fabre says, "Experimenting in dialogue and dialect it is a farcical novel about the working and housing conditions of the black immigrants in London" (122). The immigrants, Indo-Caribbeans and Afro-Caribbeans, displaced and dislocated, have a hard time in finding a house in London due to the stringent enacting of the policy 'Keep Britain White'. The dichotomy in the attitude of the mother country is apparent but goes unnoticed and unquestioned. In an interview Selvon remarks, "I had troubles finding a place to live. I had doors slammed in my face. I had difficulties finding a job, odd jobs here and there, because of my colour, because the prejudice and discrimination against this 'invasion' as they called it in England, of Third World people coming into the Country, and taking up jobs, and looking for accommodation, and things like that" (96). As a writer and an immigrant he has voiced the problematic issue faced by the people from the Caribbean. Jana Evans Braziel posits that "race is a cultural construct that is historically malleable and differently deployed at different moments in time and in varying national contexts". It is "deployed as a discriminatory rubric across multiple geographical settings and historical periods" (133). How do the diasporans carve their histories within the national history of so-called the mother country, Britain?

Making a critique of Kitchener invading England with his calypsos, Hugh Hodges presents the prominent problem of the days, "Refused housing in better neighbourhoods by the extremely unsociable English, West Indians were crowded into the most run-down parts of Brixton, Notting Hill, Hammersmith and Bayswater" (25). He continues that they had to pay four, even five times more than the actual rent. Naturally what they saved to send home to Jamaica or Trinidad disappeared into the pockets of their landlords. Bat, Syl, Poor and all the boys face the problem of housing in Britain where the policy of "No Kolors, sorry!uropeans only" (29) is followed.

Paradoxically the islanders land up in London not of their own volition but on demand, once again for the gain of the Empire. Susheila Nasta, corroborates that over 40,000 West Indians immigrated to Britain. "Originally invited to the 'mother-country' by the post-war government as an attempt to solve the immediate labour crisis following the Second World War and commonly known as the 'Windrush generation' these islanders moved to Britain expectant to improve their standard of living" (78). On arriving, they face disappointment and disillusion. Racial discrimination is so sharp that they feel thwarted. Economic deprivation, social ostracisation and unemployment feature their lives that they appear to be aimless wanderers and perpetual hunters and remain caught up in a tangle of troubles.

Helen Tiffin, besides drawing a parallel, dwells upon the ostensible distinguishing features between the European migration and the Caribbean migration. Two primary motivations geared the massive migrations in the last four centuries. Europeans undertook the voyage to the Caribbean because they had the impelling force of economic gain. The mass migration of the colonised to Europe in the twentieth century, were similarly 'sponsored by a hope of economic improvement'. Two powerful myths underpinned both the migrations. The English were in the quest of EL Dorado in the Caribbean islands. The Caribbeans were after the imperial myth that the streets of metropolis were paved with gold. Both underwent the experience of demythologising their in-built myths. However, the Europeans economic gain and extension of territory are rewards that they reaped beyond the scale.

The Caribbeans, on the other hand, suffered loss beyond redemption at political, economical and social levels. They undergo pschyic trauma and violence even after the Empire departed. Helen Tiffin conjoins 'But a second imperial mythology underlay colonial migrations to 'Britain—the myth of the 'mother' country with all its implications of welcome and affiliation which had been sponsored by the nineteenth and twentieth century rhetoric of empire (mother and children, sisters and brothers) and deliberately fostered in the twentieth century in the educational curricula." Naturally, it ensues that the empire's ideology does not promote the practice of racial differences. "But as the colonial chickens came home to roost in the imperium, however, their experience was, well, a horse of a different colour". (135) The continual clamour of the white people for maintaining purity of race has got spearheaded. They receive the children as unwelcome and uncivilised colonials. The colonials are strangers, foreigners to be wary of and rough people to be kicked. They cannot be accommodated for fear of invasion. Manipulating ideology for its gain and conveniently throwing it overboard at confrontation but at the same time exercising ideological power have become the reigning force.

Some West Indians talk with their English friends about "the waves of immigration and deplore the conditions immigrants live in" (109). However, they try to win the favour of English people at the cost of despising their own people but they never succeed. Their trustworthiness is exploited and their simplicity is taken advantage of. Fearing that Battersby may drop him out of the scheme of buying a house, Gallows goes out to spy. He chances to meet Alfy who leans on a wall with a camera strap on his shoulder. An Englisher has told him that he made plenty of money on selling a snap of an accident to the newspapers and so he is on the lark now. When Alfy attempts to verify it with him, the Englisher says, "I don't tell lies like you people" (51). The stereotypical image of the colonised pervades. The situation is cleverly contrived for without any further implication it is apparent who the liar is in the context.

Alfy has been duped and walks around with the camera with an undying hope of making money. The Englisher's illusion falls upon him permanently. At another occasion, the boys discuss on how hard life is for them. Alfy expresses a wish to be back home. Another responds that life is too hard in London and all the time they have "to live hand to mouth" (125). Life is so harsh for them that one even thinks of life in jail that may supply meals regularly. As the conversation prolongs, someone suggests to Syl to go back to India, his mother country. Syl, unwaveringly ascertains "Brit'n is my country" (126). Another teases him for not wearing the south Indian costume of dhoti and turban. At the next instant, he doubts whether the Indian High Commissioner will help him if ever he gets into trouble or he will send him back to the Trinidad office. Belonging neither here nor there they are in the Trishanku position, always floating upwards. The claim they make on Britain denotes their loyalty only to interpellate the disloyalty of the Empire. They have been coerced and conscientized all along to look upon the mother country but in experience they see the dark reality behind the facade of magnanimity.

The concept of mother country envisages evergreen memories, cherished ideals and abiding values. Markarand Paranjape remarks, "the tug of the Motherland is subtle but powerful. It is almost obsessive and mystical in some cases" (92). The assimilationists and the traditionalists carry the motherland either in imagination or in a toolbox. Imaginary home has its origin in the land. But the Caribbeans both the Africans of slavery and the Indians of indentured labour have neither known nor seen the motherland except for their feeble and fragmented knowledge of it. In Selvon's terminology it is 'the third race', be black or Indian, that grew up Westernized and "who have adopted a way of life which tries to work and operate between the two races and who are Creolized as it were, and who see themselves more as West Indians than as perhaps belonging to people who originally came from India" (120) and they are in a strange position. As they have been dominated by the benevolent coloniser, they possessing no history of their own, for it has been consciously obliterated or the mother land itself has at times deserted them, they have been cultivated to believe in the image of Britain as the mother country.

The dilemma arises particularly for people from Third World countries because of their colour who move into white society to settle and they cannot "build a future without using the past" (121). Sylvester cannot go back to India for history tells us that the Indians in the Caribbean islands clamoured to return to India on its Independence. The then Prime Minister, Jawaharlal Nehru wrote to the West Indian official that the Indians remain there and build up the Country and India is in its formation process after a long spell of imperial regime. Yet, they cannot but have passing glimpses of India. All the histories intertwine in the lives of people, especially the West Indies immigrants in London.

History travels, along with the travellers. As the different histories meet, the juxtaposition of differing worlds emerges with the benevolent and malevolent growth. Susheila Nasta words it well: "somewhere between the two on a continuum alongside" there is "a place of resistance deeply embedded in the process of history" and she clarifies that she does not refer to "history as possession of space or place but as a possession of time and the migrant is not travelling as light as might sometimes appear" (42).

Histories have been embedded in history of the West Indies. To go back to its origin, the Caribs and Arawaks are fossilized in the land. At the next stage, colonisation calls in the middle passage and kala pani. Grace Eche Okereke writes, "The history of the West Indies has been characterized by a lot of violation and trauma, consequent upon colonization and latifundia which insured the economic enrichment of the colonialists and the degradation of the slaves and indentured labourers. This has presented the West Indian as a victim, rather than a maker of history". However each writer has tried to depict the West Indian man as a unique "creator of history in his own right" (35). Africans, brought as slaves, occupy a place and leave traces of their own history. The brutal attacks and the inhuman treatment they have faced can never be sunk in the sea of oblivion. Songs bemoaning their alien primitive soil, hearts whispering in pain and the daily ordeal of life suck them in but their hope is their succourer.

Indians arrived in Guyana in 1838 and in Trinidad two years later. Helen Tiffin narrates, "By 1879 the era of European empire slavery was over, but in the 1840s both the psychic memory of slavery and its institutional apparatuses were immediately available to the indentured labourer, and Indian labour was expected to occupy the old slave niche in the plantation economy. The Indians of Trinidad thus inherited a system designed centuries earlier for African slaves" (88). The Indians, subjugated under the white masters, have also to face the inimical attitude of the blacks or to adjust with the social life of the blacks. Severance from the mother country and dislocation disrupt the life of people. They have to adopt willingly or enforcedly the history of the ruling class. It is no more a distinct or separate history but a collective history of its peoples. The boys in the Housing Lark, though they are blacks and Indians do not fanatically cling to their roots. Instead, they look upon themselves as West Indians. As West Indians, they have their own petty prejudices and do not maintain an all embracing gesture towards one another. Battersby wants a Trinidadian to share his room to lessen the rent but not any other. Charlie Victor suggests that a Jamaican is on the lookout for a place and preaches to Bat, "We have so much of prejudice with the white people and them, and don't like a fellow-country man in Brit'n". Bat, of course, replies that he could be a "missionary to the white races if it pay off " (17). Harry Banjo, a Jamaican Calypsonian, has a promising future. When Nobby asks if Harry is in the housing lark scheme Harry confronts them boldly that it is he who gives the idea and all Trinidadians cannot think for themselves. All the same he is generous to pay the rent for the basement room and buying rations too for Bat. Consequently, Bat is free of worrying about rent and food. Gallows accuses Poor, "you send Harry Banjo to jail. Harry was a nice fellar, nicer than you, don't mind he was a Jamaican. The man only in the country a short time and you get him in trouble and save yourself" (116). In the alienating and hostile atmosphere, they have not made an erasure of their differences but assert it as the occasion arises.

In an interview Sam Selvon emphasises that a national feeling needs to be cultivated and attributes the fall of the Federation in the late forties to the following cause: "There was all this bickering. Trinidad feels that it's a better island than Jamaica, and Jamaica feels it's the biggest English-speaking Island. They want everything to happen over there, and Barbados doesn't want to have anything to do with it. That sort of petty rivalry that goes on has been keeping us apart for years" (124). The historical background gets manifested in the characters. But, as

Selvon points out, there is a shift in attitude that the islanders tend to overlook such differences and work towards nationhood. The immigrants too express their differences with each other but come together inevitably as they float in the sea of loneliness.

As the narrative progresses they discuss the land's history, which stays silently as a silhouette. Makarand Paranjape reviews that the Caribbean islands derive their name from the Caribs and they have been practically wiped out. "Other indigenous populations that were decimated in the wake of European colonisation include the Ciboneys and the Arawaks" (126). The Caribbean history has been, as Helen Tiffin affirms "at least since European contact long, bloody and spectacular. The virtual extermination of the native Caribs and Arawaks, the rapacious race between the European powers to find the legendary EL Dorado, and the subsequent rise of the slave plantation system gave the area 'a history' long before the arrival of Indian indentured labour' (89).

The boys surprise others with their `historical knowledge' but one remarks it is mixed up and it is English history. One refers that they were not taught any other history in school. Another responds, "That's because OUR PEOPLE ain't have no history" (125) and doubts when they have history whether the children in English schools will be under compulsion to learn it. Some other person refutes the established notion of the West Indies having no history and says, "Who say we ain't have history? What about the Carib Indians and Abercomby and Sir Walter Raleigh?" (125).

Helen Tiffin comments on this passage that the English history is so humorously, ironically, yet lovingly and familiarly presented (92) but the infusion is rather ironic. The massacre of the natives by the coloniser that has resulted in almost wiping off a race from the face of the earth comes alive. Two indigene groups, the peaceful and the aggressive known as Taino and Carib respectively have been the original dwellers. The Arawaks are mainly agriculturists. The Carib drive out The Antillean Arawak or Taino out of the Lesser Antilles shortly before the appearance of the Spanish (480).

Peter Hulme specifies "the native Caribbean diaspora which is a not a glorious story of survival but a desperate story of trauma and adaptation in which many hundreds of thousands died but out of which emerged a recognizable Carib nation forged in the crucible of colonial struggle" (297). The West Indians cherish the Caribs's indigeneity and are consciously aware of the land's birth pangs. Resistance against the oncoming onslaught, even threatened extermination, has coursed its way through the soil and the land has buried the agonising cries of the people.

Conquest causes destruction and one man's gain is another man's loss. Juxtaposing Raleigh and Abercromby, representative of imperialism against the Caribs, excavates the ruthless hunting after lives. The encounter evolves in endless struggle and resistance. Sir Walter Raleigh (1552-1618), favourite of Elizabeth I, imprisoned for life in the Tower of London gets released in 1616 to find a gold mine in Guiana. Of course, the expedition fails in its gold quest. It signifies the covetous heart of the king of England and also the people's adventurous spirit and the dream of discovering and conquering new land. The renaissance trend of individual's uniqueness and his/her potential gets unleashed in such crossing over seas and entering unknown territories. Sir Ralph Abercromby (1734-1801) was "appointed to the command of British forces in West Indies when he seized the French sugar islands" (20). The two soldiers represent warfare and invasion, which ring death knell to the islanders, both the natives and the settlers. The historical stereotypes are reinstituted to acquiesce with the master narrative with the underlying purpose of throwing it back. While Syl hunts for residence, Bat directs him to an English landlord who takes Indians and not any West Indian. Though Syl protests that he is a West Indian and prefers not to live with an Indian, Battersby quietens him. Helpless in his search, he approaches the landlord who looks at him suspiciously. In a foolhardy manner, much to the amusement of the reader, he blurts out, "I am straight from the banks of Ganges". "I am a student from the orient seeking a roof over my head"(30). The landlord plies him with queries for not wearing national garments, he philosophies that when one is in Rome he has to be a roman and claims to hail from 'West India' and he is a student of life as all are and identifies himself as Ram Singh Ali Mohammed-Esquire. And that reaches the climax. When they both stand there talking, an Indian tenant, Ram, with a big beard and wearing a turban gets inside. Syl succeeds in his endeavour of getting a room. But he cannot rest at peace after the wild hunting because he has to avoid Ram who may get him into trouble. Syl, to guard his safety, goes to the landlord and confesses that Ram is not from India. Besides, he chants all the time and creates a nuisance to the other tenants. The Englisher verifies and knocks at his door. Syl hurries to the corner to prove his Indianness, stands in the corner on his head and asserts to him that he practises his 'yoghourt'. However, the Englisher accuses that he is "flying under false colours and he is from West Indies and gives him a week's notice to vacate. Once again Syl reiterates that he is a born Indian who grew up on the banks of the Ganges and worked on the rice and tea plantation" (32). Later, when he discusses it with Battersby, he identifies Ram by his costume and shocks Syl that he sent him there and he is from Jamaica. The Ganges meanders in the residual memory and the cult of 'Yoghourt' stands aloof signifying the mystical aspirations of a human being in the land of the East. Out of desperation to get a room both Syl and Ram have duped the Englishman. One mimicking certain strategies claims to be an orient and the other alters his appearance to conform to the oriental outward look in order to move around unscathed. But it is in constructing these images the irony gets sharpened. It indicates the image fixity of the Englisher who is unable to see through the pretentious acts for his preconceived and unaltered notions of the East block his perception.

Unearthing of the past in a rather flippant way exemplifies the dexterity of the narrators', who are not professional historians, in alerting the memory and knowing the history of the coloniser. The dominant's imposing of history, from the narrator's view, shows ambivalence and claims sense of superior culture and thereby provides space to show resistance and colonial struggle. Jean expresses a wish of going on a picnic back home. Battersby implements and executes that the party looks like they are setting off for an expedition to the North Pole or something. With all possible pandemonium, they reach Hamdon Court, a historical site, which becomes a space for the immigrants to dehistorcise the historicity of place and people. As the boys near the palace bedroom, the narrator visualises as if King Henry stands there: "the old bird watching his chicks as they stroll about the gardens, studying which one to behead and which one to make a stroke with" (117). The narration continues that he had about three Catherines, two Annes, one Jane and others and when he called out 'Catherine' how the three of them would have wondered which one he was going to send to the Tower for beheading. Fitz warns Teena, his wife, who tries to teach their children some history there, "Don't teach the children no wicked things! Henry Eight was an evil character living with ten-twelve woman" (118). And he ascertains that this place does not belong to him but Wosley has built and given it to him as a present. Further he tells her not to shout for Anne of Cleves might be "catching up on some sleep after a heavy night" (119). It is said in Britannica that King Henry VIII was a "despot under the forms of law' and 'had elastic conscience which was always at the beck and call of his desires and he cared little for principle". The immigrants lovingly mixing with a note of humour express their opinions and resistance to the historical record. The Englishers may not be able to distinguish the territory of Jamaica from that of Trinidad yet the colonised possess an accurate knowledge of the coloniser's history of even remote past.

Talking of mediaeval period, they reminisce alout the great days of the Knights of the Round Table and Richard with a lion heart. Another interjects about Robin Hood and the Merry Men and travel over to the Battle of Hastings when the man looked up in the air, an arrow fell and damaged his eye. Immediately another, as if in a quiz competition, answers that was William the conqueror (1026-1087), who, as the annals say in Senlac, with his Norman army, defeated the English in 1066 which came to be known as the Battle of Hastings and he became the king of England from 1066. The reference to one-eye person reminds them of Nelson and one jumps up with the Battle of Trafalgar and concludes with the current news that Charles Laughton, who as an actor proved his brittle when he acted as Nelson. Horatio Nelson won crucial victories in the Battles of Nile and Trafalgar and is still regarded as Britain's most appealing national hero, and from 1784 to 1787 he commanded a frigate in the West Indies. He was killed by the enemy fire during the Battle of Trafalgar, which established "British naval supremacy for more than a century" (298). In the above narration, history is revisited. Royalty and commonalty alike emerge. The truly valiant and the kind-hearted traverse through. The despots and the chivalrous chart their life. The turbulent period of battles and the ordinary cowardly time commingle. It occurs in flashes but carry within the potency of historical trauma and glorious moments. Bill Ashcroft postulates that the postcolonial discourse adopts three modes in transforming history, namely, rejection, interjection and interpolation (100-102). Sam Selvon does not refuse to recognize history. Instead, he incorporates, thereby avoiding the problem that arises with such exclusivity which results in a kind of 'group insularity'. When it comes to the point of West Indian history whose experiences are omitted from imperial history, he inserts them, which is termed as interjection. Caribbean mind, which he has consciously wanted to develop and project to the world, comes afresh through his writing.

Paul Ricoeur turns on Augustine's concept of time in confession to solve the problem of any narrative having the essence of history and speaks of human time as a threefold present. Bill Ashcroft analyses it thus: a present of things past (memory), a present things and a present of future things (expectation) (87). The temporal experience structures for a slippage of the past into the present and the present of the future into the present and makes the present of the present come alive. The West Indian immigrants bring back the past, and the past of Caribs and Arawaks slip into the present and the past monarchs and great warriors with full gusto spring up and the past routine life of people evinces two geographical boundaries collapsing. In addition to these, there is also an expectant future that forms part of the narrative, The Housing Lark. Engaging the strategy of narrativity, the postcolonial discourse can reinscribe the historical representation and also interpolate history. Interpolation of history is as Ashcroft explains, not "an oppositional discourse but a tactic which operates from the fractures and contradictions of discourse itself" (102). It becomes a tool to insert and revision history. It offers room for contestation, radical perspective and disrupture of history. In fact, "it turns its status as a record to the task of self-determination and cultural empowerment" (92). Histories of different nations echoing the disrupture and difference progress towards distinct identities.

In colonial situations, Helen Tiffin attests "history frequently becomes the source of psychic affirmation and continuity, or, as group genesis, becomes the focus of a developing communal self-consciousness. History and cultural self-consciousness are necessarily aligned, and the idea of history is often closest to the hearts of those whose tradition and legends have been disrupted" (89). She points out five ways of a colonial tackling history. First he looks back to his ancestral homeland and then has either willingly or enforcedly adopted the history of the ruling class. He/she has been transported to another land which causates to opt for the history of the new place and to go in for the collective history of its people. Another is a resistance mode of establishing the history of the race. Finally, the colonial invokes the legends and traditions of the new land and tries to close the gap between his own exile and that of the people of the land. In the case of Selvon's characters, they look upon England for shared roots of West Indian history, which of course does not offer a promising scope. They tend to adopt European and African history of the Caribbean as their own and also at the point of having a shared Indian and black history. However, there evolves the Caribbean history that is racially collective through its complex relationship between British history and the Indian indentured labourers and their generation and the black slaves with their progeny in integration in the islands and in England.

The glowing tribute paid by Ismith Khan comes in adequately. He records that the Caribbeans lack in possessing a record of its past and writes, "The great gap of historical past has not yet been filled in by historians or social scientists, it has been filled in by our writers of fiction, poetry and drama. Sam Selvon was the first writer to fill those empty spaces of history not as historian or social scientist but as novelist, poet and dramatist. While his early works give us a picture of the roots and origins of our culture, his later works—the Moses novels—trace, with accuracy not only where we come from but where we are headed" (59). He adds that it takes a writer like Selvon to crystallize their 'complexity'. Indeed he has woven histories within history dexterously and in a masterminded way that does not descend to bitter cynicism but maintains a genial humour. Pain and laughter parade, gentle humour and sordid pathos permeate and irony and details tend to subvert and interrogate to portray the truth, the facts which add up in the colossal construct of history.

Works Cited

Ashcroft, Bill. *Post-colonial Transformation*. London: Rouledge. 2001

Braziel, Jana Evans. *Diaspora: An Introduction*. Malden: Blackwell Publishing Ltd., 2008.

Clarke, Austin, Jan Carew, Ramabai Espinet, Ismith khan with Frank Birbal Singh. 'Sam Selvon: A celebration'. *Ariel*: A Review of International English Literature, 27.2 April 1996. 49-63.

Collins Biographical Dictionary of English Literature. Glasgoue: Antony Kamm Harper Collins Publishers, 1993. 388-389.

Encylopaedia Britannica. Chicago: Encyclopaedia Britannica Inc. 1960. Vol-I 20,480,879. Vol-II . Vol-VII 248. Vol-X 679.

Fabre, Michel. Samuel Selvon. *West Indian Literature*. Ed. Bruce King. London: The Macmillan Press Ltd., 1979. 111-125.

Hodges, Hugh.'Kitchener Invades England: The London Calypsos of Aldwyn Roberts'. *Wasafiri, 45, Summer* 2005. 24-30.

Hulme, Peter. 'Survival and Invention: Indigeneity in the Caribbean'. *Postcolonial Discourses*. Ed. Gregory Castle. Maiden: Blackwell Publishers, 2001. 294-308.

Mandal, Somdatta. "Home and Abroad. The Politics of Asian-American Representations: A Conversation with Makarand Paranjape". *The Diasporic Imagination: Asian-American Writing*. Vol. I. Interviews of Creative Writing. Ed. Somdatta Mandal. New Delhi: Prestige Books, 2000. 85-98.

Nasta, Susheila. 'Setting up Home in a city of words: Sam Selvon's London Novels'. *Kunapipi* 17.1,1995. 78-95.

Okereke, Grace Eche. "Samuel Selvon's Evolution from A Brighter Sun to Turn Again Tiger: An Expansion of Vision and a Development of Form". *Kunapipi* 17.1, 1995. 35-50.

Paranjape, Markarand. 'The Fragmented Experience'. *CRNLE Journal*, 2000. 126-127.

Reinventing Britain: A Forum. *Wasafiri* 29 Spring, 1999. 37-44.

Roberts, Kovin Thakur Andra. 'Christened with Snow: A conversation with Sam Selvon'. *ARIEL: A Review of International English Literature*, 27.2, April 1996. 89-115.

Selvon. Samuel. *The Housing Lark*. Washington: Three Continents Press, 1965. Interview with Reed Dasenbrock and Ferroza Jussawalla. *Kunapipi*. 17.1, 1995. 114-125.

Tiffin, Helen. 'History and Community Involvement in Indo-Fijian and Indo-Trinidadian writing'. *Reworlding: The Literature of the Indian Diaspora*. Ed. Emmanuel S. Nelson. New York: Greenwood Press. 1992. 87-98.

______. 'Under the kiff-kiff Laughter': Stereotype and Subversion in Moses Ascending and Moses Migrating'. *Kunapipi* 17.1, 1995. 130-139.

12

"Re-"visioning Intertextualities in R.K. Narayan's Novels: Comparative-Cultural Critique

Anand Balwant Patil

The concepts of revisiting, redoing, rethinking, re-imagining, re-visioning, rereading, reinterpreting, rewriting etc. imply improvisations or new dimensions added to the earlier knowledge. The wavering loyalties of the colonized reader are not yet theorized in India (see Nancy Hogley). So reading *A Passage to India* or *The English Teacher* in the light of postcolonial or cultural theories will certainly not only deconstruct but discard hegemonic intra-colonial judgements of Indian comprador class of imitators of Anglo-American New Critics. R.K. Narayan is the cultural product of Anglo-American "regional modernism", British colonialism and indigenous elitism.

Meenakshi Mukherjee's brahminical concept of "twice born" fiction falls short in contrapuntal analysis of cultural hybridity in Indian English novel. It is multi-toned, faced, and layered. Owing to the, in Michael Echeuro's words, "culture conditioned imagination" in a peculiar Indian way, a researcher, the victim of Anglo-American critical theories of autonomy of text, is first shocked by mere title of the English Doctoral thesis of Hyacinth Cynthia Wyatt "R.K. Narayan as a Brahman Novelist" (1997) in Germany. We cannot imagine of the first paragraph of the conclusions in this work in any caste and culture conditioned

Indian criticism. The first sentence is: "Throughout this study, it has been shown that Hindu culture and Narayan's Brahminical beliefs and preparation constitutes the substratum of his novelistic work"(172). It is far better than Indian run-of-the-mill "R.K. Narayan's Life, and Works."

Reading of Edward Said's *Culture and Imperialism* or Homi K. Bhabha's *Nation and Narration* will lead us to new comparative perspectives on RKN's fiction. It is not an accident that similar Brahminical "innate nativism" (see Chomsky) can be traced in *The English Teacher* and "distand Diaspora-immigrant nativism" in Vidyaprasad Surajprasad Naipaul's *The House for Mr Biswas* Not only poetics but also international cultural politics of recognition has influenced both the selection of *The Guide.* To be brief, rereading of RKN's fiction with rich Interdisciplinarity and multiple approaches will certainly produce new knowledge. A great difference is not noticed between the Indian and NRI critics' interpretations of RKN's novels. Alpana Sharma Knipping's (1993) comments on British colonialism and imperialism in *The English Teacher* are more or less in the tone of Meenakshi Mukherjee and Arunprabha Mukherjee. Does Narayan really "write back to the empire"? Why? W.B. Yeats wrote, "What Next" asked Plato's Ghost." The Seminars and Conferences are meant to debate such questions.

Time for a pause, right there. I'm beginning to do exactly what I've always criticized the Naipauls for doing: drawing grand, sweeping conclusions from the flimsiest of anecdotal evidence. After all, one cannot be unaware that in trying to paint even an impressionistic portrait of contemporary Indian society and culture, one is recalling a concept to undefinable that T.S. Eliot was curious enough to call his book on the subject: *Notes Toward the Definition of Culture* and George Steiner, two and half decades later, could do no better that subtitle *In Blue-beard's Castle* as Notes Toward the Redefinition of Culture. I have neither the desire nor the ability to attempt to define or redefine this slippery term; one cannot entirely forget the pro-Nazi poet Hanns Johst's declaration, "When I hear the word 'culture', I reach for my gun." Shashi Tharoor. "India at Forty-nine: Notes Toward an Impression of Indian Society and Culture Today". *Midnight to the Millennium and Beyond*. New Delhi: Penguin Books, 1997: 278.

Much water has flown under the bridge than what Tharoor means by "Indian society as culture" in terms of "the social heritage and contemporary life of Indians". Tharoor's title exhibits the echoes of intertextuality of Salman Rushdie's controversial *The Midnight's Children*. Moreover, revisiting any colonial text from the postcolonial comparative cultural perspectives would reveal a number of unexplored contradictory aspects than what is seen through the elitist "blue" eyes of Tharoor in *Midnight to Millennium*, R. K. Narayan in *The English Teacher* and Meenakshi Mukherjee in *Realism and Reality: Novel and Society in India* or M.K. Naik in a host of articles and books on Indian writings in English. Tharoor's sibling relationship and "family romance", in Sigmund Freud's famous terms, with Naipaul's *The Area of Darkness* or *A Wounded Civilization* and Rushdie's *The Midnight's Children* is apparent in this essay. Similarly the fiction of the first famous trio i.e. Raja Rao, Mulk Raj Anand and Narayan needs to be "revisited" with not only new strategies of reading their texts as a symbolic political unconscious act but also as products of Western, in Edward Said's phrase, "culture and imperialism."

Stepping back and looking comparatively with post-colonial and postmodern perspectives at R.K. Narayan's fiction and contemporary reality after nearly seventy years is more or less similar to what Chinua Achebe did in his *An Image of Africa: Racism in Conrad's Heart of Darkness* (1972) and Henry Louis Gates in his *Race, Writing and Difference* (1995). Elsewhere I (2011) have coined the term "castealization" based on Western "racialization" of literature to study national and international affiliations of intertextualities in Indian literature

So concepts of revisiting, redoing, rethinking, re-imagining, re-visioning, rereading, reinterpreting, rewriting etc. imply improvisations or new dimensions added to the earlier knowledge. In Harold Bloom's terms all reading is misreading and revisions lead to new creations. Intertextual relations are determined by the anxiety of influence and in Sigmund Freud's concept "the family romance of writers". The pre-text makes the posttext possible. The author child is the father of stalwart "writerly" writer. Which R.K. Narayan do we want to revisit, from which perspectives? Does he represent the rich, in Bakhtinian terms, "carnivalization and heteroglossia", of diverse Indian cultures and languages? For whom did he write? In order to answer such pertinent questions we have to take the descriptive term "revisiting" to the deeper analytical conceptual level. For the intellectuals undernourished by colonized traditional curriculum of mono-literary studies it is still a greater challenge to reinterpret colonized texts with pseudo-secularism and cultural illiteracy without Raymond William's vision and commitment to challenge Leavisian Great Tradition of critical thought.

In the new millennium of internationalization of literatures it demands postmodern interdisciplinary approaches; but our criticism is stuck in the mire of Anglo-American modernity. See the simple dictionary meanings of the word "revisit" in the title of the theme of the seminar. The dictionary meanings are many: To visit again, A second or repeated visit.(*The American Heritage® Dictionary of the English Language*, Fourth Edition copyright ©2000 by Houghton Mifflin Company. Updated in 2009. Published by Houghton Mifflin Company). revisit (Verb)-visit again; "We revisited Rome after 25 years". return-go or come back to place, condition, or activity where one has been before; "return to your native land"; "the professor returned to his teaching position after serving as Dean" (Based on WordNet 3.0, Farlex clipart collection. © 2003-2008 Princeton University, Farlex Inc).

Our "revisit" to Narayan with ideology of Namwar Singh's preaching to decolonize Indian mind and prior to him Ngugi wa

Thing'O's battle cry for decolonizing African mind would certainly bring new revelations and rewards. It is Ngugi's "homecoming" (1972) and the agenda of "abolishing Departments of English" (1976) might help us more than our too subjective and impressionistic caste conditioned Indian criticism. It should be noted at the outset that the wavering loyalties of the colonized reader are not yet theorized in India (see Nancy Hogley).

In "re- examination" of Narayan's *The English Teacher,* 66 years after its birth, by the post-Independent Indian readers fed on Anglomerican postcolonial theories and affected by indigenous, in Edward Said's word, "affiliations" of regions, religions, class and caste, needs new cultural approach today. For example, reading *A Passage to India* or *The English Teacher* in the light of postcolonial or cultural theories again enriches our understanding. But for this we have to read Harold Bloom's "introduction" to the first and compare the latter with Naipaul's *A House for Mr. Biswas* in Fanonian terms. Such revision is bound to deconstruct and discard hegemonic intracolonial judgements of Indian comprador class of imitators of Anglo-American New Critics; but also take us to their resistant counterparts in Black aesthetics. In fact, R.K. Narayan's oeuvre is the cultural product of Anglo-American "regional modernism", British colonialism and indigenous elitism.

In this sense, Meenakshi Mukherjee's brahminical concept of "twice born" fiction falls short in contrapuntal analysis of cultural hybridity in any Indian English novel. Its is confined to, in Edward Said's term, the "worldliness" of the earliest sociological twin process namely Anglicization (modernization) and sanskritization (brahminization) used for analyzing the process of acculturation after the elitist cultural contact with Europe.

But why only "twice born"? Has it not projected the monolithic brahminical image of Indian literature to the Western world? What about indigenous "native" cultural transformations?

Why are they excluded both from *Kantapura* and *The English Teacher,* albeit both are set in the villages? Hence the cultural representation of "the Other's double" in Indian English fiction is yet to become the subject of discussion. In this cultural sense the terms such as "Indianness", Indianize", nativize" etc. are very deceptive. We may be able to trace how old wine in new bottle may be more poisonous, if we understand why Americans always condemn the French theories of structuralism, deconstruction and intertextuality as "poisonous".

Moreover, in our literary image building cultural industry, to use Fanonian theory, "the battle for reciprocal recognition" is determined by hierarchical cultural capital and degree of illiteracy. Consequently, this dominant Orientalist (British-brahminical) image of earlier Anglo-Indian, later Indo-Anglian-Commonwealth and the latest Indian writing in English by the Indian elitist writers with traditional, in Pierre Bourdeu's sociological concept, "cultural capital" must have led the German scholar Hyacinth Cynthia Wyatt to undertake the research topic for the doctoral degree "R.K. Narayan as a Brahmin Novelist" submitted to Universitat Rovira I Virgili in 1997. We hardly find such cultural materialism and semiotic approach in our double colonized Indian critical thought. No one can dare to think of such inflammatory cultural area of research where devils fear to tread in a pseudo-secular environment. This shows how and why the term "culture" is considered not only the most difficult word among three English terms but also the most inflammatory of all as demonstrated by George Huntington in *Cultural Clash.*

It is necessary to study any Indian literary text as a Walmikian as well as Homerian cultural battlefield. In the tsunamis of globalization it is a right time to rethink of not only the relevance of true contributions of our stalwarts but also device new strategies of rereading colonialisms of various kinds and replacing literary theories for survival in the new competitive literary market of the global village. I hope this seminar is a welcome beginning in this direction. But we should think of its concrete returns in terms of marketing new knowledge by producing books to be sold all over the world. Of course, there is the ending in the beginning itself. As a creative writer and comparatist-culturalist, I limit this discourse only to the intercultural and international intertextualities in two novels.

It is necessary to demonstrate comparatively, with the help of theory of intertextuality, how literature in all formerly colonized countries is Eurocentric, two-toned, multi-faced, and multi-layered. Owing to, in Michael Echeuro's words, "the culture conditioned imagination" in a peculiar Indian systemic way, a researcher, the victim of Anglo-American critical theories, and local structures of culture and imperialism. Let us juxtapose two samples of the titles and conclusions of the doctoral theses carried out in the same year in India and Germany. Ramesh Dnyate's *The Novels of R.K. Narayan: A Typological Study of Characters* (1996) was completed in University of Pune under the guidance of a " reputed Marxist interpreter of literature" and published with a bibliography which includes only 80 books but any periodical. The contents do not show least awareness of Interdisciplinarity and the conclusions remain at very superficial levels. The final paragraph runs as follows:

> In short, the typological approach may be regarded as a strategy to focus on the essentials in the craft of Narayan's novel. The essentials seem to have been reflected (a) in Narayan's presentment of the epic of the ordinary conceived on the stage of the middle-class Malgudi; (b) in his bifocal vision of comic irony perceiving the essentially illusory nature of the life and (c) in his positive vision of life despite its predestinate or karmic conception (170).

This title seems to be a misnomer and we do not know how Narayan's characters are "cultural products", which are determined by double binds of imperialism. The majority of Indian doctoral works on Rao and Narayan, excluding Anand, exhibit salient features of "culture and imperialism" and project the image of their novels as "prose epics of India"(see M.K. Naik). Elsewhere, I (1997) have demonstrated how *Kanthapura* is "a bogus prose epic" of anglicized elitist India. What is consciously or ignorantly ignored by Indians is objectively analyzed by the foreigners. Hyacinth Cynthia Wyatt's *R.K. Narayan as a Brahmin Novelist* (1997), in Germany, is a simple cultural study, which demonstrates once again how foreigners have studied Indian languages and literatures better than Indians. We cannot imagine of the first paragraph of the conclusions in this work in any caste and culture conditioned Indian criticism. The first paragraph runs as follows:

> Throughout this study, it has been shown that Hindu culture and Narayan's Brahminical beliefs and preparation constitutes the substratum of his novelistic work. This study has also called attention to the strong presence of Narayan's Brahmanical heritage and erudition as revealed by the recurrence of cultural symbols and allegorical tendencies that appear at different levels of understanding in all his novels. It has been demonstrated that the myths and teachings continually influence the psychology and behaviour of Narayan's protagonists, many living out roles similar to the mythological, some even with the same names, such as Chandran in *The Bachelor of Arts* (the myth of the King Chandran), Savitri in *The Dark Room* (the myth of Savitri), Vasu in *The Man Eater of Malgudi* (Vasu, the King of the Sudras), and Nagaraj in *The Wounded Nagraj* ((another name for Shiva when he is the King of Dance). Others have similar names such as Krishnan in *The English Teacher* for *Krishna,* the avatar of *Vishnu,* Bharati in *Waiting for the Mahatma* for Bharat (another name for India) and Raman in *The Painter of Signs* for Rama the hero of *Ramayana.* (172).

Now, crossing the boundaries of one language and literature is inevitable in anglobalization. Let us study comparatively Narayan's *The English Teacher* and Naipaul's A *House for Mr. Biswas to* illustrate interculturalism and both poetics as well as politics of culture in fiction. What structures of literary feelings did go in making of Narayan's and his counterpart immigrant

Naipaul's novels? Naipaul's *A House for Mr Biswas* is a fine example of continuation of "distant nativism" of a different kind by the immigrants, especially diaspora writers of the original Brahman caste in majority. The names of his characters such as Mr Mohun Biswas, Shama, Tulsi, Ganesh, Jairam, Govind, Leela etc., have distinct myths and legends associated with them and they are deeply rooted in Indian ethos. Even the names of houses, places and stores such as a Hanuman House, a Tulsi store, a Tulsi shop etc. remind us of, in Derek Walcott's compliments used in his Nobel lecture, "the fragments of the great epic culture" on that distant island in the British colony. William Walsh has cited Gordon Rohlchr's observations to show how: "The book can be interpreted on several levels. There is the obvious surface level where Biswas can be seen as a second generation Indian who, although rebelling against his own decaying Hindu world, cannot compromise with the Creole world of Trinadad" (65). Walsh has not commented on the impact of British "high" culture and literature on Mr. Biswas. As an outsider, Walsh cannot claim adequate cultural literacy of India also, but recommends it Naipaul's masterpiece and further points out:

> ...The members of the community in *A House for Mr. Biswas*, even those like the Indians who were exempt from formal, historical slavery, carry about with them in their attitude and posture, in their management of life and feeling, the indelible mark of the slave, who is supremely the unnecessary man.... Mr. Biswas constructs the proof of his necessity...that he becomes a model of man, just as the history and situation which formed him are seen to be a metaphor of the process which constitutes any man (30-31).

It is not the coincidence that Nayarayan's protagonist is constituted in the same mould of the Brahmanical Vedic culture with very few local differences. I (2005) have demonstrated how a single "sign" like "bell" plays a significant semiotic role in the cultural structure of a novel. Wyatt has analyzed Narayan's protagonists in terms of four *ashramas.* Like his Raju (*The Guide*),

Raman (The *Painter of Signs*), Mr Biswas acquires knowledge through books and learns to help people as well *sarvadharma*. Mr Biswas represents *grihastha* also. But he is the product of more hybridized culture which is reflected in a ritual meal described by Ganesh:

> "Open a tin of salmon," Ramlogan ordered. "And get some bread and butter and peppersauce and some avocado pears". And he went himself to look after the preparations, saying, "We have a author in a family, a man, girl..."

After quoting these lines Theorux writes, "In the first year of their marriage Ganesh beats Leela considerably. No brutality is attached to beating; on the contrary, they are a source of pride for traditional Hindus.Mr. Biswas, not a wife-beater reflects...." (58). The interdisciplinary exploration of such Hindu culture specific structures in both the novels and the degree of westernization illustrate the significance of comparative culture studies. The problem of creative tension in representation of the colonized needs to be studied with reference to theories expounded by Frantz Fanon, Edward Said, Homi K. Bhabha and others. For example, Said argues:

> Think the narratives through together within the context provided by history of imperialism, a history whose underlying contest between white and non-white has emerged lyrically in the new and more inclusive counternarrative of liberation. This, I would say, is the full situation of postmodernism, for which Lyotard's amnesiac vision has been insufficiently wide. Once again *representation* becomes significant, not just as an academic or theoretical quandary but a political choice.
>
> How the anthropologist represents his or her disciplinary situation is on one level, of course, a matter of local, personal, or professional moment. But it is in fact part of a totality, one's society, whose shape and tendency depend on the cumulatively alternative or deterrent and oppositional weight made up by a whole series of such choices.... The main point is that anthropological representations bear much on the presenter's world as on who, or what is represented (224).

The sources of this interculturalism and internationalism should be traced to the Anglo-American project of high modernism and aestheticism. The Joycian trend of modernization of myth had reached the Gateway of India as well as the shores of West Indies along with other Western, to use Edward Said's term, "travelling theories" of novel. The Anglo-American "Project of Modernity and Aesthetic Experience" was designed in the 1920s immediately after the First World War. Narayan wrote his fiction in the next decade. Of course, he amalgamated Indian reality and "cultural heritage" in Western technique. Apart from Narayan's alien technical devices, Wyatt's mastery of deconstructing "Indian" myths from the *Vedas* to modern "Bharata" can be hardly found in the corpus of Indian criticism on Narayan's novels. So his objective semiotic cultural interpretation of Narayan's novels is a novel intervention in Indian critical thought. Albeit not comparative, his cultural materialistic approach is so neutral and scientific that there is not a single casteist tinge that spoils the image of any caste. It is a very illuminating thesis of less that two hundred pages and not voluminous duplicate compilation like Indian *A Critical Study of R.K. Narayan's Life, and Works.* If similar myth making is traced to in V.S. Naipaul's *A House for Mr Biswas* set in a village in the West Indies, it will be more revealing and rewarding comparative cultural study. The semiotics of names of persons and places carries with it not only their religion, markers of identity; but also history, politics and what not. Perhaps Shakespeare wanted to ignore them when he said, "What is there in a name?" His characters and plots of the plays were structured by the Western culture and society. It matters most as to how the creative writer uses or misuses/subverts these classical texts in his own fiction. Walsh has explored several "personal matters" in Narayan's life which reveals the texture of hybridity of Indian and Western elements of culture. His wife used to play tennis with white women in the club. Walsh observes:

> An Indian child of this class and caste was introduced to the classical Indian tales, myths, and Vedic poetry very early in life (11).

> ...He went first to the Lutherian Mission School (Madras) where he was one of the few non-Christians and the only Brahmin boy in his class. Scripture classes were devoted to lampooning the Hindu gods and ridicule was poured on the Brahmins, who, it was said, while claiming to be vegetarians sneakily ate fish and meat in secret and were probably responsible for the soaring prices of those commodities (12-13).
>
> ...In addition, a priceless privilege for someone like Narayan were the amenities he enjoyed both in his father's library crammed with Carlyle, Ruskin, Walter Peter, Wordsworth, Browning. Byron and Shakespeare, and in the school library, particularly during the summer vacations. He read any book that he liked and all the magazines, of which there seemed to be copious supply, from *Little Folks* to *The Nineteenth Century and after: a Monthly Review* and *The Cornhill Magazine.* Through *The Strand* he became familiar with Conan Doyle, P.G. Wodehouse, W.W.Jacobs, and Arnold Bennett, and *The Bookman* introduced him to the library figures of those days, Shaw, Hardy, Ibsen, Chesterton and Belloc. He loved the literary gossip in *Johnson's London Weekly*, *The Spectator* and the *Times Literary Supplement.* He was another library cormorant, and certainly a fiction and romantic poetry cormorant, and he developed some extraordinary enthusiasm at this time, in particular, for example, for Marie Corelli and Mrs Henry Wood's East Lynne (13, 14).

All such autio/biographical references helped the earlier comparatists in traditional studies of literary influences, imitation, mutation, echo, adaptation, translation, offshoots, echoes, plagiarism, and so on. But in new comparative cultural study it is more important to analyze the structures of writer's literary feelings in terms of the interculturalness, interliterariness, internationalness and intertextualities at the microscopic levels. The concept of regionalism in *The English Teacher* is guided by contemporary "aesthetics of regionalism" depicted by William Empson in the essay of the same title. Our comparative culture criticism has to give equal importance to the study of both poetics as well as politics of cultural productions. In the age of information traditional umbrella term "autobiographical approach" has taken a new avatar of "literary biography" In the introduction to a recent book aptly titles as *Built of Books: How Reading Defined the Life of Oscar Wilde*, Thomas Wright observes:

> Wilde's reading was the chief inspiration for his writings. He was essentially a pre-modern author who adapted and conflated the books he read, rather than a Romantic writer concerned with originality and self-expression. His works are saturated with allusions from his vast and miscellaneous reading: they form a little library of exquisite echoes.... Wilde knew how to use books—the traditional symbols of authorship and learning in Western iconography—to convey his culture and his literary achievements.(6-7).
>
> Wilde devoured and luxuriated in books. ...
>
> Wilde talked of books and often talked like books; he talked so well that he seemed to talk books away. He told stories based on books and countless anecdotes and jokes about them; in his writings, his characters are frequently compared to kooks... (7).

Narayan (and also by 'heritage of loss' Naipaul) belonged to the priestly class and culture traditionally known for monopolized classical learning. He was a son of the Headmaster of the Secondary School, and William Walsh, like Wright, has used Coleridge's famous phrase, a true 'library cormorant' to show how was fed off a varied diet of books in the school.

Certainly the above cited references, albeit exclude any reference to Indian books; have contributed to the shaping of spirit of The *English Teacher* (1945) which we will consider later. In addition, a comparitist, like monoliterary critic, should not believe the authorial confession cited by Walsh as follows:

> 'After Scott I picked up a whole row of Dickens and developed his London and the queer personalities therein. Rider Haggard, Marie Corelli, Moliere and Pope and Marlowe, Tolosti, Thomas Hardy- an indiscriminate jumble; I read everything with the utmost enjoyment (14).

It is very interesting to compare literary intertextuality in these sample texts. Narayan's protagonist is a teacher of English in the pre-independence phase of the freedom struggle, which gives rise to the resistant literature of, to use Fanon's phrase, "fighting phase". It is neither the product of Fanonian violence nor of Gandhian non-violence but rather of a priestly ideological "return to the village", especially Malgudi coloured by American aesthetics of regionalism.

Krishna is a college teacher, but the literary intertextuality is neither exhaustive nor illusive in Wildean sense. The absence of Indian texts, both *deshi* and *margi*, shows how Western cultural imperialism had been alienating our intellectuals from their own roots. It is the first person narrative which reflects the dialemma of Krishna caught between two pulls: indigenous rustic and alien modern. His family is in the village and he stays in the college hostel and engages four lectures per day. The colonized life is full of paradoxes. Krishnan who once "devoured" English books and hopes to write poetry and later fiction by following British models ad by reading books on creative writing in English now begins to hate the white master's language and literature. This Prospero-Caliban Complex needs to be illustrated in detail. The monotony of this exercise in, to use a strong term in black aesthetics, 'daffodilization' of minds and dislike of teaching profession strikes the reader in the opening paragraph itself: some sort of vague dissatisfaction, a self rebellion" (5). Like Mr Biswas, the dominant presence of British texts in his consciousness is noticed in the next paragraph. The married teacher tells:

> I took stock of my daily life. I got up at eight every day, read for the fiftieth time Milton, Carlyle and Shakespeare, looked through compositions, swallowed a meal..(5).

He teaches *King Lear* to B.A. Junior students. Four lines from the stormy scene are quoted. The teaching of grammar and composition provides another but for a mild satire. He writes further:

> I spent the rest of the period giving a general analysis of the mistakes I had encountered in this batch of composition—rather

> very, as such for hence, split infinitives, collective nouns, and all the rest of the traps that the English language sets for foreigners ... Then I set men on Exercise in essay writing on the epigram 'Man is the master of his destiny'. "An idiotic theme," I felt, "this abstract and confounded metaphysics' but I could not help it. I had been ordered to set this subject to the class (5, 6).

Further there is a pun on' Kant' and 'can't', American spelling and domination. The father in law of the protagonist provides one more model for him to rise up in arms against the British education system and tender the resignation to return to the village. He bring out the contradiction in the life of his father-in-law: "He was a B.A. of the olden days brought on Pater, Carlyle and Scott and Browning; personally looked after by Dr. William Miller, Mark Hunter, and other eminent professors in Madras... refused to enter Government service, settled in village...." (19)

Two theoretical aspects might explain some aspects of intra and inter-national colonialism and imperialism. The love and hate relationship with the ruler's culture and education takes us to the sources of comparisons in *Miseducation of Negroes, The Pedagogy of the Oppressed, Masks of Conquest: Literary Study and British Rule in India.*

Unlike Rao in *Kanthapura*, Narayan has not mentioned M.K. Gandhi's name that was the fountainhead of nationalism in those days. Here steps in the intra-cultural clash in India. So the resistant elements in this novel need to be studied at two levels: national and *international.* The latter is illustrated by the following intertextuality: "I picked up *Taine's History of Literature* and leaned the glass against it." "Taine every time, I muttered" (22). But it is a very meek resistance which fits well into the pattern of the flexibility of the comprador class. Later Jane Austen's *Pride and Prejudice* is mentioned as a text for non-detailed study. However, nowhere there is a deeper psychoanalysis of such literary responses. It seems that Narayan consciously guarded himself against British stream of consciousness techniques which had penetrated into Rao's novels. For locating such elements in a text we have to take into consideration several factors such as place of writing, implied readers, publishers, critics, local creative tensions etc.

Krishna's creative urge is the only oasis in this desert. When he becomes introspective he thinks loudly:

> 'Nothing to do, Why not write poetry? Ages since I wrote anything?' My conscience had the habit of asserting itself once in six months. Some pieces written in English and some in Tamil... He hopes to publish them. Wordsworth's "She was the phantom of delights and Keats", "A thing of Beauty"... are cited.

The Ode to the West Wind gives the ironic touch to the letter of resignation submitter dramatically to Mr. Brown. The intertextuality of *Golden Treasury* (p.47) opens the Pandora's Box of pre-Independence plagiarisms in Indian poetry. Finally, before protagonist's declaration in the resignation that "I am up against system"... "The whole system of education" "insensible Shakespeare's sonnets or the ode" are referred to in passing. The soft corner for the twin process of Anglicization and Sanskritization does not allow Narayan to resist the Western tradition of education just like Achebe in Africa and Braithwaite in Caribbean islands. There is some nationalist spirit which entered through the freedom struggle movement. But it remains at the superficial level.

Although the similar name of both protagonists invoke cultural signs associated with Lord Krishna, the degree of their literary acculturation differ in few ways. But similarities are many. Hindi texts and Jairam's teaching influence Mr. Biswas less, but British texts play vital role in making him a journalist of *Trinidad Sentinei. Bell's Standard Education, Volumes of Comprehensive Knowledge, Collin's Clear-Type Shakespeare* other Western, especially British, texts mentioned by Naipaul speak volumes for his more dialogic imagination and richer cultural hybridity in his novel. Paul Therous writes:

> His marriage is not a secret in a gotes, he is welcomed tearfully by his mother, pestered for details by his relatives, who have the same awe for Mrs Tulsi that Joe Gargery has for Havisham in *Great Expectations.* Mr Biswas's confusion (how to explain to these simple people the ways of those in that great house?) is similar to Pip's, but he must admit to himself that what he has done cannot be undone: 'He was married. Nothing, now, except death, could change that' (62).

Mr. Biswas, reading the *Meditations* of Marqcus Aurclius and Samuel Smiles, is trying to be different from the Tulsis, from the people he knows, from his own parents. He is trying to escape from tedium (64).

In this way, both the protagonists "rise up against" two distinct systems in two different regions of the British colonies. Yet the structures of their literary feelings are not much different like those in the French or Portuguese colonies.

What changed Krishna's love of European literature into hate of western education and dislike to enter into the machine of otherness and made Krishna resign the post of the teacher of English in a college in the nineteen thirties? Narayan graduated in 1930 and after his MA in literature made "half-hearted effort to teach". This "love and hate" relationship needs to be studied in terms of Albert Memmi's *The Colonizer and The Colonized* (1957).He has theorized how the slave slowly internalizes the master's model and becomes Europe-America-centric. His resistance to the colonized wears different masks. For example, "the colonizers always create the class of bourgeois" of their own colour, taste and culture, from among natives Frantz Fanon in his revolutionary *The Wretched of the Earth* and *White Skin, Black Mask* presented the psychoanalysis of their violence which led to the apartheid movement in Africa as well as the Black Panthers' movement in the States of America. We cannot have the violence of that kind in the Gandhian era of non-cooperation and non-violence in which Narayan conceived *The English Teacher* and other novels. Thus the major theme of resistance and nationalism, which is much hyped by formalist critics, needs to be reconsidered. "The white man's burden" was shifted to the "whitish/wheatish" highest class/caste among browns in India. Narayan's writings represent that bourgeois class/ caste which must have provoked "leftist students at Madras", as Walsh reports. Narayan's as well as Raja Rao's elitist nationalism in their novels needs to be reinterpreted in terms of the literary representation of the subaltern. Ranajt Guha opens his article, "On Some Aspects of the Historiography of Colonial India" as follows:

> The historiography of Indian colonialism has for a long time been dominated by elitism-colonialist elitism and bourgeois-nationalist elitism. Both originated in the ideological product of British rule in India, but have survived the transfer of power and been assimilated to neo-colonialist and neo-nationalist forms of discourse in Britain and India respectively. Elitist historiography of the colonialist or neo-colonialist type counts British writers and institutions among its protagonists, but has its imitators in India and other countries too. Elitist historiography of the colonialist type or neo-colonialist type is primarily an Indian practice but not without imitators in the ranks of liberal historians in Britain and elsewhere (1).

According to Alpana Sharma Knippling, the period of the 1930s and1940s display show "the alliance of nationalism and colonialism produced India's modern 'moment' and now the writing of a certain kind of fiction participated in this inauguration of modernity" (170). Further she observes:

> R. K.Narayan (b.1906) and Raja Rao (b.1908), two early Indian writers in English, productively demonstrate how the literary project participated in the modern 'moment' inaugurated by the complicitous embrace of the discourse of the discourses of nationalism and colonialism. Narayan's *The English Teacher* (1945) and Rao's *Kanthapura* (1936) are novels produced at a time when the most volatile political imperative concerned the need for Indian subjects to position themselves vis-à-vis British colonialism and Indian nationalism. But with the exception of *Waiting for the Mahatma,* neither colonialism nor nationalism occupies a central

> position in Narayan's novels of this or. for that matter any later period. Conversely, questions regarding colonialism and nationalism do occupy a large part of Raja Rao's *Kanthapura*, but they are treated in such a way that they are deterred rather than addressed in both Narayan's *The English Teacher* and Rao's *Kantapura*, the, aspects of colonialism and nationalism are engaged in a sidewise fashion, indirectly and obliquely (170,171).

She has pointed out how *Kanthapura* does a lip service to Gandhism, it fails to explain: why did it happen? Why did M.K. Naik laud *Kanthapura* as "a prose epic of India"? How to decolonize such extensions of Anglomerican projects of modernism and aesthetics which demand, in Immanuel Kant's words, production of "ignorance' for retaining hegemony of aesthetics of 'forms and culture.' Our colonized curriculum produces much ignorance. It is necessary to take into consideration the second part of Kantian aphorism for gaining better comparative perspectives on all "Indian Writing in English" and the big process of internationalization of literature. My (1999) works have brought out some hidden aspects of this intra- as well inter- colonialism. The different nature of colonialism and imperialism in Portuguese Goa still awaits explorations. Hence I am asked to translate my Marathi book *British Bombay ani Portuguese Govyateel Wangmay* (1999) into English (literature in British Bombay and Portuguese Goa) by the German publisher.

In order to understand this complex creative process we have not only to master Blooming aesthetics of influence, Venetian theories of intertextuality, recent medical concepts of "textual intercourse" and K. K. Ruthven's long list of terms such as faking, remaking, retailoring, prefabricating, etc. In addition to this it is necessary to define double colonized Indian reader as Nancy Hogley had done in case of Irish reader. From the new historicist perspectives is necessary to trace the significance of the relationship between culture and imperialism in Indian fiction.

Since this talk focuses on intertextualities in a novel on the English teacher is befitting to cite some lines from Ngugi wa

Thingo's' *The Writer in a changing Society* (1969). He himself is a committed writer and a teacher of English. He writes:

> I too must have changed since I started writing in 1960.
>
> I was then a student at Makerere University College...I had read a number of writers, African and West Indian, and I knew that what they told, the song they sang, was different from what I had heard from the British writers who had been crammed down my throat in schools and at the University....I grew up in a small village...One day I heard a song. That song I heard as a child then spoke of things past and things to come. I was living in a colonial situation but I did not know...
>
> I believe that African intellectuals must align themselves with the struggle of African masses for meaningful national ideal...Perhaps, in a small way; the African writer can help in articulating the feelings behind this struggle (7-50).

I believe our revisit to RKN and his Malgudi threatened by the Special Economic Zone in Americanization "can help in articulating the feelings behind this struggle". Keep it up!

Works Cited

Achebe, Chinua. *Hopes and Impedements: Selected Essays 1945-1987*. London:Heinemann International, 1988.

Adiga, Aravind. *Between the Assassinations*. London: Picador, 2008.

Bhabha, Homi K. (ed.) *Nation and Narration*. London: Routledge, 1995.

Guha, Ranajt (ed) "On some aspects of the Historiography of Colonial India". *Subaltern Studies I: Writings on South Asian History and Society*. Delhi: OUP, 1982:1-8

Memmi, Albert. *The Colonizer and The Colonized*. 1957, trans. Howard Greenfield. New York: The Orion Press, 1965.

Naipaul, V.S. *A House for Mr Biswas*. London: Russell Edition, 1961.

Narayan, R.K. *The English Teacher*. Great Britain: Eyre and Sportiswoode, 1945, reissued by William Heinemann, 1978.

Patil, Anand. "A Comparative Study of Nativistic Intertextuality in Indian Fiction", in Paranjape, Makarand.ed. *Nativism: Essays in Criticism*. New Delhi: Sahitya Akademi, 1997: 177-210. Reprinted in *The Whirligig of Taste: Essays in Comparative Literature*, New Delhi: Creative Books, 1999.

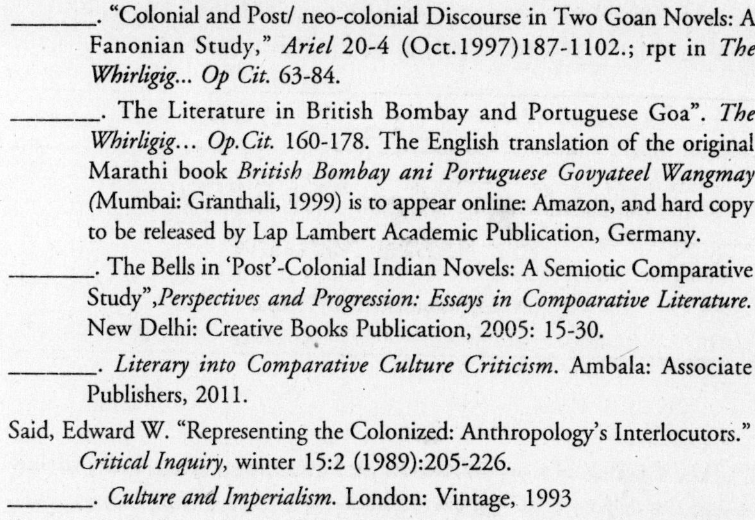

_______. "Colonial and Post/ neo-colonial Discourse in Two Goan Novels: A Fanonian Study," *Ariel* 20-4 (Oct.1997)187-1102.; rpt in *The Whirligig... Op Cit.* 63-84.

_______. The Literature in British Bombay and Portuguese Goa". *The Whirligig... Op.Cit.* 160-178. The English translation of the original Marathi book *British Bombay ani Portuguese Govyateel Wangmay* (Mumbai: Granthali, 1999) is to appear online: Amazon, and hard copy to be released by Lap Lambert Academic Publication, Germany.

_______. The Bells in 'Post'-Colonial Indian Novels: A Semiotic Comparative Study",*Perspectives and Progression: Essays in Compoarative Literature.* New Delhi: Creative Books Publication, 2005: 15-30.

_______. *Literary into Comparative Culture Criticism.* Ambala: Associate Publishers, 2011.

Said, Edward W. "Representing the Colonized: Anthropology's Interlocutors." *Critical Inquiry*, winter 15:2 (1989):205-226.

_______. *Culture and Imperialism.* London: Vintage, 1993

Sharma, Knippling, Alpana. "Fiction of the Indian subcontinent". *Modern Fiction Studies*, 39:1, (Spring 1993) 169-186.

Theroux, Paul. *V.S. Naipaul: An Introduction to His Works.* London: Hienemann, 1972.

Walsh, William.*V S. Naipaul.* Edinburgh: Oliver and Boyed, 1973.

Thing'O, wa Ngugi.*Homecoming: Essays on African and Caribbean Literature, Culture and Politics.* London: Heinemann Educational Books 1872.

_______. *Narayan: A Critical Appreciation.* New Delhi: Allied Publishers 1982.

Wright, Thomas *Built of Books: How Reading Defined the Life of Oscar Wilde.*New York: Henry Holt and Co. 2009.

Wyatt, Hyacinth Cynthia. "R. K. Narayan as a Brahman Novelist" Thesi Doctoral, Universitat Rovira, i Virgili (1997).

13

Rushdie to Adiga: The Edifice of the Indian Narrative

G.A. Ghanshyam Iyengar

Indian English fiction enlivened and attained a stature of its own with the advent of Salman Rushdie's novel *The Midnight's Children.* A novel that broke all conventions and rules to create a new genre that was revolutionary in its use of theme, literary techniques and linguistic variations, it has remained one of the best fictions ever to have bagged the prestigious Booker Prize in 1980. *Midnight's Children* transformed not only the face of Indian English fiction but also the very genre of fiction on a global scale. The trend set by Rushdie was a tall order to follow but young Indian writers took up the challenge and proved their mettle not once but thrice since Rushdie's achievement. Arundhati Roy's *The God of Small Things* (1997), Kiran Desai's *The Inheritance of Loss* (2006) and more recently Arvind Adiga's *The White Tiger* (2008) have won the coveted prize keeping the Rushdian legacy alive and kicking with their talent and expertise.

The present paper traces the excellence achieved by these Booker Prize-winning novelists and their novels, which have generated the image of Indian English fiction as the hot new cakes of world literary scenario. The novelty of expression and representation inherent in the works will be taken up for analysis in the paper as the required merit of achievement on a global scale as well as their influence on the whole gamut of Indian and world literature.

Indian English fiction owes its grandeur to the literary experiments and innovations of its stalwarts like the path breaking genius of Salman Rushdie, the panache of regional flavour in Arundhati Roy, diasporic consciousness in Kiran Desai and social critique in Arvind Adiga. The experiments in language, theme and technique have engendered their art as exquisite pieces of literature that has prompted the whole world to stand up and take notice. In the present paper the novels of the four Booker Prize winners will be studied focusing on the narrative skills and expertise in the select novels: *The Midnight's Children (MC)*, *The God of Small Things (GST)*, *The Inheritance of Loss (IL)* and *The White Tiger (WT)*, respectively.

In the year 1981 was published a novel that has continued to win laurels even after two decades. Salman Rushdie's groundbreaking novel *The Midnight's Children* was a pioneer of sorts in the history of Indian English fiction. It heralded a new beginning for the genre that had seen the likes of such literary geniuses as the celebrated trio of Indian English fiction amongst a plethora of so many others. His novel proved to be the beginning of a new era with its unabashed expressions, use of language, extravaganza and multitude. A saga of a country's journey from inception to partition and freedom, it juxtaposed the realms of personal with public, history with fiction, realism with magic; a trend that influenced the coming generation of writers and is visibly reflected in their art. The contemporary structure of Indian English fiction; its edifice rests assuredly on the capable shoulders of its new generation of writers who have followed in the footsteps of Rushdie. In 1997, Arundhati Roy bagged yet another Booker Prize for an Indian, with her novel that centred on the representation of the patriarchal Indian society, the class structure and gender discrimination. Drawing up a regional picture of rural Indian society in South India, Roy reveals glimpses from her own life through the eyes of the young twin.

Kiran Desai, the next Indian to win the coveted prize in 2006, is a diasporic writer like Rushdie. It's the characteristic backward look of the Diaspora that finds an expression in her works that are based on Indian society, culture and ethos. Her narratives are the portrayal of small town India with all its idiosyncrasies, beliefs, and social and cultural life that gives a charm to her fiction. Unlike Desai's nostalgia for her home that finds an expression in her choice of themes and settings for her novel, Arvind Adiga, the winner of 2008 exposes the underlying dark belly of Indian society, culture and politics. The novel is a harsh indictment of India and the Indian way of life and ethos. It attempts to represent the other darker side of 'India Shinning', hitherto neglected and ignored in contemporary fiction. All the novelists and their literary art are winners and have richly contributed to the development of the genre, giving a shape and form to the edifice of the Indian narrative. Literally speaking, a narrative is a story that tells a tale through images, pictures, characters, dialogues, verse, etc, as per the genre. In other words apart from fictional narrative, poetry, drama as well as non-fiction can also employ the narrative structure as its mode of representation.

Edifice of Indian Narrative

The narrative style that has evolved and developed from Rushdie to Adiga is characterized by the postmodern technique of an amalgamation of various narrative voices within the story. The narrator is often the protagonist of the novel around whom the action revolves, not only on the personal front but the public as well. In Rushdie's *The Midnight's Children*, Saleem Sinai's life is closely intertwined with the life of the nation. He is born at the time of midnight when India achieves independence and this uncanny fusion of personal and public becomes an integral part throughout his life. The narrative in Roy's *The God of Small Things* though not akin to that of Rushdie does represent the Indian social and cultural life through the life of its characters. It does not mingle the personal with the public explicitly but provides a comment on the public through the personal. The treatment that Ammu faces in the hands of her own family and from society at large, the exploitation and suffering of Velutha are all examples that reveals the prevalent social prejudices and evils. In her novel, Desai wraps up her representation of the diaspora 'within' and 'without' through the characters of the Judge and Biju along with the contemporary north-eastern situation plaguing India. Her narrative presents a perspective on the social, cultural, psychological and political situation of present-day India. Adiga's narrative is the continuation of the style conceived and conceptualized by his predecessors as well as a deviation from their technique. In his narrative style there is a strong influence of his journalistic experience that brings in a dash of investigative approach to a social and cultural issue.

The postmodern condition in literature is preoccupied with the idea of representation of life: knowledge, history, and reality through the employment of the meta-narrative. Meta, which means beyond and narrative that refers to the story merge to form the distinctive literary style of the meta-narrative. The meta-narrative is in fact an attempt to give a voice to the different stories hidden within the narrative of one single story. It is an endeavour to comprehend life in all its variedness and complexity, and also bring into focus the neglected and marginalized perceptions of knowledge and experience.

In the emerging narrative techniques a discernible reader can easily notice the double consciousness of the narrator. Since 1990 the narrators in Indian English fiction speak in the language tinged with a deep anguish for the motherland. There is deep-rooted awareness of the belonging to the periphery. (Bhandari)

In Saleem's voice is heard the voice of a generation marginalized and tormented by the partition and disillusioned by the post independent India. The story of Ammu is an expression of the women pushed to the peripheries of existence by a patriarchal society, while the plight of Velutha reveals the deep tentacles of casteism in the Indian society, administration and politics. The hierarchy implied by the class structure is given a new expression in the social structure wherein resides Judge Jemubhai, his cook and the cook's son, Biju. Balram Halwai is again the voice of the migrant workers and servants, the exploited and the homeless suppressed by the caste system and people in power. In building up the edifice of the Indian narrative, the writers have employed the technique of the meta-narrative to represent the voices from the periphery. It in fact is an aid to another postcolonial literary technique of dismantling the hegemony of power structures by lending space to the 'others'. In all the novels mentioned, the narrative forms a story that liberates and asserts all the various stories within. They are the meta-narratives; a fusion of multiple voices and stories.

In each of the narratives, either the first person narrative is employed through one of the characters or the third person narrative, fused with dialogues or monologues, multiplicity of voices, fragmented trajectory of time and stream of consciousness, linguistic experiments, and satire. The writers employ one or the other literary technique to give credibility to their stories, yet in their employment of techniques they differ in style and temperament. The Indian narrative tradition inherent in the oral tradition of storytelling and enactment of tales in the folk theatrical tradition has a significant influence on the art of the writers. Their fictional narrative is tinged with these traditional techniques of story-telling and also literary tradition from the West.

Influence on the narratives: Rushdie's narrative in *Midnight's Children* displays a strong influence of the oral tradition of stories in India. In his novel, the narrator is performing the role of the Sutradhar in a traditional folk tale/play, often digressing from his tale, re-inventing facts and mingling elements of fantasy with them. Saleem Sinai narrates the story of his family, spanning three generations. It is through his voice that the tale of his life and the nation unfolds. Rushdie alludes to "Scheherazade" (*MC* 9) of *The Arabian Nights* while referring to the role of the narrator. In Roy's *The God of Small Things*, the narrator is the omniscient author/narrator who gives a voice to adult Rahel returning from the U.S. Written in the third person narrative it is a versatile narrative style; the past recreated through her memory as a child and as an adult living in the present. In her narrative can be found the traces of the oral tradition of rendition as found in the traditional art of the Kathakali dancers. The story unfolds through Rahel's perspective that introduces us to Ammu, her life, desires and her tragic end. The oral tradition of storytelling in the manner Rushdie employs in his novel is missing in Desai's *The Inheritance of Loss*. Like Roy, here it is the omnipresent, invisible narrator/ author again, who introduces the setting, the characters and theme of the novel. The characters and themes unfold before our eyes through the narrative of the author. It is Desai who gives a glimpse of her characters and their thoughts, likes and dislikes. In her employment of the third person narrative she follows the traditional narrative mode predominantly in use since the inception of the genre itself. The narrative style employed by Adiga is unique and quite different from those of his contemporaries. In *The White Tiger* Adiga follows the epistolary tradition of writing, representing his story through a series of letters written by the protagonist Balram Halwai to the Chinese Premier.

Stream of Consciousness: Contemporary fiction adheres to the postmodern technique of non-linearity and time jumps. In a world where borders and boundaries are fast disappearing, time leaps in consciousness is common and central to the narrative structure. The employment of flashback, stream of consciousness and digressions marks the narrative style of these writers. Rushdie's Saleem relives the history of his entire family through his memory. Stories are an ancient means of preservation of history, experience and knowledge. Saleem, awaiting the final disintegration of his self, tries to preserve the story of his family and his self through his narrative that he pens down while recounting it to Padma. He also merges the political history of the nation with his personal one, often prompting his own unreliability as a narrator. Arundhati Roy takes up the string from Rushdie and lends her Rahel the memory of her life as a child in Ayemenem, "She has . . . memories . . . . She remembers . . ." (*GST* 5). Like Rushdie's Saleem, Rahel takes the readers on a journey to her past and presents a, "life reconstructed out of the memories of the past" (Sodhi 42). She recreates the life and trials of her mother Ammu and draws up the other characters as well, often giving an expression to the views of the young Rahel. Roy follows a non-sequential narrative mode, tagging along her character's narrative and her perception of the life and society. In Kiran Desai, the narrative is based in the present with Sai coming to stay with her grandfather, the Judge, Jemubhai. Her arrival, interaction and assimilation into her new surroundings take the story forward while it drives the Judge on a trip down memory lane. The reminiscences of the Judge display Desai's use of stream of consciousness and flashback in the narrative. In Adiga's novel, the stream of consciousness or flashback technique is self-evident as the entire narrative rests on the memories narrated by Balram. It is through his memory that cast-ridden India; corrupt and unscrupulous comes to life.

Magic Realism

All the novelists represent the contemporary creed of writers who are known for their penchant for portray of realism in their fiction. However contemporary realism is an idea subject to varied interpretations and perspectives. In Rushdie's *Midnight's Children,* realism portrayed through symbols and metaphors; it is a realism that gives space for alternative aspects of realism to come forth from the periphery and assert their presence. The extensive use of the postmodern technique of magic realism lend a unique charm as well as complexity to the novel that endeavours to satirize and present an ironical picture of India's political history thereby breaking the structure free from the hegemony of the centre, as such the voices from the periphery: Saleem, Parvati, Picture Singh and all the other subdued voices can be heard. The technique is expertly employed by Rushdie through the characters of the midnight's children and their magical powers. In Arundhati Roy the technique is less obvious than Rushdie and is employed primarily through the hallucinations and dreams of Rahel and Ammu. Rahel imagines Sophie move in her coffin and hears her scream when being buried. Likewise, ". . . Ammu travelled upwards through a dream in which a cheerful man with one arm held her close by the light of an oil lamp. He had no other arm with which to fight the shadows that flickered around him on the floor" (*GST* 205). The technique of magic realism that has come to characterize contemporary narratives is however not employed by Kiran Desai and Arvind Adiga. The narratives of Desai and Adiga are marked by their direct and explicit approach to reality that undermines the possibility of their usage.

Metaphor/Imagery and Other Features

Rushdie's fiction abounds in the use of metaphors and images, myths drawn from religion, caricatures of political figures, facts and fantasy. Saleem is the metaphor employed to symbolize the birth, illusion, hopes and disillusionment of India as a nation. Political allegory, fragmented and complex narrative, multitudinous, vast, extravagant, etc are some of the features that describe his legendary novel that refers to facts as the Partition, War, Emergency, and Widow, and juxtaposes them with the magical powers of the midnight's children. Arundhati Roy is an activist-novelist and the strains of her calling can be seen in the social realism of her novel. Feministic in approach she exposes the prevalence of castism and gender discrimination, a prominent theme that she best expresses through the metaphor of the 'Laltern' and the 'Mombatti'. In Desai can be found strains of similar realism and social concern; evidenced in her choice of setting that highlights the north-eastern situation of India. Her characters are more than individuals; the Judge, an anglophile stands for the 'ridiculous Indians' while Biju symbolizes the average Indian person enamoured of the West and its illusory greener pastures. The marginalization of the natives is recreated in the plight of the Gorkhas who are denied an equal existence and their resultant frustration is portrayed through Gyan and the violence of the insurgents. Adiga supplies a very striking metaphor of 'Darkness' and 'Light' in his novel that echoes the employment of similar images by Roy and that best illustrates the major concern of both the works with the theme of power structures; the 'centre' and the 'other', "Men with Big and men with small Bellies" (*WT* 64). Adiga's extensive use of animal imagery reminds of Orwell's *Animal Farm*. To describe the landlords and the powerful men in his village he names them after animals, the Buffalo, the Wild Boar, the Stork and the Raven, while he groups the servants in one category and calls them the 'Rooster Coup' for their servile attitude.

Language

Experimentation with the language has been an area of expertise for all the writers concerned. Tracing its development from the early novelists, it has matured greatly in the hands of the contemporary novelists like Rushdie and his fellow writers. In *Midnight's Children*, Rushdie has made a liberal use of the Hindi and Urdu words and expressions. Sometimes he has employed the word as it is: Baap-re-baap, Kali-yuga, Gandharva, falooda, etc., while at others he has given a literal translation: "Piece-of-the- Moon" (*MC 9*). Expressions like "Godown, gudam, warehouse, call it what you like" (*MC 71*) presents the peculiar fusion of language variants by Rushdie. The form of Indian expressions employed in the regional tongue lends a native flavour to the language. Roy's use of the vernacular is an example of Indianization of the English language: "Aiyyo kashtam" (*GST* 169), "Ividay!" (*GST* 68), and so is Desai's use of the influence of the regional tongue portrayed in the conversation of Biju or the cook, "Ai aaa, ai aaa . . . please, I'm a poor man . . ." (*IL* 5), "Shopping ke liye jaenge, bhel puri khaenge . . . dollars me kamaenge, pump um pump um" (*IL* 298). Adiga also follows the lead and employs the language along with its regional flavour, 'paan', 'vada', 'daal', 'hahn', 'pooja', 'ghat', etc. His language is conveyed in various tones, in tune with the class, education, profession and background of the character; Balram's attempts to articulate terms as Mall or Pizza result in, "Moool . . . . Mowll. Malla." (*WT* 147), "Pijja. Pzijja. Zippja. Pizja." (*WT* 155).

Conclusion

The pioneering work that was started by the early phase writers of Indian English fiction has come of age in the present scenario. Rushdie, Roy, Desai and Adiga are the proud and capable flag-bearers of the genre who have contributed immensely to the enrichment of the edifice of the Indian narrative. In their talented hands, the genre has matured and attained an identity of its own within the nation as well as on an international scale. Diverse and multifaceted the genre has its own distinctive Indianness in the choice of themes, settings, characters, and language. The story that it endeavours to represent; the narrative style that it gives shape to is rich, vibrant, traditional as well as contemporary, fresh and fascinating. Its uniqueness lies in its perfect blend of ethnicity with modern modes of expression and representation. Rushdie and Adiga's narrative is laced with satire that is an indictment of the social and political situation prevalent in the nation. Roy and Desai on the other hand represent the social, cultural and political in a realistic tone. The famous four Indian Booker Prize winners have carved a niche for themselves and for the genre of contemporary Indian English fiction, thereby strengthening further the edifice of the Indian narrative.

Works Cited

Bhandari, Supriya. *Emerging Narrative Techniques in Indian English Fiction Since 1990* September 19, 2009. Literary Shelf. http://www.boloji.com/literature/00145.htm.

Rushdie, Salman. *Midnight's Children* (MC). London: Vintage, 1995.

Roy, Arundhati. *The God of Small of Things* (GST). New York: Harper Perennial, 1998.

Sodhi, Meena. "The God of Small Things: Memory and Art." In *The Fictional World of Arundhati Roy*. Ed. R.S. Pathak. New Delhi: Creative Books, 2001. 39-50.

Adiga, Arvind. *The White Tiger* (WT). Noida: Harper Collins Publishers, 2008.

Desai, Kiran. *The Inheritance of Loss* (IL). New Delhi: Penguin Books India Pvt. Ltd., 2006.

14

Fugitive Histories: A Reading in New Historicism

A. Marie Josephine Aruna

> All my novels and stories look at power politics in some way or the other. Fiction has a thousand ways of giving us a new take on the dynamics of power relations.
>
> —Githa Hariharan

Githa Hariharan's fiction *Fugitive Histories* lends itself to a new historicist reading in terms of its thematic and narrative technicality. Writing in this postmodern/postcolonial era, Hariharan centres her text on the issue of communal disharmony embedded in the post independent nation-state that India is with its claims of secularism as its democratic principle.

Fugitive Histories deals with the aftermath of the communal violence of 2002 in Godhra which results in the dislocation of a whole community that is marginalized within its own country. Sara the protagonist records the testimonials of the women who are the worst sufferers of the historical event so as to recreate the actual situation in the perspective of the victims. Hariharan in the process attempts at reconstructing history that has been written by those in power, challenging its ideology that is defined so finitely as the single truth. She seems to say that there are several other perspectives to history, that it is fugitive and shifting.

Githa Hariharan's latest oeuvre, *Fugitive Histories* (2009) subtly opens up the presence of all the differences, given within a postcolonial nation-state as India. Staring us starkly in the face is the 'reality' that the colonial world bequeathed to us a legacy-that of the Partition, the one historical/ political event the ghosts of which haunt us in our personal, social, and cultural conduct of every day life. That India is a secular country, in that it recognizes and acknowledges the different identities of its subjects might be true, but the underlying issue, however, is the internal power structure in a multi-cultural social set up, that is most often ignored.

New Historicism is an approach to literary criticism and literary theory based on the premise that a literary work should be considered a product of the time, place, and historical circumstances of its composition rather than as an isolated work of art or text. New Historicism developed in the 1980s, primarily through the work of the critic Stephen Greenblatt, gaining widespread influence in the 1990s and beyond. New Historicists aim simultaneously to understand the work through its historical context and to understand cultural as well as to investigate the intellectual history and cultural history through literature. In other words, New Historicism aims at interpreting a literary text as an expression of or reaction to the power-structures of the surrounding society.

Fugitive Histories can be read by applying the tenets of New Historicism, which discourse is informed by the Foucauldian concept of power and Louis Montrose's 'historicity of the text' and 'textual history'. The text deals with the particular historical event of 2002 (the Godhra incident in which a whole compartment of Hindus were burnt down). What the writer does is to look at this past incident not only to recreate it but also to rebuild/ reconstruct the entire event through various other viewpoints mainly those of the victims, thereby reinstating the New Historicist theory that history is not homogeneous, it is rather fleeting, shifting and constructed by those in power. The textual discourse therefore does not exist in a vacuum, but is influenced by the discourses of historical /social/ cultural/ political milieus that are drawn into its context. Received history is tampered with and rewritten from a women centreed perspective. For history has it, that in any kind of war or unrest it is the women and children who are the worst sufferers. It is but inevitable that Hariharan weaves her tale through her women characters.

The text is divided into three parts with significant titles 'Missing Persons', 'Crossing Boundaries', and 'Funeral Rites'. At the surface level the author speaks of the death of Asad, an artist, missed by his wife Mala, who ruminates over their hybrid marriage (Asad a Muslim, and Mala a Hindu). She tries to reconstruct their past life and Asad the person himself through some of his drawings which she has unearthed only after his death. Mala is yet to come to terms with the missing husband from her life, though this is only the result of natural death. Theirs is a marriage that signifies the post independent secular state that the nation is. On the other hand, we have the missing persons from the aftermath of the godhra incident, innocent people like Akbar who simply disappear from their homes probably arrested by the state police on the pretext of terrorism, or killed in orchestrated encounters. As Yasmin, Akbar's sister reflects about her missing brother: "Missing is not so bad, it is better than dead . . . . It's the first time Abba saw that being dead meant being cut. It meant missing a body part —an arm, a leg, even a head" (*FH* 136-137). The incident as such is brought to us by Sara's friend Nina who makes a documentary script which reconstructs the past of how on the fatal day the Sabarmati Express was attacked in Godhra station. The Hindu activists inside the train were burnt alive. This happens in a Muslim locality; therefore the Muslims of Gujarat become the target of brutal violence. As a result,

To this day the dispossessed of Gujarat live in 'safe areas'—Muslim Ghettoes—without civic amenities. In Ahmedabad, for instance, people who used to be part of the city's life-bakers, autodrivers, shopkeepers, engineers, schoolteachers—are now refugees in their own city. (42)

Nina's documentary in reconstructing history takes into account the stories of some of these people in their own voices, what the state has done or didn't do to change their situation, and how these people are now trying to rebuild their lives. This leads us into the second part of the text where Sara, Maya and Asad's daughter accompanies Nina in her field trip to Gujarat, where they record the multiple voices of women victims who witnessed the violence in the aftermath of Godhra. These are the women who have either been raped by perpetrators of violence, or have totally lost their brothers, sons, husbands, or find them missing. Their homes have been burnt and they have been uprooted from their living places to Ghettoes for safety. Hariharan also refers inadvertently to another past incident that of the 1992-93 Mumbai riots when her friend Laila and her husband were burnt to death. Laila, Sara's childhood friend is described by her in this ironic manner:

It was as if her parents had unknowingly typecast her by naming her Laila, starting her on the road to romance. Laila took the name to heart, built fantasies around herself; it was impossible for her to be anything but a romantic heroine. In the end, of course, her name made her someone else; someone in whom the men who lit the fires saw nothing romantic or heroic; all she had, in their eyes, was a religion. (53)

The name that meant one thing to Laila and her parents meant something else for others. To those others 'Laila' symbolized the religion they hated, representing the postcolonial 'other', the marginalized within the nation-state. The process of making of the nation-state involves the shaping of the 'self' on the one hand as well as defining of the 'other'. In such a given situation then hostilities and prejudices are not only hardened but get deeply embedded.

In 'Crossing Borders', at the personal level again, we have Mala and Asad who form the resistance from within the powerful structures of neatly divided religious borders, and yet who have been successful. They are the subversion that power contains within itself. On the other hand we have Sara and Nina literally crossing borders within the nation/ state/ district, moving from the Hindu area to the Muslim area where lines/ borders are drawn to demarcate/ discriminate/ distinguish and separate the two peoples/ cultures/ based on religion. This very fact serves to undermine the idea of a secular state.

According to Stephen Greenblatt, New Historicism draws heavily on ethnography and also storytelling wherein people's experiences are recorded. In this case Sara's own interpretations and involvement with the issue is described with great sensitivity. Yasmin is the young girl, with whom Sara identifies, understands that stories are of different kinds as are the storytellers. But on this occasion the story she narrates to Sara is real, a story in which she has to live for the rest of her life. A host of women gather in Yasmin's small one room home—even after five years of the actual incident these women keep it live in their memories, the trauma, the pain and the suffering. Reshma, Zulekha, Razia, Nasreen, Najma, Mariam, Farida, Zahida, Salma, Abeda, Sabiya, Mumtaz are some of the representatives of the powerless community who face the brunt of the powerful Hindu state. Githa Hariharan uses this technique of thick descriptions which forms a significant element in the recreating of history, deftly weaving political events into private lives.

India Today describes the text so aptly, "the daily lives of individuals and those of history appear to blur and seep through time and memory till they... become all of a piece. It's a measure of Hariharan's tenacity as a writer that even while moving from the very same cut-rate story of communal hate and horror that has been played so many times in the media by social activists and documentary film-makers, she is able to colour it with her own brand of fierce integrity that we are able to look at it again..." This integrity of literary representation makes it so evident that history is fugitive, that it is shifting and that there are other perspectives to it. History cannot be a 'single truth' as constructed or manipulated by those in power.

In reconstructing past lives through the medium of memory and documentary, Githa Hariharan brings alive the hoary situation of the terror torn Gujarat. Sara could imagine the worst when she listens to the women pouring out their experience with such frenzied emotions:

> Now they are in the deep smoky pit of the story. It's not a pit with imaginary terrorists or imaginary Pakistans.... It's a pit with closed windows and locked doors, then broken windows and doors. It's a pit where it only rains stones. It's a pit where everyone is running-women, children, men, everyone.... It's a pit full of corpses, the maimed dead. It's a pit full of the maimed living. (157)

In narrating her own story each woman gains a kind of identity that creates a sense of 'self' in her. Here Sara and Nina almost play the role of ethnographers who would later interpret/retell/ reproduce these narratives or incidents. Noor points out rightly in her article, that "women ... the only survivors of the carnage... recreate the horrors that people have gone through, horrors that have bruised their bodies and souls" ("*Fugitive Histories* as fiction" 2). Yasmin soon realizes that these women like her are only bodies whose souls are missing because they have experienced only rape, murder and death. Ironically, Hariharan conjures up the ghost of Gandhi who has to fight the mob that has just gangraped, murdered, burnt people and houses, but seems to remain staunch in his battle for freedom.

The third part is titled 'Funeral Rites', where Sara's own identity is created and affirmed:

> Sara could acknowledge her great grandfather's choice, his faith in home, and say she is Muslim Indian. Or Indian Muslim, since great- grandfather Mulla chose Nehru's republic while merely inheriting the republic of God. Sara could acknowledge a choice

> made closer to her time and say she's her parents' daughter, she's secular. But given her last name, this may now only mean she's a Muslim who knows how to live with other people, she won't take to jihad if she's angry or unhappy. (180)

The funeral rites of Asad is performed by Mala as she comes to terms with his death on the one hand and on the other we have Yasmin trying to bury the hoary past, her missing brother, and decides to move forward, out of the confined territory to greener pastures to pursue education, to taste freedom. She foresees an optimistic end to her troubles from her political and historical past which she symbolically decides to bury. It is ironical however that the whole event has happened in Gujarat, Ahemedabad, and the place where Gandhi's ashram is founded. People like Asad are in the mainstream while Akbar still a minority, unaccepted. Asad's own son Samar (Sara's brother) chooses Islamic fundamentalism for he strongly believes that there's no room for him as a Muslim, "whatever I am, whatever I believe and however I live, I am an M. Samar too is just another Muslim, a potential terrorist" (206). While women like Sara and Yasmin are positive and work towards rebuilding their lives, men like Samar lose faith in the idea of nationhood and democracy. Therefore, the nation/ state is being rejected and questioned for all that it stands, though it professes to be a secular state, which speaks for its failure as a system in the postcolonial canvas.

The text thus speaks at different levels of representation of the personal lives of Mala, Asad, Yasmin and Sara, on the one hand, and the political, historical, social and the cultural on the other. Hariharan represents a highly polarized world in spite of its proclaimed multicultural, multilingual and multi-religious space. She concedes that 2002 was the culmination of this polarization. In her re-reading/ reconstructing of the past Githa Hariharan has certainly conceived of a literary text that is "situated within the institutions, social practices, and discourses that constitute the overall culture of a particular time and place, and with which the literary text interacts as both a product and a producer of cultural energies and codes"(Abrams 183). In reading Fugitive Histories in the light of the new historicist perspective not only serves to grapple with the reality of the subcontinent but at the same time it also brings to the fore the literary astuteness of the writer to handle such a subject matter that has been deeply thought out and subtly represented.

Works Cited

Abrams, M.H. *A Glossary of Literary Terms*. 7th edition. India: Harcourt, 1999. Print.

Gallagher, Catherine, Greenblatt, Stephen. *Practicing New Historicism*. USA: University of Chicago Press, 2000. Print.

Hariharan, Githa. *Fugitive Histories*. New Delhi: Penguin Books, 2009. Print.

New Historicism. New World Encyclopedia, August 2008. Web. 11 October. 2010.

Zaheer, Noor. *Fugitive Histories as fiction*. Infochange. Women's Feature Service, February 2009. Web. 25 September. 2010.

15

The Fluid and the Fixed: Subject in Lacan and Deleuze

Bilal

The paper proposes a threefold comparison and contrast between the Lacanian and the Deleuzian views on the subject. First, I argue that both Lacan and Deleuze problematize the Liberal Humanist Cartesian notion of an autonomous, transcendental subject that the Humanists so valued and took for granted. Second, Lacan highlights and focuses the lack in the constitution of the subject while Deleuze's focus is on the productive desire. Finally, Deleuze's project in Anti-Oedipus is to attain the production of desiring-machine through scrambling and demolishing Lacan's Oedipal triangulation of Daddy-mommy-me.

One of the most intriguing questions haunting the literary theory in the wake of poststructuralism is that of identity and the definition of subjectivity. Poststructuralist thinkers as various as Roland Barthes, Jacques Lacan, Michel Foucault, and Jacques Derrida argued, not so long ago, that the autonomous subject of the humanist tradition, a subject capable of knowing both the world and itself, was a utopian dream of the European Enlightenment. Humanism believed in what is now called the "transcendental subject", the long standing belief that "individual (the subject) is antecedent to, or transcends, the forces of society, experience and language" (Barry 18). This view of human subjectivity was severely questioned and revised in many different ways in a period that recognized the existence of an unconscious mind, the opacity of language, and the role of discursive practices in the dissemination of social power. This revision of the idea of subjectivity has had important reverberations for the conception of knowledge generally and the notion of history in particular. If subjectivity is conceived of as something unstable, groundless, fluid and changing rather than stable, transcendental, fixed and constant, then human knowledge can no longer be viewed as something fixed and permanent.

Instead of regarding knowledge as an edifice to which positivistic scholarship could continue to contribute so that the scope of its insights might continue to expand and evolve according to generally accepted universal principles, we live in an age that questions the very basis on which that structure was erected. It is these doubts about the traditional premises on which the knowledge-producing activities of the humanist disciplines were once based that have provided the justification for varied interpretation of human subjectivity.

In this paper, I propose to compare and contrast the Lacanian view of subject with the Deleuzian subject. The contrast and comparison is aimed at three levels: first, I argue that both Lacan and Deleuze problematize the Cartesian notion of an autonomous, transcendental subject that was at the centre of humanist tradition. Second, Lacan highlights and focuses the lack in the constitution of the subject while Deleuze's focus is on the productive desire. Finally, Deleuze's project in *Anti-Oedipus* is to attain the production of desiring-machine through scrambling and demolishing Lacan's Oedipal triangulation of Daddy-mommy-me.

(Mis)Treating Cartesian Transcendental Subject

Bruce Fink (43) proposes that Descartes employs the graph of two overlapping circles to illustrate his idea of the subject, in the midst of the *cogito.* Being and thinking coincide temporarily when the Cartesian subject asserts to himself, *cognito, ergo, sum*, that "I am thinking." (*Figure 1*).

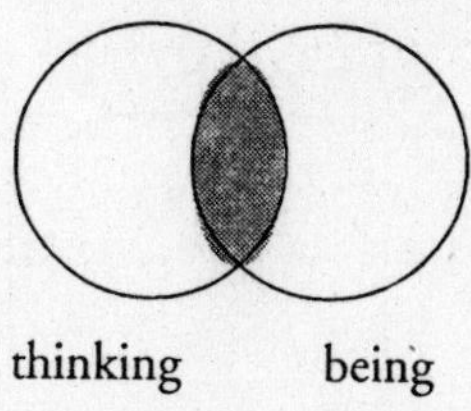

Figure 1

Jacques Lacan, to the humanist's surprise, turns "Descartes' subject inside out, employing everything the *cogito* is not" (Fink 45). Unlike Descartes', Lacanian notion of the subject is essentially split, alienated and subject to the locus of an impossible identity. For Lacan it is "true that the philosopher`s *cognito* is at the centre of the *mirage* that renders modern man so sure of being himself even in his uncertainties about himself" (Ecrits 167). However this essentialist fantasy, reducing subjectivity to the conscious ego, cannot sustain itself any more: "the myth of the unity of personality, the myth of synthesis... all these types of organization of the objective field constantly reveal cracks, tears and rents, negation of the facts and misrecognition of the most immediate experience" (Lacan, III 8).

This "misrecognition" was first discovered by Sigmund Freud in this theory of the unconscious as the main cause determining human personality and it is precisely this discovery that Lacan hails as more radical than Copernican and the Darwinian discoveries in that they both left intact the belief in identity between human subject and conscious ego(Ecrits 296). The Lacanian subject is devoid of any given essence. If there is any essence it is precisely "the lack of essence" (Chaitin 196). *Figure 2* shows the possible schema of the Lacanian subject (Fink 44).

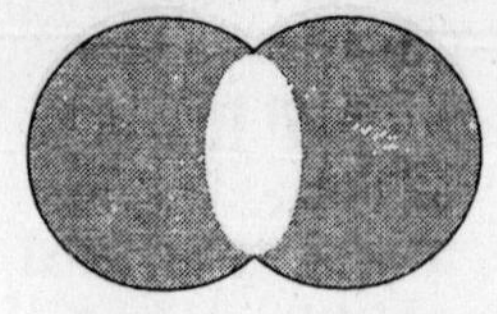

either I am not thinking   or I am not being

Figure 2

The left side is the ego, the false self while the right side is the unconscious. The splitting of the I into ego (false self) and unconscious is termed "split subject," "divided subject," or "barred subject", all represented by the same symbol, the barred S (symbolized by an *S* marked by a slash—a character unfortunately untypeable). S for "subject," / for "barred": the subject as barred by language, as alienated within the other) (Fink 41). Lacan considers that the ego or "I" self is only an illusion, a product of the unconscious itself and that "ego thinking is mere conscious rationalization" (Fink 44). In Lacanian psychoanalysis, the unconscious is the ground of all being. The ego is constructed like an onion: "peeling off layer after layer of identification in search of the substantial kernel of one's personality, one ends up with a void, with the original lack" (Nobus 175). Instead of identifying with the ego, the subject learns to desire as the Other and hence identifies with the Other. Lacan further proposes that "the subject is nothing here but a split between two forms of otherness—the ego as other and the unconscious as the Other's discourse," (qtd. In Fink 46).

Thus the subject is split between "an ineluctably false sense of self and the automatic functioning of language (the signifying chain) in the unconscious" (Fink 45). The advent of the split subject marks a corresponding division of the Other into lacking Other ( ) and object *a*. Through this, one realizes that there is no longer the idea of a Whole subject or Other but that of a lacking and barred one. Deleuze also problematizes Cartesian idea of subjectivity and proposes his own conception of the subject. For Decartes, as Fink notes,the thinking subject mapped out the material world through the axis in rectilinear fashion and the ego (at the intersection of the diagonals of a surrounding square) conquers the world through the order and process of the Quincunx (41).

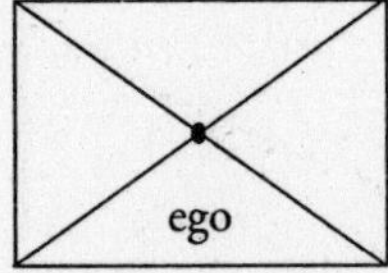

Figure 3

Whereas, for Deleuze, "there is no ego at the centre... but a series of singularities in the disjunctive network, or intensive states in the conjunctive tissue, and a transpositional subject moving full circle" (Deleuze and Guattari 88). The idea that "humans stand as triumphant subjects among inert objects no longer holds" (Deleuze xiv) since the difference between organic and inorganic materials is no longer determined by a wall but only by a way of a vector. The ideal of mastery couldn't persist if the imbrication of subject and object becomes the norm. Once the nostalgia for a substantial, core self fades away, the choreography between the subject and the object dazzles us with its infinite enfolding and unfolding. Without the ego-grounded assumptions, a subject gains reciprocity from the world through operating in a rhizomatic system of heterogeneously becoming relationships that breeds cross-fertilization. Moreover, Deleuze argues that there is nothing but desire—the flow and break of desire that escapes coding. He even claims that "the only subject is desire itself on the body without organs" (Deleuze and Guattari 72).

Lack and Desire

Like Plato, Lacan argues that desire is constituted as a lack. "Lack and desire are coextensive for Lacan. The child devotes considerable effort to filling up the whole of the mother's lack, her whole space of desire" (Fink 54). He endeavours to seek out the boundaries of the Other's lack and fills it with himself. The attempt of totally super-imposing the mother's lack and the child's is shown in *Figure 4* as described by Fink, where their desires completely coincide.

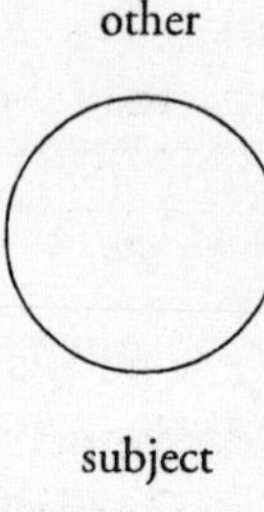

Figure 4

Thus, "man's desire is the Other's desire" and "man learns to desire as an Other" (54). However, the unity of mother-child relationship is challenged by the appearance of the third term, the Name-of-the-Father, which results in the expulsion of the subject from the other. The father's castration threats result in the break away of the child from the mother. And since the castration is linguistically rather than physically done, language protects the child from a potentially dangerous dichotomous relationship with the mother through the substitution of a name for the mother's desire Lacan symbolizes the Name-of-the-Father as S ( ), which is usually read "'the signifier of the lack in the Other' but, as lack and desire are coextensive, can also be read 'the signifier of the Other's desire'" (Fink 58). In this sense, "the subject is caused by the Other's desire" (Fink 50). Therefore, for Lacan, lack is considered as primary for the germination of the subject; in *Seminar XI*, alienation and separation are "linked to the twofold lack and they install the subject in a never ending pulsating process of appearing and disappearing" (Nobus 180).

On the one hand, in Lacan's concept of Alienation, the child, through giving up himself to the Other, gains the opportunity to enter the zone of language and becomes a subject 'of language' or 'in language.' The child, through alienation within language, disappears beneath or behind the signifier, S. The substitution of a signifier, S, for the barred subject, ( ), inaugurates the vicissitudes of the transient subject(Fink 49) The signifier:

> functions as a signifier only to reduce the subject into being no more than a signifier, to petrify the subject in the same movement in which it calls the subject to function, to speak, as subject (Colette203).

The Subject is alienated once he is spoken by language and becomes a function of language. It is language that preexists and determines subjectivity. Therefore, "the process of alienation conducts the subject toward the signifying chain of the Other" (Nobus 180). The subject appears not as a static subject, but as a fleeting irruption or pulsation, expressing itself through the endless chains of signifiers. The signifier substitutes for the subject who has now vanished beneath or behind the signifier. Thus, the subject transforms from a register of imaginary fusions with the world and with others (the Imaginary) into language (the Symbolic). The vel of alienation can clearly illustrate the inevitable loss of the subject in the end. The logic of the vel of alienation is that:

> Whatever the choice operating may be, has as its consequence a neither one, nor the other. The choice, then, is a matter of knowing whether one wishes to preserve one of the parts, the other disappearing in any case (Colette 211).

If one chooses being, the subject will disappear and fall into non-meaning. Contrarily, if one chooses meaning, the meaning will survive "only deprived of that part of non-meaning that is, strictly speaking, that which constitutes in the realization of the subject, the unconscious" (Lacan, *The Four* 211); that is, the result of choosing meaning will be the Other eclipsed by the disappearance of being. Thus, the choice is provided, but predetermined. Whatever you choose, you will lose the most precious part, your being (subject) irrevocably. The initiation of the subject into the symbolic order, represented by the-Name-of the-Father, inescapably severs him from the primal unity with the mother. As Zizek notes:

> By means of the word, the subject finally finds itself, comes to itself... in the Word, the subject directly attains itself, posits itself as such. The price for it, however, is the irretrievable loss of the subject's self identity; the verbal sign that stands for the subject, that is, in which the subject posits itself as self-identical, bears the mark of an irreducible dissonance; it never 'fits' the subject. (Zizek 43)

The failure of its own symbolic self-representation is the condition of possibility for the emergence of the subject of the signifier, for representation in general. Therefore in Lacanian subject the notion of fixed identity is not possible, "identity is possible as a failed one; it remains desirable exactly because it is essentially impossible" (Stavrakakis 29).

Desire in Deleuze, unlike Lacan, is a positive concept had is understood as a primary active force rather than a reactive response to unfulfilled need. Desire is productive in the sense that it produces real connections, investments and intensive states within and between bodies. In this sense "desire produces reality" (Deleuze, Nomad 30). This basic difference in the point of departure sets the Deleuzian theory of desire apart from the whole tradition of thought surrounding desire, from Plato through Hegel to Lacan. Desire in Deleuze attains a constructivist sense in that desire always requires a machine or assemblage. "Desire is present in a given assemblage in the same way that, in a musical work, the principle of composition is present in the silence as much as in the audible sounds"(Patton 70). Thus "lack refers on a positivity of desire and not desire to a positivity of lack" (Deleuze and Parnet 91).

In Deleuze and Guattari's initial outline of their theory at the beginning of *Anti-Oedipus*, desire is treated as a process of production. What desire produces, in the first instance, is a machine or circuit of libidinal energy which they call a desire machine (Patton 71). First, Desire as desiring-machine represents not a static entity but a process, the production of production. Second, "desire as desiring-machine has no subject and no object" (Hardt) and is completely invested in the process of desiring production. So Deleuze believes in the power of the positive desire and proposes that "the three errors concerning desire are called lack, law, and signifier" (Deleuze and Guattari 111).

Since desiring-machines only emphasize on the production of production, there is no object of desire and thus no lacking Subject and Other as in the framework of Lacan and Freud. Deleuze suggests that "from the moment lack is reintroduced into desire, all of desiring–production is crushed, reduced to being no more than the production of fantasy" (Deleuze and Guattari 111).

He criticizes the concept of the lack and tries to situate the desiring machine as the dynamo. Ever since desire is welded to the law, the circle of prohibition and transgression, taboo and incest operate its eternal repression. Deleuze considers that "the sign of desire is never a sign of the law, it is a sign of strength (puissance)" (Deleuze and Guattari 112). It signals the incessant flows and breaks among partial objects and different machines. According to Deleuze:

> An organ-machine is plugged into an energysource- machine: the one produces a flow that the other interrupts. The breast is a machine that produces milk, and the mouth a machine coupled to it. The mouth of the anorexic wavers between several functions: its possessor is uncertain as to whether it is an eating-machine, an anal machine, a talking-machine, or a breathing-machine (asthma attacks). (Deleuze and Guattari 111)

The flows and breaks among the different machines weave a dynamic matrix, within which the myth of a lacking subject is replaced by the productive interaction among partial objects and different machines. Even the nursing child is "already caught up in an immediate desiring-production where the parents play the role of partial objects" (Deleuze and Guattari 100). For the infant, there is no longer the whole image of daddy and mummy, but the partial images that connect and disconnect with his organs. Furthermore,

> "the sign of desire is never signifying, it exists in the thousands of productive breaks-flows that never allow themselves to be signified within the unary stroke of castration" (Deleuze and Guattari 111).

Deleuze, in *Anti-Oedipus*, tries to subvert the concept of the Oedipus Complex, which puts everything, including desire, under the sway of the Phallus. This will be discussed in details later. Within the framework of Deleuze, the advent of the subject is instated not before desiring-machine but only after as an effect or residue of production. The radical demolition of subjectivity is operated through his three syntheses: the connective synthesis of production (desiring-machine), the disjunctive synthesis of recording (Body-without-Organs), and the conjunctive synthesis of consumption-consummation (subjectivity). According to Deleuze, Body-without-Organs serves as a surface for recording the entire process of production of desire. It is a cosmic egg, traversed by "bands of intensity, potentials, thresholds, and gradients" (Deleuze and Guattari 09). Body-without-Organs represents the force of anti-production (repulsion) while desiring-machine symbolizes the force of production (attraction), connecting and disconnecting partial-objects. And the interplay of the forces of production and anti-production gives birth to a wide range of forms of subjectivity. The following quotation capsules the germination of the subject within the framework of Deleuze's three syntheses—desiring-machine, Body-without-Organs, and the subject:

It is a strange subject, however, with no fixed identity, wandering about over the body without organs, but always remaining peripheral to the desiring –machines, being defined by the share of the product it takes for itself, garnering here, there, and everywhere a reward in the form of a becoming or an avatar, being born of the states that it consumes and being reborn with each new state. (Deleuze and Guattari 16)

It's not a theater of representation but a factory of desire that allows the multiplicity of subjectivity to be born and reborn. Thus, the map that records the complex relationship between the Cartesian thinking subject and the world that he creates is redrawn. For Lacan, "the unconscious is the discourse of the Other;" (Lacan, Ecrits 16) therefore, it is language, Unconscious, or the lacking Other that give birth to and situate the subject. For Deleuze, it is desiring-production and Body-without-organs that engenders the subject.

Oedipus Complex

The Oedipus Complex is just as important for Lacan as it is for Freud, if not more so. The difference is that Lacan maps that complex on the acquisition of language, which he sees as analogous. The process of moving through this complex is the way of recognizing the need to obey the social strictures and to follow a closed differential system of language in which one understands "self" in relation to "others". For Lacan, the Oedipus Complex impels the passage from the imaginary order to the symbolic order and represents the paradigmatic triangular structure. The passage is marked by three 'times' of the Oedipus complex. The first time of the Oedipus complex is characterized by "the imaginary triangle of mother, child, and phallus" (Evans 128). The triangle represents that a purely dual relationship between the mother and the child never exists and that there is always the third term, the phallus. The child finds out that both he and the mother are marked by a lack. Thus, he seeks to completely satisfy the mother's desire, the imaginary phallus. The second time of the Oedipus complex is characterized by "the intervention of the imaginary father" (Evans 128). The father exerts the operation of privation through denying mother's access to the phallic object and forbidding the child's access to the mother. The third time of the Oedipus complex is indicated by the intervention of the real father.

The child (subject) is castrated by the real father since the father's phallus thwarts any hope of his attempt to be the phallus for the mother. Thus, the subject is initiated into the symbolic order and falls from the imaginary fusion with the world and with others. The Oedipal triangulation of Daddy-mummy-me is omnipresent and "Oedipus has as its formula 3+1, the one of the transcendent phallus without which the terms considered would not take the form of a triangle" (Deleuze and Guattari 73). The triangle of Daddy-mummy-me is anchored by the phallus as the third term.

In *Anti-Oedipus,* in contrast to Freudian and Lacanian interpretation of Oedipus Complex, Deleuze and Guattari deny any "primal lack" or yearning for a pre-oedipal, instinctual desire for unity. The Oedipus complex, they maintain, does not involve the resolution of problems created by pre-existing, instinctive desires; it is first and foremost the territorialization of desire, the differentiated "desiring production" that is the essence of human reality. The various "desiring machines" that make up the unconscious are first organized by the parents, by society and then "resolved", that is further territorialized into a social body, a corporal form of representation. As such for Deleuze, "there is no Oedipal triangle: Oedipus is always open in an open social field. Oedipus opens to the four winds, to the four corners of the social field (not even 3+1, but 4+n)" (Deleuze and Guattari 96). The phallus as the detached complete object is replaced by detachable partial objects. The breaks and flows of desire among partial objects and different machines crack open the structure of triangle. Deleuze proposes the possibility of the schizoanalysis, which aims to schizophrenize the domain of the unconscious in order to "shatter the iron collars of Oedipus and rediscover everywhere the force of desiring-production" (Deleuze and Guattari 53). One is impelled to learn from the experience of the psychotic how to subvert the Oedipal yoke and kindles the politics of desire, The anti-oedipal forces—the schizzes-flows-forces that escape coding, scramble the codes, and flee in all direction: orphan (no daddy-mummy-me), atheists (no belief), and nomads (no habits, no territories) (Deleuze and Guattari xxi).

The unconscious is no longer conditioned by the eternal triangle of daddy-mummy-me. It is freed from the Oedipus complex and initiated into the zone of desire, where the distinction between subject and object is crashed and the only survivor are desiring-machines traversing on body-without-organs in a nomadic way. Therefore, Deleuze asserts that the desiring-production shouldn't give way to a simple representation since it is a factory of desire rather than a theater of representation. The productive unconscious should never make way for an "unconscious that knows only how to express itself-express itself in myth, in tragedy, in dream" (Deleuze and Guattari 54).

To sum it up, both Lacan and Deleuze contribute important perspectives for criticizing the traditional concept of the transcendental subject and for rethinking and reconceptualizing subjectivity. Lacan claims that "the subject is split from its real being and forever tossed between eventually contradicting signifiers coming from the Other" (Nobus 179) while Deleuze's subject is the nomadic subject which exists temporarily in an ever shifting array of potentials as desiring machines distribute flows across the body without organs. Moreover, though both of them consider that desire lacks an object and is conceived of as an incessant movement, Lacan argues that the subject is constituted through lack because "one can only desire what one does not have," (Nobus 6) while Deleuze tends to focus on the power of productive desire. Furthermore, Deleuze employs the schizophrenic desire to subvert the Oedipal triangulation, whose operation on the subject is as if "a tablecloth were being folded, as if its 4(+n) corners were reduced to 3 (+1), to designate the transcendent factor performing the operation" (Deleuze and Guattari 101). Through an incessant process of territorialization, deterrtorialization, and reterritorialization, Deleuze aims to set free the production, reproduction and anti-production of desire.

Works Cited

Barry, Peter. *Begining Theory.* Manchester & NY: Manchester University Press, 2007.

Chaitin, G. *Rhetoric and Culture in Lacan.* Cambridge: Cambridge University Press, 1996. Deleuze, G and Parnet, C. *Dialogues.* Trans. Hugh Tomlinson and Barbara Habberjam. London: Athlone Press, 1987.

Deleuze, G. & Guattari,F. *Anti-oedipus: Capitalism and Schizophrenia.* Minneapolis: University of Minnesota Press, 1983.

______. "Nomad thought." *The New Nietzsche: Contemporary Styles of Interpretation.* Ed. David B. Allison. Trans. David B. Allison. MA: MIT Press, 1977.

______. *The Folds: Leibniz and the Baroque.* Trans. Tom Conley. Minneapolis: University of Minnesota Press, 1993.

Evans, Dylan. *An Introductry Dictionary of Lacanian Psychoanalysis.* New York: Routledge, 1996.

Fink, Bruce. *The Lacanian Subject: Between Language andJouissance.* Princeton, New York: Princeton University Press, 1996.

Hardt, Michael. *Reading Notes on Deleuze and Guattari C a p i t a l i s m & S c h i z o p h r e n i a.* 1 0 J a n u a ry 2 0 09 <http://www.duke.edu ~hardt / Deleuze&Guattari.html>.

Lacan, Jacques. *Ecrits,A Selection.* Trans. Alan Sheridan. London: Tavistock Publications, 1977.

______. *The Four Fundamental Concepts of Psycho-Analysis.* Trans. Alan Sheridan. Harmondsworth: Penguin, 1991.

______. *The Seminar. Book III. The Psychoses, 1955-6.* Ed. Jacques- Alain Miller. Trans. Dennis Porter. London: Routledge, 1992.

Nobus, Dany, ed. *Key Concepts of Lacanian Psychoanalysis.* New York: Other Press, 1999.

Patton, Paul. *Deleuze and the Political.* London and New York: Routledge, 2000.

Soler, Colette. "The Subject and the Other." *Reading Seminar XI: Lacan's Four Fundamental Concepts of Psychoanalysis.* Ed. Richard Feldstein, Bruce Fink and Maire Jaanus. Ithaca. NY: SUNY Press, 1995.

16

The Politics of Economic Power and Exclusion: A Critique of Charles Dickens's *Hard Times*

Sandeep Kumar Sharma

The present paper is an attempt to scrutinize the relevance of Foucauldian concept of power/knowledge discourse in Dickens's celebrated novel *Hard Times* (1854). It will be very significant to mention here that *Hard Times* belongs to the Victorian era after the Industrial Revolution in England. So far, this text has been analyzed from the traditional point of view by critics. For example, Percy Marshall says that *Hard Times* is "a savage attack on Capitalism and on those who kept on working in the general disadvantage and in defiance of the laws of charity" (Marshall 42).

F. R. Leavis opines that "the adult mind does not as a rule find in Dickens a challenge to an unusual and sustained seriousness. Dickens, the moralist always distinguishes between good and bad and he always indicates some evil of this era of rapid industrial expansion but in no other book as harshly and consistently as in *Hard Times*" (Leavis 18). Earle Davis says that *Hard Times* is "of all Dickens's books the clearest in its statement of his economic belief. Its thesis is a satire on Utilitarian philosophy" (Davis 27). J. Hillis Miller says that "In *Hard Times*, Dickens dramatizes in strikingly symbolic terms the opposition between a soul destroying relation to a utilitarian, industrial civilization in which everything is weighed, measured, has its price, and in which emotion is banished, and the reciprocal interchange of love" (Miller 226). Lionel Stevenson remarks, "*Hard Times* is more strictly centreed upon a single social theme than his other novels, and that he had not absorbed this theme through his pores from childhood onward. He began with the conscious purpose of examining the relationship between industrialists and workers in the new manufacturing cities, and of discrediting the utilitarian philosophy which has the ideological basis of current capitalism" (Stevenson 312). Dickens felt that a dependence upon capitalistic practicality without reference to sympathy and human understanding causes continued difficulties in the relations of capital and labour. Thus we observe that the existing criticism of *Hard Times* is based on the traditional point of view. In the modern times when literary theories have become so much prominent, Foucault's theory of power/knowledge is quite relevant and another valuable and significant way of understanding the text and major thematic concerns.

Michel Foucault is an outstanding and distinguished French philosopher, historian, and a renowned thinker who has given a kaleidoscopic view of man's condition, is known for having made the exploration and the operations of power. There is no doubt that the issue of power and knowledge has occupied a central position within sociological analysis in recent times. Above all, Michel Foucault believed in the freedom of the people. He also realized that as individuals, we react to situations in different ways. He used his books as a vehicle to show the various factors that interact and collide in his analyzation of change and its effects. As a philosophical historian and an observer of human relations, his work focused on the dominant genealogical and archaeological knowledge systems and practices, tracking them through different historical eras, including the social contexts that were in place that permitted change – the nature of power in society. He wrote that power is "always already there, that one is never outside it" (Foucault, *Power/Knowledge* 140). He further argued that "A society without power relations can only be an abstraction" (Dreyfus and Rabinow 222).

Foucault believed that knowledge is a form of power, but he took it a step further and told us that knowledge can be gained from power, producing it, not preventing it. Through observation, new knowledge is produced. In his view, knowledge is always connected to power, and often wrote them in this way: Power/ Knowledge. Foucault's theory states that knowledge is power because knowledge linked to power, not only assumes the authority of the truth but has the power to make itself true. All knowledge, once applied in the real world, has effects, and in that sense at least, becomes true. Knowledge, once used to regulate the conduct of others, entails constraint, regulation and disciplining of practice. "Power and knowledge directly imply one another; that there is no power relation without the correlative constitution of a field of knowledge, nor any knowledge that does not presuppose and constitute at the same time, power relations" (Foucault, *Discipline and Punish* 27). For Foucault, power exists everywhere and comes from everywhere; it is a key concept because it acts as a type of relation between people, a complex form of strategy, with the ability to secretly shape another's behaviour. "Power refers to the degree to which individual or groups can impose their will on others, with or without the consent of others." (Haralambos 24).

Foucault did not view the effects of power negatively. For him, power didn't exclude, repress, censor, mask and conceal because Foucault saw it as a producer of reality, The importance for him always lay in the effect that power has on entire networks, practices, the world around us, and how our behaviour can be affected, not power itself. "We must cease once and for all to describe the effects of power in negative terms: it 'excludes', it 'represses', it 'censors', it 'abstracts', it 'masks', it 'conceals'. In fact power produces; it produces reality; it produces domains of objects and rituals of truth. The individual and the knowledge that may be gained of him belong to this production" (Rabinow 205).

One of the techniques of power/knowledge that Foucault cited was the Panopticon, an architectural design put forth by Jeremy Bentham in the mid-nineteenth century for prisons, insane asylums, schools, hospitals and factories. Instead of using violent methods, such as torture, and placing prisoners in dungeons that were used for centuries in monarchical states around the world, the progressive modern democratic state needed a different sort of system to regulate its citizens. "Panopticon is the spontaneous exercise of power without noise, often without any need of intervention at all and the constant power of one mind over many" (Crimmins 74). The Panopticon offered a powerful and sophisticated internalized coercion, which was achieved through the constant observation of prisoners, each separated from the other, allowing no more interaction, no communication. This modern structure would allow guards to continually see inside each cell from their vantage point in a high central tower, unseen by the prisoners.

In the view of Foucault, power and knowledge comes from observing others. It marked the transition to a disciplinary power, with every movement supervised and all events recorded. The result of this surveillance is acceptance of regulations and docility– a normalization of sorts, stemming from the threat of discipline. Suitable behaviour is achieved not through total surveillance, but by panoptic discipline and inducing a population to conform by the internalization of this reality. The actions of the observer are based upon this monitoring and the behaviours he sees exhibited; the more one observes, the more powerful one becomes. The power comes from the knowledge which the observer has accumulated from his observations of actions in a circular fashion, with knowledge and power reinforcing each other. Foucault says that "by being combined and generalized, they attained a level at which the formation of knowledge and the increase in power regularly reinforce one another in a circular process" (Foucault, *Discipline and Punish* 224).

Hard Times deals with industrial power, but it is not so much a picture of its ramifications as a presentation of its underlying principles. It is an analysis and a condemnation of the ethos of industrialism. There is no mistaking Dickens's violent hostility to industrial capitalism and its entire scheme of life. Here, he is proclaiming a doctrine not of individual but of social sin, unveiling what he sees as the real state of modern society.

As the novel stands, its thesis is a satire on utilitarian economy. In *Hard Times,* Dickens assailed industrialism, utilitarianism, new education and difficult and costly divorce laws in Victorian England. He believed that industrial progress cannot solve human problems by power and knowledge alone. The novel fiercely attacks industrialism and utilitarianism because it maintains a huge gulf between the rich and the poor where the poor become victims of discourse of power because they are powerless and these aspects receive a telling expression at the hands of Dickens in *Hard Times.* Thus, as the novel's plot and narrative form convey, the whole Victorian atmosphere is knitted in power relations. In the words of a critic, "Power is not possessed or appreciated as a commodity or piece of wealth, rather it has the character of a network, its threads extend everywhere" (Smart 83).

Thomas Gradgrind, the major character in the novel, serves as an embodiment of the beliefs of utilitarianism and industrialism. Through his narrative and characterization, Dickens expounds the ideals, evils and effects of industrial utilitarianism. Dickens felt that a dependence upon capitalistic practicality without reference to sympathy and brotherly understanding causes continued difficulties in the relations of capital and labour. "Here you will find, no more villains and heroes, but only oppressors and victims, oppressing and suffering in spite of themselves, driven by a huge machinery which grinds to pieces the people it should nourish and ennoble and having for its directors the basest and most foolish of us instead of the noblest and most farsighted. Dickens has spread the indignation into a passionate revolt against the whole industrial order of the modern world" (Shaw 126).

In *Hard Times,* the utilitarian principle finds its exponents and champions in the two leading characters, Gradgrind and Bounderby. Gradgrind's theory of education is evidently an offshoot of this utilitarian attitude to life. This man emphasizes the importance of facts, and fails to attach any importance to feelings and emotions.

Hard Times opens, significantly in a schoolroom where the children are to be indoctrinated in the tenets of practicality, encouraged to think of nothing except in terms of use, crammed full of information like so many "little vessels ... ready to have imperial gallons of facts poured into them until they were full to the brim" (1). Now what I want, Mr. Gradgrind tells the schoolmaster, 'is, Facts. Teach these boys and girls nothing but Facts. Facts alone are wanted in life. Plant nothing else and root out everything else. You can only form the minds of reasoning animals upon Facts: nothing else will ever be of service to them. This is the principle on which I bring up my own children, and this is the principle on which I bring up these children. Stick to Facts, sir!"(1).

In the world of Gradgrind, there is to be no imagination, no fancy, no emotion, only fact and utilitarian calculus. "No little Gradgrind had ever learnt the silly jingle, twinkle, twinkle little star; how I wonder what you are!"(10). So this is convincing from Foucauldian perspective that the discourse of a powerful man cannot be challenged who is the representative of the society. "Power demands obedience. Power, ultimately, is repression; repression, ultimately is the imposition of the law, the law, ultimately demands submission"(Boyne 125). Here Bentham's plan for the chrestomathic school is finally realized, these schools like 'factories, panopticon style, turning out finished products under the eyes of monitors, were never built, but Dickens erects a Chrestomathia in Coketown. But the fact in which Gradgrindary is interested are only the cut and dried facts of intellectual definition, not the facts of living and breathing reality.

However, the fancy, the love, the compassion which Dickens brings to his picture of Coketown workout to erupt spasmodically, but they do finally and forcefully make themselves felt, win their small victories.

The novel ironically subverts this complacent picture of an invincible Gradgrindian system, of course, for it is Sissy who functions as the principle of juxtaposition of Sissy Jupe and Thomas Gradgrind, the novel sets heart against head, loving compassion for the particular human heart against soul deadening uniformity, uniformity that it represents as the product of the mid-Victorian social movements and reform efforts. *Hard Times* represents a system of disciplinary scrutiny, a hierarchical system of multiple hazes that enforce docility and obedience. The circus serves as a figure in small for the pervasive, multiple-layered system of surveillance at work in the novel as a whole, for the representation of the circus makes that system highly visible. As Gradgrind approaches Sleary's horse riding establishment at the circus, he is horrified to see that his own children are peeping at the circus people through a hole in the tent. As he admonishes the children, they tell him that they wanted to learn more than they had at the lecturing castles. Tom and Louisa talk about the rebuking to "never wonder"– as Dickens writes, the keynote of Gradgrind's educational system. Tom is disgusted with his education, indeed, he writes that he could use gunpowder to blow up the doctrine of 'Facts and Figures', but he says instead that when he leaves home to work for Bounderby, he will take revenge for enjoying life. Here we see the reflection of Foucault's notion of resistance that "where there is power, there is resistance" (Foucault, *The History of Sexuality,* Vol.1 95).

In contrast to these, Sissy Jupe, the strolling juggler's child, also resisted the utilitarian education system of Gradgrind that she could not be filled with facts only. She has vitality, generosity and uncalculating goodness. It is significant that she has been born and nourished among a people whose activities are not dominated by pure utility, but have at least some association with those of art, self-fulfilment, and self-satisfaction. Sissy, like a character in a morality play, illustrates all the ideas opposite from the utilitarian philosophy. The contrast between her 'dark-eyed and dark haired' warmth and Bitzer's cold eyes and colourless hair renders in pure sensation, as F.R. Leavis points out, the opposition between "the life that is lived freely and richly from the deep instinctive and emotional springs and the thin blooded, quasi-mechanical product of Grandgrindery" (Leavis 231). So utilitarian is Gradgrind that, even in the matter of his daughter Louisa's marriage, he does not need to take into account Louisa's feelings. The interview between Gradgrind and Louisa, when he puts before her Bounderby's proposal of marriage, is fraught with irony, and is a powerful attack on Gradgrind's utilitarianism. So this is convincing from Foucauldian perspective that the discourse of a powerful man cannot be challenged who is the representative of the society. It is also evident that our social fabric is knitted by power relations and the web of power is spread everywhere and it has effected the most intimate relations in the society, as we observe in the case of Gradgrind's relations with his son, daughter and wife.

The principles that dominate Mr. Gradgrind's school are the principles that dominate Coketown and its industry. His hard-facts philosophy is only the aggressive formulation of the inhumane spirit of Victorian materialism. In Gradgrind, though repellent, it is honest and disinterested. In Bounderby, its embodiment in the business world, with his bragging self-interest, it is nothing but the greed of power and material success, Victorian rugged individualism in its vulgarest and ugliest form. He is described as a "man perfectly devoid of sentiment"(15). While Gradgrind does show some signs of human feeling by taking the abandoned Sissy under his protection and he certainly changes his outlook upon life by the time the story ends, Bounderby shows no sign of any human feeling and remains till the end what he is at the beginning—cold and impervious to human needs. Bounderby is a man made out of a coarse material who constantly boasts of his being self-made. He looks upon his workmen as tools by using which in the proper manner he can enrich himself. He is frankly contemptuous of the needs, requirements, and demands of his workmen. His treatment of Stephen, both when Stephen seeks his guidance in the manner of his domestic life and when he is called upon to supply inside information about the activities of the workers' union, shows his utter callousness. He dismisses Stephen Blackpool from employment without realizing the enormity of the damage he is doing to a man whom he himself recognized as a "steady hand". Here we see the reflection of Foucault's hypothesis that where there is imbalance of power, one person will surely try to dominate the other. The exercise of disciplinary power of Bounderby is also apparent here as he wants to assert his authoritative attitude on whosoever comes in his contact whether he is Tom, Sissy, Louisa or Stephen Blackpool.

Tom, reacting against the rigidity of his utilitarian upbringing and in order to compensate himself, takes to evil courses, going to the extent of robbing the bank in which he is an employee. His life is a wreck too, and the manner in which he explains his conduct shows how, as in the case of Louisa, Gradgrind's philosophy has rebounded upon himself. Tom says to his father, "So many people are employed in situations of trust; so many people, out of so many, will be dishonest. I have heard you talk, a hundred times, of it being a law. How can I help laws? You have comforted others with such things, father. Comfort yourself" (286). Thus the sinister system is once again exposed and derided when Gradgrind finds his son Tom to be a thief. It is rather ironical that the utilitarian Gradgrind's public façade and personal beliefs should end at the hands of Bitzer. Bitzer, a truly successful pupil and the real triumph of the Benthamite system intercepts the guilty Tom's flight to clinch his own promotion to Tom's job in the bank. Conclusively, we see that *Hard Times*, one of the masterpieces of the Victorian era can justifiably be analyzed from the point of view of Michel Foucault's theory of Power/Knowledge Discourse. Though the novel has been set up in Victorian surroundings and the existing criticism is based on this text from the traditional standards, yet Foucault's analysis of power/knowledge has set in motion an entirely new way of examining power relations in the Victorian society. In the sphere of modern literary criticism, Foucault's theory of Power/ Knowledge is quite prominent and significant which is another alternate and valuable approach to understand and peruse this Victorian text.

Works Cited

Boyne, Roy. *Foucault and Derrida: The Other Side of Reason*. London: Unwin Hymen, 1987.

Crimmins, E. James. *On Bentham*. Canada: Wadsworth, 2004.

Davis, Earle. *The Flint and the Flame: The Artistry of Charles Dickens*. London: Gollancz, 1964.

Dickens, Charles. *Hard Times* (1854). New Delhi: Peacock Publications, rpt. 2008.

Foucault, Michel. *Discipline and Punish: The Birth of a Prison*, trans. A. Sheidan. New York: Pantheon,1977.

______ *The History of Sexuality, Vol.1 An Introduction*, trans. Robert Hurley, New York: Pantheon, 1978.

______*Power/Knowledge: Selected Interviews and Other Writings* 1972-1977, ed. Gordin Colin, New York: Pantheon, 1980.

Haralambos, Michel. *Sociology: Themes and Perspective*. Delhi: Oxford University Press, 1980.

H Dreyfus, and P Rabinow. eds. *Michel Foucault: Beyond Structuralism and Hermeneutics*. Great Britain: The Harvester Press, 1982.

Leavis, F.R. *The Great Tradition*. London: Chatto and Windus, 1948.

Marshall, Percy. *Masters of the English Novel*. London: Dennis Dobson, 1962.

Miller, J. Hillis. *Charles Dickens: The World of His Novels*. Cambridge, Mass: Harvard University Press, 1958.

Rabinow, Paul. The Foucault Reader. New York: Pantheon, 1984.

Shaw, G.B. *Introduction to Hard Times*. London: Waverly, 1912,

Smart, Barry. *Michel Foucault*. London: Routledge, 2002.

Stevenson, Lionell. *The English Novel: A Panorama*. Boston: Houghton Miffin Company, 1960.

17

Encoding and Decoding Auxiliaries in Amitav Ghosh's *Sea of Poppies* for the Semantic Interpretation

A. Sathikulameen

One of the most enduring issues in the analysis for semantics is the nature of an auxiliary system that helps a main verb for thematic interpretation. The issue of this paper is to analyze how the auxiliary helps the main verb to give the interpretation of a writer. I have culled out some usages of Amitav Ghosh's Sea of Poppies for this analysis. He expresses his semantic ideas with the aid of auxiliaries. The usefulness of a primary auxiliary verb for stylistic analysis may depend on the aspectual function it serves in relation to the lexical verb: for example, whether an action is still going on, no longer functioning etc. These verbs may be of concern in relation to the accuracy of our analysis of time in the literary work.

Introduction

The verbs in English can be generally categorized in terms of auxiliary and lexical. The auxiliary verbs perform their function only in relation to the lexical verbs sometimes also known as function verbs. Auxiliary verbs, unlike lexical verbs, are sometimes described as a closed category, as their total number is limited, and has not changed very much in the recent history of the language. Due to their limited number, all the auxiliary verbs in

English, unlike the lexical verbs, can be conveniently listed in a typical grammar of English. Some of the auxiliary verbs are categorized as modal, whereas the others can be categorized as primary. The primary auxiliary verbs in English are do, have, and be. The modal auxiliary verbs are can, could, may, might, shall, should, will, would, must, used to, need, dare. One must be careful with these examples, because some of them can function as lexical verbs. All the primary auxiliary verbs for example, depending on their meaning, can function as lexical verbs, and this is also true for some of the modal auxiliaries, such as need and dare. In order to see whether a verb functions as an auxiliary, we have to see whether its essential function is to modify another verb; if the verb stands on its own, then it should be regarded as a lexical verb. For example, the verbs in the following clauses are all lexical:

'He needs some money'.

'He has two houses'.

'She is a teacher'.

However, the same verbs are auxiliary in the following examples, because they modify other verbs:

'He needn't do it'.

'He has done it'.

'She is doing it'.

In linguistics, an auxiliary is a verb functioning to give further semantic information about the main verb following it. The auxiliary verb alters the basic form of the main verb to have one or more of the following functions: passive, progressive, perfect, modal. In this paper, the study would be made on exploring how Amitav Ghosh communicates his ideas with the help of auxiliaries that gives the meaning of the novel. One can analyze the meaning of sentences, as well as, how one can trace out a part of an initiation process of a writer by analyzing two meanings in the given literary work, firstly, the word meaning and secondly, sentence meaning. The writer usually reveals semantic ideas with the help of the main verb, and even subtle ideas with the aid of auxiliaries which interface between syntax and semantic interface. For example,

> Relieved to be out of the sun, Deeti squatted beside her oven and thrust an armload of firewood into last night's embers, which could still be seen glowing, deep inside the ashes. (Ghosh 4)

In the above sentence, starts with the main verb 'relieved' and further it interfaces with primary auxiliary 'to be', then 'could' also conveys some meaning that some suggestion 'still be seen glowing' for this sentence besides 'squatted' and 'thrust'.

In this novel, he uses this particular primary auxiliary in a unique way; he combines this primary auxiliary with 'be' verb like 'is', 'are', 'was' and 'were'.

> The Ibis is to be his last command. (Ghosh 97)

'are'

> It is in keeping with these precedents that this court pronounces its sentence, which is that all your properties are to be seized and sold, to make good your debts, and that you yourself are to be transported to the penal settlement on the Mauritius Islands for a period of no less than seven years. (Ghosh 111)

'was'

> Many days passed with no word being received about when exactly Neel was to be moved to the jail at Alipore, where convicts were usually sent to await transportation. (Ghosh 123)

'were'

> And 'roti' was indeed the name by which these poppy-petal wrappers were known although their purpose was entirely different from that of their namesake: they were to be sold to the Sudder

> Opium Factory, in Ghazipur, where they would be used to line the earthenware containers in which opium was packed. (Ghosh 4)

He uses 'be' verb and 'perfect' verb followed by the primary auxiliary 'to be' throughout this novel, which functions as an adjunct to give further semantic information about the arguments. He adopts this particular technique throughout the novel. Generally there are two main functions in English auxiliary verbs which are follows:

The first, the auxiliary verb 'be' is used with a past participle to form the passive voice; for example, passive= is written (Present), is being written (Present Continuous), has been written (Present Perfect), was written (Past), was being written (Past Continuous), will be written (Future).

The second, the auxiliary verb 'be' is used with a present participle to form the progressive aspect; for example, "I am reading a book." describes what the speaker is doing at the very moment of utterance, whereas "I read my book." is a temporally broader statement.

Initially, I have traced out this question, what are all the components that make us to understand his language? The writer expresses, what he means to convey to readers. One can analyse sentences from this novel that renders his emotions, ideas and intentions with the help of auxiliaries. Language is a complex phenomenon and it is difficult to define the intended meaning of the writer. The writer communicates his intended meaning with the help of a sentence and we can derive the meaning from the sentence by analyzing contexts in which language is used. The sentence is a construction of words in a particular sequence that reveals the ideas of the writer. If one analyze the structure of sentence properly, this would help to find out the utterance of the writer.

> Kabutri, in the meanwhile, had kneaded some atta and rolled out a few real rotis. (Ghosh 4)

The above sentence, he uses 'had kneaded' which is a perfect auxiliary that joins with main verb that clearly indicates a past perfect event. He constructs the sentence in the following order:

NP+ PP+ VP+NP+VP= S (Sentence)

This sentence is not constructed properly according the generative grammar which defines that "the grammar will generate all the well-formed syntactic structures (e.g. sentences) of the language and will not generate any ill-formed structures. This has been called the 'all and only' criterion, that is, all the grammatical sentences and only the grammatical sentences will be produced" (Yule 87).

So, it is clear that the writer follows different techniques to represent his ideas, in which the primary auxiliary 'to be' plays a vital role in conveying arguments in sentences. He starts with 'was', 'is', 'are' and 'were' then followed by 'to be' throughout this novel.

He also uses 'has to be', 'have to be' and 'had to be'

> This here mud is good akbarry: has to be eaten whole. (Ghosh 210)
>
> There's some who just can't take it and have to be sent home. (Ghosh 36)
>
> The sahib's pregnant wife was in great pain and in desperate need of a white doctor; there were none to be had on this side of the river, so she had to be taken to Calcutta, on the other bank. (Ghosh 31)

The sentences above state that the usage of two auxiliaries together in the sentences; he follows that throughout this novel and he proceeds with the utterance which is "an act of speech or writing that describes a specific event, at a particular time and place and involving at least one person, the one who produces the utterance, but usually more than one person" (Kreidler 26-27). For example,

> Paulette to Annabel: 'Of course not! It is only that I feel I should not let down your family at such an important evenment.' (Ghosh 115) 1
>
> He feels thirsty. 2

In the first sentence, Paulette utters that 'I feel I should not let down your family' which is the act of speech that describes a specific event. But in the second, 'He feels thirsty.' is the complete sentence which gives us the meaning with the help of syntactic and semantic construction.

According to Kreidler, "The utterance is often part of a larger discourse like conversation, a formal lecture, a poem, a short story, a business letter, or a love letter, among other possibilities" (Kreidler 27). 'I feel thirsty' is spoken discourse, the act of speech that occurs in a given place and during a given period of time. A written discourse may be the record of something that has been spoken, or it may originate for the purpose of being performed aloud, like a play or speech, or it may exist without ever having been spoken or intended to be spoken, like most articles and books.

According to Noam Chomsky, "Language is a set (finite or infinite) of sentences, each finite in length, and constructed out of a finite set of elements". (Chomsky,. *Syntactic Structures* 13). For example, the utterance 'I feel thirsty' is produced with the help of a certain grammatical structure like I (NP), feel thirsty (VP*Adv), therefore NP*VP=S (Sentence), i.e. language is described by a particular grammar as the set of all the sentences it generates. The set of sentences may be, in principle, either finite or infinite in number. For example, the sentence:

> This is the tiger that chased the fox that killed the deer. ... 3

The sentence will be finite if we look it as it can be expanded by making proper insertions in the place of the ellipsis (...). Ellipsis is one of the main properties in English Auxiliary Verb, which says that auxiliaries can appear alone where a main verb has been omitted, but is understood:

> I will play cricket tomorrow, but she will not." ...4
> 'The judge does so enjoy your company, Puggly!' she said. (Ghosh 97) 5

In sentence 5, 'does' is the auxiliary verb which can stand alone where a main verb has been omitted, but the sentence gives us meaning, according to Falk who says in *The English Auxiliary System Revisited* that there are two types of analyses, the aux-predicate (5) and aux-feature (4) which conveys that 'does' plays a role of aux-predicate, but in sentence 4, 'will' plays a role of aux-feature.

Before we analyze the auxiliary which helps to present intended meaning in the sentence or utterance, we distinguish these two components:

I don't believe you!—— (Utterance)

He doesn't believe him.——(Sentence)

Uterances	*Sentences*	*Page No.*
'Six nine-pounders, sir'	Neel *lay* on his back.	81
'Going back?'	Neel *stared* at the bird.	112
'Amiable, was he?'	Paulette *snatched* the tablet	210
'But Mr Reid'	from the Bee Bee.	252
'No can *do*,' said Zachary.	He *whispered* to Paulette.	12

The utterance clearly indicates what a certain individual meant by saying such-and-such in a particular place, at a particular time, and to certain other individuals. When we have to analyze the utterance properly, then we need the help of context, but the sentence reveals the particular pieces of language with a syntactic component, which specifies how to combine words together to form phrases and sentences. If we try to characterize this ability of decoding any new utterance which is mingled with the auxiliary verb then we can find out the creativity process of the writer which is the problem of knowledge. For example:

> 'I *do* apologize, sir,' said Zachary, stepping forward. (Ghosh 13)
>
> Paulette looked quickly away, for she harboured a great dread of attracting the attention of Mrs Doughty, who tended to speak, at length and with exceptional rapidity, about matters she *could* not quite comprehend. (Ghosh 119-120)

> '*Can do,*' said Serang Ali, handing him the Dosootie shirt. (Ghosh 25)
>
> 'It does,' she said.(Ghosh 120)

Auxiliaries play a vital role in the utterance as we see in the above utterances where 'could' stand alone and give a semantic interpretation without main verbs. But the sentence will be finite if we look it as it can be expanded by making proper insertions in the place of the ellipsis. For example:

> "Why so it does," he said. "So then tell me, sir," I asked, "how often have you heard anyone say in Hind. (Ghosh 259)

He said that he does. . . .

We can remove 'does' and by adding proper insertions, we can make an infinite sentence as suggested by Chomsky before.

In the syntactical structure, subject comes first, then verb and finally objects. For example:

> Kalua lived in the Chamar-basti, a cluster of huts inhabited only by people of his caste. (Ghosh 25)

But in this novel, the writer uses a different sentence pattern with the help of the rules of recursion because rules have the capacity to be applied more than once in generating a structure. For example:

> In her last days, when her mind was wandering she often referred to Deeti as 'Draupadi'; when asked why, she would murmur drowsily: Because the earth has never seen a more virtuous woman than Draupadi, of the *Mahabharata*, wife to five brothers. (Ghosh 119)

One prepositional phrase describing period (in her last days) in the sentence, he develops the sentence by using 'Wh' pattern and auxiliary as a recursive tool. Instead of following the rule that creates a prepositional phrase over and over again. He uses 'wh' pattern 'why' and then auxiliaries like 'would' and 'has' to change the pattern of traditional syntactical structure of the sentences. We can take one more sentence for this linguistic analysis,

> At that time, help had come to Kalua from an unexpected quarter: one of Ghazipur's most prominent landowning families had three young scions, thakur-sahibs, who were much addicted to gambling. (Ghosh 26)

Thus, we can say that he follows the distinctive pattern in conveying his ideas in this novel which clearly portrays his creativity process which shows that the pattern is syntactically constructed even though phrases differ in the sentence, he utilizes auxiliaries and 'wh' type pattern to extend his creative ideas.

In this particular juncture, we need to discuss negation which is one of five properties in English Auxiliary Verb which take 'not' (or n't) to form the negative, e.g. cannot (can't), will not (won't), should not (shouldn't), etc. In certain tenses, in questions, when a contracted auxiliary verb can be used, the position of the negative particle n't moves from the main verb to the auxiliary, but Amitav Ghosh has used a distinct type of narrative techniques in this novel which he used 'no' in the place of auxiliary 'hadn't' and 'haven't' as a replacement for expressing negation. We can clearly analyze negation 'no' with the past perfect and present perfect which we have traced out in this novel, which are follows:

> Deeti had no difficulty in ignoring his jibes: turning her back on him. (Ghosh 4)

> The knowledge of this terrified her, for she had never set eyes on anything that remotely resembled this apparition, and had no idea what it might portend. (Ghosh 5)

> If I may say so, your youthful Queen has no more loyal subject than myself, and none who is more keenly aware of the rights that are enjoyed by the people of Britain. (Ghosh 56)

> To put the matter simply: there is nothing they want from us – they've got it into their heads that they have no use for our products and manufactures. (Ghosh 53)

> 'The truth is you have no option. Your debts to my company would not be covered even by the sale of the estate. I am afraid I cannot wait much longer. (Ghosh 58)

Conclusion

The above empirical analysis shows that Amitav Ghosh's novel is unique. He communicates his ideas with the help of auxiliaries which play a vital role in bolstering arguments in semantic or syntactic information about the main or full verb following it. He also uses 'no' in the place of auxiliary 'hadn't' and 'haven't' as a replacement for expressing negation. It clearly explicates that he follows a distinct narrative techniques in combining auxiliaries with the main verb.

Works Cited

Chomsky, Noam. *Syntactic Structures.* The Hague: Mouton, 1957.

Ghosh, Amitav. *Sea of Poppies.* New Delhi: Penguin Books, 2008.

Kreidler, Charles W. *Introducing English Semantics.* London: Routledge, 1998.

Yule, George. *The Study of Language.* Cambridge: Cambridge University Press, 1985.

18

Self-revelation: Crossings and Ethnicity in the Selected Travelogues of V.S. Naipaul

Jayshree Singh

Naipaul's travels mould his displaced self and his desperate morality into an ecstasy. He mystically associates himself with the subjects that belong to his lost inherited past. His archetype feelings towards moral and social relativism explore the dimensions of memory and his conscience's voice. His perception during the waking visions of the stations that he travels especially in India retreats him into his childhood in which he imagines the casteism in his family and racism in school, that regression of his primordial instincts is transformed into creative work. This paper intends to focus on: (1) How Naipaul in his travelogues evolves his self and readers' selves through the process of dialogue and perceptual selection and defence; How he tries to demystify misrepresentation, prejudices, religious manifestations and orientations in his creative art and in reality.

Naipaul's Psycho-dynamics in the Literary Urge

Naipaul in his travel accounts intends to bring out psychological and literary perspective as regards being homeless due to immigration of inhabitants from their native country, their loss of belongingness not only to the place where they exist as outsiders but also as expatriates in those countries where their ancestors belonged. Their conflicts towards their roots have slipped into oblivion, because their living conditions and environment in their existing inhabited place have acquired the wings of flight from their native tradition, memories, rituals and religion. Naipaul searches for psycho-dynamics that are motivated from perception of the expatriates, immigrants or from the reaction of the natives towards those who migrate abroad. In this context it is apt to understand the manifestation of one's emotional outburst psychologically:

> *Perception* is a psychological process very much related to both sensation and memory that stores lot of information and generates sense of the multitude stimuli or variables that influence our selection of stimuli from the environment and personal factors and characteristics of the perceiver. The intensity of the stimuli decides the selection, contrast and processing as well as the mental set. (Gerow 159)

Naipaul's travel accounts express his reaction to multitude stimuli that he cherished while on his visit to many areas of the world, and indeed his art and imagination seem to juggle with the perceptual selectivity and the contrasting situations of his personal mental set and characteristics that processed his reasoning and sensibility to derive the reality that has deep-rootedly ingrained in the natives of the regions he visited during his conversations with them. Naipaul as a writer, as an outsider and an insider felt that it was his cultural juxtaposition, cultural hybridity and cultural crossings that made him awakened to regard self-actualization in the different environments. In order to unite one's mind and body with the diverse variables, the perception transcends the experiences obtained through senses; as a result it stimulates consciousness, curiosity and complacency to receive changes both inside and outside the human mind and body towards the given environment. To understand the blending of emotions, reactions, perceptions with self-consciousness, it is described that:

> *Consciousness* arises out of the awareness of the environment and one's own mental processes. It is a state of mind—the active

> awareness of all thoughts, feelings, memories and perceptions. It is changing, based on personal experiences, continuous i.e. it is apt to refer here William James 'stream of consciousness' and lastly consciousness is selective. (Gerow 160)

Naipaul's consciousness undergoes through all these stages because his memories when struck with real experiences, his perceptual constancies, depth and motivation gets an outrageous emotional distancing with the illusions that he has in his subconscious mind and in his unconscious behaviour. He sometimes gets so ecstatic, ridiculous, sensitive and cynical in his observations that it appears he has one-sided view, but the re-reading of the text consciously suggests that how the people of different regions, due to imperial designs of colonialising the subaltern areas, lost their roots of belongingness; nevertheless their native culture, religion and rituals attached wings of roots in their memories, thoughts, feelings and that same happened with Naipaul too as an expatriate writer of Indian diaspora. Although his writings denote emphasis on certain religious communities, regional inhabitants and community cultures, but simultaneously he portrays their mental process and shift from sensation to perception to memory and back again to selective information and consciousness. Therefore his literary creativity till date leaves immense scope for the scholars to delve into his self-consciousness that perceives lopsided habitants of subaltern regions – South Asians, Africans, Blacks in America and Latin American, who suffered due to deportation, migration and immigration during the colonial and post-colonial period.

Naipaul's travel accounts explore dialogically the political and cultural causes and effects of colonialism on the different societies. He opines that it is relevant to understand the categorization of homogeneous groups into different communal and racial segments. He has craftily interpreted and recreated the context and constructions of myths, history, language and landscape which is mostly controlled by imperial discourse. There is no resistance, yet the writer tries to represent the repression, regression and suppression of the oppressed, the colonised and the indigenous people of South American Islands (Caribbean Islands) and South Asian countries since eighteenth century. In this regard the literary urge of a writer like Naipaul assimilates Mikhail Bakhtin's interpretation of the theory of language and consciousness of the writer in his writings. Bhaktin says:

> Dialogue is a means for revealing, for bringing to the surface the already-made character of a person; no, in dialogue a person not only shows himself outwardly, but he becomes for the first time that which he is, not only for others but for himself as well. To be means to communicate dialogically. (Childs 52)

V.S. Naipaul's travelogue do comprise direct dialogues and conversations with the native inhabitants, but it can be counted as the empirical observations to collect the information, to view the situations and to select those memories as per his level of depth, perception and consciousness and then to transliterate those moments and experiences of his travels into dialogic expression that is revelation of his self introspection, retrospection of past images, illusions and experiences and lastly his observations 'constitute inter-subjectivity (therefore social) and logically precedes subjectivity' (Childs 53), this we can say as how he reaches to his prospective creative flight.

Manifestation of Crossings and Ethnicity

Naipaul's writings portray dichotomies of his self-revelation. In spite of his personal voice and conscious sensitivity towards the natives of his travel stations, his vision presents his sense of 'the otherness' that is the imperial gaze towards the colonised. Second his place of birth and job-place are foreign to his root-native culture therefore his sense of belongingness as expatriate and diasporic writer expresses undertones of impersonal metamorphosis. Thirdly his dialogic literary language discusses aspirations, conflicts and predicaments of the natives who were considered primitive and savage by the European culture, yet his exhausitive study of travel stations implies traditions, assumptions, choices, plans, individuality, illusion and last but the least contexts and origins of religiosity and rituals among the emigrants (deported and transported natives of South Asia, Caribbean Islands, Africa and Latin Americans to Europe and America or vice versa). A critic writes in context of Naipaul it is hard to understand a Caribbean mind who due to creolization and transculturation got into a state of emotional dissatisfaction:

> The Caribbean experience therefore, implies a double diaspora: a migration to the Caribbean from else – where between the sixteenth and nineteenth centuries, and from the Caribbean to other parts of the globe, beginning in the middle of the twentieth century. (McLeod, 96)

Naipaul's self and his creative process emerge in three dimensional perceptions in response to postcolonial failings that still could not mitigate the inner activity of faith, religion, rituals and taboos of the people constituting the homogeneity or the hegemony of cultural relativism. He discusses the displacement and sublimation which is the outcome of negative and positive emotions. For examole he writes about the Negroes of Charleston town in Caribbean islands who had passed through slavery and civil war since eighteenth century, yet "the themes of sermon were religion as a binding together of people". (Turn of the South 80)

He continues to explain that in the American South "religion is to them a shared emotional experience rather a shared doctrine" (Turn of the South 232). The singers who connected the audience with the mythical religious values relieved the audience of their demons and they identify with the struggles, thus making audience human, receptive and loyal.

While the same situation do arises for Trinidad Indians, but they valorised their narrow loyalties because of being cut off from their roots. Their religion reduced to rites in order to establish themselves in a materialistic society. Negroes of the Port of Spain or Trinidad or of British Guiana lived in bitterness, wanted to assert dignity due to racialism, but their values became the values of white imperialism which became myths and prejudices among them. Here he means that even after the independence of the commonwealth colonies there prevail cross-cultural complexities and cultural fantasies. Secondly we find Naipaul's sensitivity to the religious and social norms affecting the psychological and physiological variables of different communities:

> The West Indies Indian despises the Negro for not being a West Indian, because Indians have taken over all the white prejudices against the Negro. Thus the two races became apart in Trinidad and their antagonism would have reached to peak, had their not the white imperialism ended in West Indies. Again he emphasises that the world of Indians in Trinidad was taboo-ridden, their own value system, their family organisation that aborbed them through their religious rites and rituals, hence no outsider could penetrate nor the members of the family could escape from the protection of heirarchy or religion. (*The Middle Passage* 59)

He further describes that unlike social rivalry between Negroes and whites in Trinidad or British Guiana, there was social complexity among Hindus and Muslims in bonding together due to different values; yet they were non-western type so they mingle with each other in British Guiana, that could be visualised in their architecture built by them in British Guiana.

He comments that Indians of Martinque in Caribbean Islands unlike the Indians in British Guiana, Trinidad and Surinam came from South India, a single depresed Hindu Caste. Their physical similarity and their religious practices recreate an Indian image in miniature but the most pathetic state was that they were discriminated in Fort de France by a canal for being regarded as Indian sweepers. "It happened because the white-mulatto-blackworld presented a common front off unaccomodating frenchness, the Indian remained an outside". (*The Middle Passage* 59)

Naipaul investigates the conflicts, coercion prejudices, misrepresentation of ethics and the dynamics of attitude change in the perception of religious orientation. The author came across of the drawings done by Alexander Bertrand who showed that Martinque Indians who although Catholic converts, follow Hinduism as regards dancing practices, occasional slaughter of sheep, a degraded form of the degrading *Kalipuja* that takes place in chapel.

Similarly the fantasy and myth of African Negroes for freedom and bliss in their homeland took the form of masochism and self contempt to ignore their past, their religion. Their national life began to sum up in virtue – religion and faith-comprising of Christian Hellenic tradition. Their unconscious collectivism of being black became a myth against the prejudices of white, fusty, musty, dusty, tea, coffee, cocoa, light black and dark black. The whiteness and modernity became their religion and ritual to begin a New world of national life. But contrary to such Negroes, there were the bush – Negroes in Surinam who never married outside their tribe and were proud of their pure African descent, skills and religion and to this day the Negroes of Coronie do commercial trade among Negroes. Bush Negroes in Surinam were the major contributors to colonised colonies as coconut planters to supply oil to whites' factories. The Bush-Negro maintained their independent identity on the African pattern, but "they were isolated from the world, he remembered his African skills of carving, song and dance; he remembered his African religions, he developed his language; in the far interior it became Africanized......" (*The Middle Passage* 191)

Naipaul expostulates the existence of Indian racialism against the West Indian that was the result of harmless egoism, but there was the Negro racialism that had its origin from the advent of Amerndian in Trinidad where already the black negroes were associated with slavery, but these same became the corrupters of Amerindians and hunted them because they could not be tolerated to be termed as 'blacks' or 'Negoes' but wanted to be known as Africans. Their cheap thrill of being an African without direction could not get them to shake off their guilt and prejudices that imposed upon them by whites in British Guiana or in Trinidad. The alternative to survive among the thrills of being African was only to adapt to Christianity that was modified in their African religion and made them known as 'heathens' and in this way they sorted the distance between blacks and whites; yet the Negroes racial consciousness was kept hurt, humiliated and alive, "It is felt as a terror to menace a Negro with selling him to Dutchman. The Dutchman, however, has a like terror in reserve, and threatens to sell his slave to a free negro"(*The Middle Passage* 191). The distance between the Christian and heathen still could not be bridged; hence the myth of blackness continues to be the incredible imagination in all whiteness. That is as the African-American author describes this 'black' myth as playing in the dark till date.

Naipaul does not seem to depict communal/racial/religious polarization in his writings rather he subjectively puts forth the ignorance, the discrimination and hegemony of particular section over other in order to make the other realize the 'other's gaze' either in the form of believers in social institution, as dominant imperialists/colonisers or as cultural relativists that are found in *Among the Believers* book that portrays Khomeini's tyranny in Iran or the subversive attitude in the sub-continent caste/communal groups. Naipaul mentions that in the city of Hyderabad of India, "It was a site that called up awe. But the Hindu temples, expressions of that awe, small, pyramid roofed structures, not old, only pre-1947, had been broken, emptied, cleansed, and then deface with urdu-inscriptions; the enemy utterly cast out. And it was a famous site." (*The Middle Passage* 177)

In his travelogue *Among the Believers* he has stated an ironical and paradoxical situation of Muslims thinking about their being Muslim and following Islamic principles. When he was on his visit to Islamabad, he was told by one of the drivers, namely, Masood (a science student) that 'These maulanas,' the driver said, in Massod's translation, are using Islam as a tool. We are Muslims. We are not Muslims in their way. They want to destroy Pakistan. Our Islam is better.We are the only people who can save Islam and Pakistan'. (*The Middle Passage* 230)

But when he was in Rawalpindi, he came across a rebel and a rationalist doctor who was Shia and said "he had been strengthened, even in everyday matters, by his faith as a follower of Ali. There were five points in his faith; the oneness of God, justice, a belief in prophethood, a belief in imamhood (the reign on earth of an imam as God's regent and spiritual successor to the Prophet), jihad or holy war. Not the holy war the mullahs spoke about, the doctor said; the holy war he had in mind was "the constant struggle in yourself to fight evil" (*Among the Believers* 201). But the same doctor explains the paradox of holy war in Iran where after the revolution 'killing has not been stopped in the name of God and the executions are decreed by the Islamic revolutionary courts' (*Among the Believers* 202). Naipaul suggests his conscious perception through thought provoking, descriptive and open conversations that he had with Muslim natives of Pakistan and he comes to the reason that: "the fundamentalists, insecure, with their un-historical view, feared alien contamination. But fundamentalism offered nothing. It pushed men to an unappeasable faith; it offered a political desert. It violated the 'basics'; it could never wall out the rest of the world. And I thought it was possible, looking not many steps ahead to see how in Pakistan, by the very access of fundamentalism, Islam might be preparing its own transformation" (*Among the Believers* 206).

The author's intellectual and literary pursuit observes the relevance of his own prejudice as regards his own caste, religion and rituals as well as the prevalent faiths and practices, the hypocrisy and false beliefs of the communities in transnational context. Naipaul ironically depicts parallelism for the victims and hypocrites who 'as big fish trying to dictate a small fish with cruelty, injustice and slander'.

Self-Revelation for Crisis of Humanity

Naipaul has brought personal overtones of the people whom he met during his travel into focus along with their immigrant past. This dichotomy represents a stream of consciousness of the immigrants' predicament. His interaction with his own self, with Mr. Jagan in the British Guiana and Bush-Negro in Suriman, with Negroes of Caroine plantation, with Aziz in Kashmir explains the fire of emancipation from self-crisis that bound in conflicts of suppression, religious practices or circumstances of mythical image given to each group of society. He elaborates Hindus' (Indians) underdeveloped ego that is bound within family, social institutions and it is 'relatively tenuous', i.e., narrow loyalties and do not help them to relate to reality, instead they search in their 'meditation therapy' a way to continue life amidst the subservience, conquests, subjugation; moreover even in the modern world, their scientific temperament remains subdued and they do not let themselves changed. He agrees to Sudhir Kakkar's analysis of Hindus and he says:

> Caste and clan are more than brotherhoods; they define the individual completely. The individual is never on his own; he is always fundamentally a member of his group, with a complex apparatus of rules, rituals, taboos. Every detail of behaviour is regulated – the bowels to be cleared before breakfast and never after, for instance, the left hand and not the right to be used for intimate sexual contact, and so on. Relationships are codified. And religion and religious practices – 'magic and animistic ways of thinking' – lock everything into place. The need, then for individual observation and judgement is reduced; something close to a purely instinctive life becomes possible. (*India: A Wounded Civilization* 91)

Naipaul perceives the contemporary situation from the current perspective and do argumentative analysis not only through his inner expression or subjectivity rather he searches inter-subjectivity vis-à-vis historical, cultural, social and political influences in the conversations, details that he gathers from the people whom he came across and then he frames his literary account within the framework of present keeping in view the past (that he does not falsify or fabricate). Instead his interaction connects the possible probabilities with the logical facts that have so long fore-grounded cultural relativism and racial ghetto in the form of slavery, genocide, apartheid, wildness, violence and savagery. The author nowhere has desired to delineate the memories of discriminated or subjugated beings as absurdities, rather he projects their choice, their anguish, their predicament and their rebel to decontextualise the postcolonial failings of power, hegemony, holy wars and cruelty which were the operational structures of colonial and postcolonial framework to subjugate 'the Other' in the context of religious mission, imperial expansion and political orientation.

These savage factors are the product of cultural phenomena, which have been turning the post-colonial world to decontextualize such predicaments and crisis of humanity.

> We use the term post-colonial to cover all the culture affected by the imperial process from the moment of the colonization to the present day. This is because there is a community of preoccupation throughout the historical process initiated by European imperial aggression. (Mukherji 8)

An account from one of his travelogue pictures bad living conditions because of the most gruesome acts of slavery, racial and religious practices:

> The emphasis was on land and Negroes. Every immigrant, who had to be Roman Catholic, was to get a personal grant of thirty-two acres and sixteen acres for every Negro he bought in. A free Negro or mulatto (a dirty, Spanish, white women used as whore) would get sixteen acres for himself and sixteen acres for every one of his own Negroes. Immigrants would pay no taxes on their Negroes for ten years, and they could import Negroes duty-free for ten years. If the money was used to buy Negroes, goods could be taken out of the island and sold subject only to a five per cent tax. A Negro code would be promulgated; in the meantime every immigrant would be required to have sufficient arms to contain his Negroes. (*Loss of El Dorado* 115)

His perception and emotional contact describes "the act of blocking" (Patrick 415) while his altruistic behaviour as conformity to social norms projects his "contrary and provocative" (Patrick 415) voice in his travelogues. The whole world that Naipaul toured appeared to be segmented with this impact and his own conscience is also one among the general crowd who in his lifetime consciously, subconsciously or unconsciously has been impressed with or suffered disillusions of caste, race factors. Yet what makes the study of travelogues so appropriate and pertinent to the present global governance is that there is awareness and maturity as well as illumination of the perceptual selectivity, perceptual defense and perceptual development vis-à-vis fanaticism, fundamentaiism, ethnocentricity, totalitarianism and conservatism. Religion in the travelogue *An Area of Darkness* contains self-examination of the featureless images of his subconscious mind that has been formed in the environment provided to him in Trinidad by his parents and grandparents, but later it turns into misconception of the diaspora and expatriate writer who has been far from Indianness and has viewed India from an eye of an explorer who tries to visualize it in certain references and illusions.

Naipaul's senses not only perceive but interpret sensory inputs to make it meaningful not only to produce a piece of non-fiction, but the external impressions transform him mystically to get into his self–introspection and this process of transcendence reorders the sensory inputs obtained from external experiences and this stimulates his impulses at first. He gets into fury and becomes outrageous in his expression. The previous memories of religious consciousness, that had faded in accordance to space and time, revives in the 'Pilgrimage' chapter, his observation turns disastrously prejudiced when *India* of his fantasy apppears real after watching the spirit of the thing, i.e., *ingam* at Amarnath caves in Kashmir, that releases his outrageous spirit from illusion of being an outsider and he indulges his self into the preoccupation of being one with common Indians' religiosity. He writes:

> The spirit of the thing! Squatting in the cave, which rang continuously with the shouts, and shuffling, concentrating on the bazaar litter on the wet floor, glimpsing out of the corner of an eye ascending crowd whose numbers I could less easily grasp than I could the size of the mountains and the valleys, I had grown light-headed. A physical growth, because it was extraordinary, was a spiritual symbol. The growth failed; it became the symbol of a symbol. In the spiraling, deliquescing logic I felt I might drown. I went outside into the light. Pilgrims, their offerings made, were looking up for the two rock pigeons, followers of Lord Shiva once, before they were turned into pigeons by the anger of their Lord and doomed forever to live near Him in his cave. I did not look up. I went on down the white slope, hopping from rock to rock, and did not stop until I came to the clear stream'. (*An Area of Darkness* 170)

Naipaul through his depth perception discovers the path of self-orientation rather than the other's orientation. The author shows conformity to the social norms outwardly and inwardly. In this context it is best to quote Theroux (a nice earnest American novelist) who writes about Naipaul's image: Until I met Vidia (V.S. Naipaul), I had never known a person who recognized no one as his equal. He's a Brahmin, the local Indians said: all Brahmins are fussy like that.' (Paul, 51)

Naipaul through his own caste-ridden strict attitude felt intrinsically to withhold his attitudes against mild attacks whether of belonging to different community in India or to different race in Trinidad or in Europe. He has sublimated his negativism or biasedness through *his flight in his writings* that narrate his accounts of real-life experiences, of emotional upheaval, maladjustment or of emotional sanctity. He explains how his writing down travelling memoirs cleanses his ethnic thoughts from malign and menace for other religious communities. He writes:

> I had my own scruples, too, about eating far from home – far, at any rate, from the Taj Coromandel Hotel. But I felt ashamed of those scruples, and I accepted a little food from Kakusthan's Kitchen, and put my lips to the glass of coffee, though the breaking

> of bread (or a puri) in Kakusthan's back did make my writing fingers oily. This became hard to ignore; it called for a more than ritual washing outside – Kakusthan pouring for me, not complaining, wasting precious water from the well, one of the six evening pots he was allowed. (And there had been no need for me to feel ashamed, or to feel that I had to eat. Kakusthan was a man of the world. When I next visited him at the colony, some days later, from home, I told him straight out that I was like him, too, and didn't eat away from home. He accepted that immediately. He laughed and said, "All right, I'll be the untouchable this time. (*India: A Million Mutinies Now* 294)

Basically what Naipaul tries to suggest through his empirical experience that a person's complaints are primarily psychological or physiological in origin. Both Naipaul and Kakusthan in their respective fanatic beliefs of conserving their cultural practices and prejudices predispose heightened consciousness extrinsically and that causes conflict between unpleasant and pleasant reciprocity to moral norms, nevertheless both are also filtering their prejudicial attitudes by finding stimuli of similarity, proximity and continuity. Because of this paradigm shift in their perception, there is order and meaning on one hand, whereas at the othei end there is degree of illumination, i.e., Naipaul realizes default of his own (although he has not been into it till he had been to India) and of his brahminical community for practicing 'untouchability' against pariahs, Shudras for centuries due to holy scriptures prescriptions and he also came to know that it is the Muslims who have been a bridge between brahmins and non-brahmins. Same he has inculcated through his writing among readers the consequences of social indifferences. Moreover it is a success because through allegorical narrative of Kakusthan, Naipaul has portrayed the reality of the cultural projection, ethnocentric influence in religious manifestations that has bound different communal groups into insensitive and unsympathetic attitude. The author presents an integrative view of human liberation from the clutches of religious orientations that Mohandas Karamchand Gandhi (the father of Nation of India) idealized. He quotes Mahatma Gandhi's words:

> Identity was related to a set of beliefs and rituals, knowledge of the Gods, a code, an entire civilization. The loss of the past meant the loss of that civilization, the loss of the fundamental idea of India, and the loss therefore, to a nationalist-minded man, a motive for an action. It was a part of the feeling of purposelessness of which many Indians spoke, part of the longing for Gandhian days, when the idea of India was real and seemed full of promise, and the 'moral issues' clear. (*India: A Wounded Civilization* 60)

But in the travelling accounts of Naipaul there are ironical references of the misrepresented self-cherishing attitude of Hindus, Sikhs etc. who refute Gandhi's ideals as regards Hinduism. For example, "In Madras most of the vegetarian restaurants used to boast themselves as 'Brahmin hotels' – and the Dravidian people would erase the word 'Brahmin'. Now hotels do not have these words in the city. In those days you would have the 'Brahmin hotel' and the 'military hotel". (*India: A Million Mutinies Now* 296). Another reference mentions the idealization of identity through religious orientation, i.e., the Sikh movement aimed at creating pure Sikhs, and amrit was necessary. "After you take amrit, you don't eat food not cooked by amritdharis. People, who have taken amrit, 'that helps to control the five evils: lust, anger, covetousness, ego, family attachments'. This was initiated by the 10th Guru Gobind Singh to enable followers of Sikhism to reach God". (*India: A Million Mutinies Now* 527).

Naipaul says that the 'credibility of this myth' changed its course, i.e., the practices of idealization were deformed into cultural relativism after two or three generations because of political encouragement, political security, development in agriculture, the growth of national economy. In 1984, the Golden Temple had been occupied by Bhindranwale.

People stopped going to the Golden Temple. Both my neighbours stopped going, though they wanted to. People were Angry about what was happening in the Temple, but the Sikh political party never condemned the desecration of the Temple by Bhindranwale and his guns. The Sikh political party was fighting a joint agitation with Bhindranwale from the Golden Temple, and they were afraid of him. He was a killer. Hc didn't worry about Hindu or Sikh – once you opposed him, you would be on his hit list'. "....It's the minority fear, the persecution complex, the death wish. It's a new religion...." "It's madness, it's fanaticism...." "...He harmed the Sikhs the most, the Sikh religion the most. He harmed Punjab, and he harmed India". (*India: A Million Mutinies Now* 558)

Through such findings, Naipaul raises a very important question concerning whether individuals can change their attitude under coercion. The answer seems to be largely negative, because such characteristics do not have credibility, but may have power and attractiveness for the community. Without credibility, power cannot propagate democracy and brotherhood; it can only lead to self-laceration, violence, torments, killings, deaths, murders, terrorism, totalitarianism, authoritarianism. Such prejudices infest regionalism, communalism, social ostracism and fundamentalism. It may serve the individual or community needs to feel superior and the need to express aggression, but such feeling of hostility, aroused by frustration, according to psychologists result in *scapegoates* and finally in other's gaze it may be that the prejudice may become reinforced and continue unabated that metamorphically be termed as *scarecrow* or *scaremonger* to spread alienation, resentment, riots, violence and killing.

Naipaul has off course been so realistic in illustrating the effects of religious prejudices but his intention is to establish compatibility through his art of writing. Naipaul justifies his vision not through didactic or moral approach, rather he avoids to be directly between the devil and the deep sea, or on the horns of dilemma. His narrative style is motivational and suggests achievement of reality. Another sort of misperception is interpreted as disassociate perception or self-deception, which often is likely to lead to distortion of reality and make it difficult to make a healthy adjustment with the reality, they live in make-believe world. Naipaul writes: "There were people in Pakistan who had taken the faith to its limit. To them Islam was more than personal salvation, more that a body of belief; it had become country, culture, identity; it had to be served, at whatever cost to the individual or the state itself" (*Among the Believers* 391-392).

Naipaul through his writings has not uttered in any kind the communal division of groups or regions. He says that social crusaders and fanatics who fantasizes their faith, surpasses all extremes of emotional sublimation and forced to the path of identification and aggression, that is well analyzed in the perceived notion by V.S. Naipaul: "People develop fantasies about who and what they are; and in the Islam of converted countries" (Naipaul undertakes the journey of the countries- Indonesia, Iran, Pakistan and Malaysia), "there is an element of neurosis and nihilism" (*Beyond the Belief* 1). He further writes: "The British period—two hundred years in some places, less than a hundred in others—was a rim of Hindu regeneration. The Hinds, especially in Bengal, welcomed the New Learning of Europe and the institutions the British brought. The Muslims, wounded by their loss of power, and out of religious scruples, stood aside. It was the beginning of the intellectual distance between the two communities"(*Beyond the Belief* 265).

Conclusion

Thus Naipaul projects the predicaments of humanity in context of their own cultural coercions or cross-cultural fatalism and contentions. He has laid bare before us the suppressed histories of the third world countries of the sub-continent and has left open for us the platform to decide how much we should be sacred and secular to achieve the better prospects of global understanding and unity. He nowhere suggests any escapism rather he tries to make the reader comprehend that it is we who have to decide to have self-emancipation or self-upliftment by following the path of passive resistance not by brute force that was the path enunciated by Mahatma Gandhi in his book '*Hind Swaraj*'.

Alberuni argued that it is very important for people of one country to know how others elsewhere live, and how and what they think. Evil behaviour (of which Alberuni had seen plenty in the barbarity of his former patron, Sultan Mahmud of Ghazni, who had savagely raided India several times) can arise from a lack of understanding of – and familiarity with – other people. To supplement the argument given by one of medieval history visitor to India, it is apt to elaborate this viewpoint by the quote of Prof. Amartya Sen, who writes that moral imagination and reason are the binaries to control oneself and to think for univeral welfare:

> In trying to go beyond what Adam Smith called our 'first perceptions', we need to transcend what Akbar saw as the 'marshy land' of unquestioned tradition and unreflected response. Reason has its reach – compromised neither by the importance of instinctive psychology nor by the presence of cultural diversity in the world. It has an especially important role to play in the civilization of moral imagination. We need it in particular to face the bats and owls and the insane moon. (Sen 292)

His travelogues manifest his inward desire to transform the misconceptions as a visionary. His perspective does not disillusion the reader; rather it brings him/her closer to the reality, the darkness, the ignorance and the primitive state of primordial stream of fundamentalism in any corner of the world. His thrust is on spirituality, social order, political upheavals, emotional crisis that have taken place due to the threat to the ethnocentric identity or on the nativity. His sensibility to romanticize the images, the myths as regards the continuity, the custom and the corruption, is worth to explore to know the impact of religiosity in the local and global context.

Works Cited

Gerow, Josh R. (1993). 'Perception and Consciousness', *Essentials of Psychology*. U.S.A.: Harper Collins.

Childs, Peter and Roger Fowler (2006). 'Dialogic Structure', *The Routledge Dictionary of Literary Terms*. London & New York: Routledge.

McLeod, John (2007). 'Marxism', *The Routledge Companion to Postcolonial Studies*. London & New York: Routledge.

Mukherjee, Arun P. (1996). 'Interrogating Post Colonialism", *Interrogating Post-Colonialism: Theory Text and Context. E*d. Trivedi, Harish and Meenakshi Mukherjee, Shimla: Indian Institute of Advanced Study.

French, Patrick (2008). 'Author's Interview with V.S.Naipaul', *The Authorized Biography of V.S. Naipaul.* London: Picador.

Theroux, Paul (1998). *Sir Vidia's Shadow*, London.

Sen, Amartya (2005). 'The Reach of Reason', *The Argumentative Indian-Writings on Indian Culture, History and Identity.* London: Penguin.

19

The Fragmented Identity of Postmodern Individuals: A Scrutiny of Michael Ondaatje's *Anil's Ghost*

M. Preetha

The postmodern condition and the concomitant globalization have a great impact on the contemporary lifestyle, identity formation and the perception of life. Michael Ondaatje insinuates that the identity of the characters is a unique phenomenon in the postmodern world as it reverberates the social arena to which they belong. He adumbrates that in the postmodern age of discontinuity, fragmentation, and metamorphosis, the primarily established norms of identity have turned obsolete. In the postmodern world, the concept of identity is considered as a transitive, mutable and self-effacing entity.

Ondaatje foregrounds the fragmented nature of Anil Tissera's self which is divided between the adopted Western culture and the sense of affinity towards the homeland. He examines Anil's personal and cultural metamorphosis as she migrates from one country to another. She is initially dependent upon the cultural and individual identity given to her by her parents and though she moves temporarily away from the national identity by adopting herself to a different culture, she rejuvenates her national identity by aligning herself with the homeland. Ondaatje directs the migrants living in the adopted land to preserve their identities by taking pride in their ancestry and thereby achieve a sense of belonging. He accentuates that the national identity offers the characters to transcend the notions of homelessness and wilderness by achieving a stable identity.

In the postmodern world, the flourishing development of capitalism, the advancement of technology, the wide spread phenomenon of globalization, and the war between the different factions of society have ensued in an intense and considerable transformation in social, cultural, and economic structure as a whole. The postmodern condition and the concomitant globalization have a great impact on the contemporary lifestyle, identity formation and the perception of life. Michael Ondaatje insinuates that the identity of the characters is a unique phenomenon in the postmodern world as it reflects the social arena to which they belong.

Ondaatje adumbrates that in the postmodern age of discontinuity, fragmentation, and metamorphosis, it is hard for contemporary people to ascertain who they really are. The myriad metamorphosis in the ambiance of the world has counteracted the modernists' notion of forming a stable, predictable and coherent identity. Fredrick Jameson comments in the book *The Cultural Turn: The Selected Writings on the Postmodern* that "the modernist aesthetic is in some way organically linked to the conception of a unique self and private identity, a unique personality and individuality, which can be expected to generate its own unique vision of the world. . . " (6). Ondaatje ascertains that in the contemporary epoch of displacement and disenchantment, the primarily established norms of identity have turned obsolete. Jameson claims that the cultural turn in the late modernity has exacted the notion that "this kind of individualism and personal identity is a thing of the past; that the old individual or individualist subject is 'dead' . . ." (6).

Ondaatje reckons that in the postmodern world, the concept of identity is considered as a transitive, mutable and self-effacing entity. The condition of the postmodern world has actuated millions of people to cross the frontiers of their country. There are various reasons for migration – political upheaval including war, persecution, climate-related refugees, economic migrants, education, and family reunification. The transplanted migrants have the profoundest anxiety of identity crisis as they confront the jeopardy resulting from hyphenated identities. In the article entitled "Introduction: Who Needs 'Identity'?" Stuart Hall abduces that in the late modern times, the individuals do not have any unified identity, instead they are "increasingly fragmented and fractured; never singular but multiply constructed across different, often intersecting and antagonistic, discourses, practices and positions. They are subject to . . . the process of change and transformation" (4).

In *Anil's Ghost*, Ondaatje examines the hyphenated identity of Anil Tissera who emigrated from Sri Lanka. He adumbrates that the civil tensions in the country and the lack of educational opportunities has urged millions of people to migrate. The migrated people initially face cultural displacement in the foreign countries but the fear of facing the trauma of war belittled their cultural alienation. They learn to assimilate themselves to the new environment. The life in the alien land distances them from the cultural and linguistic patterns of the homeland; however, during the moments of social upheaval, the emigrants share emotional affinity with their homeland and its inhabitants. The conflict that arises between the contradictory forces of the postmodern world results in hyphenated identity.

Anil migrated from her homeland at the age of eighteen to study medicine in England. She had been an exceptional swimmer as a child and had won several accolades in Sri Lanka. She was known throughout her homeland as a child prodigy. Her talent became an indispensable part of her life, so she felt alienated in England when the people around her failed to recognize the talent in her. She becomes timid and reticent as she finds it difficult to open up conversation with people. She felt lost and perceived herself to be living in far ends of the world. Moreover, the contrasting ambiance of the homeland and the host country stifles her. In the tropics, the classrooms were filled with the noises of the birds, lorries, and fighting dogs whereas the intricate geography and the serene atmosphere of the English classroom astound her.

Anil experiences the problems of displacement when the ties with her homeland attenuated. Her only connection with the island was the new sarong that her parents used to send her every Christmas but with the death of her parents, she lost all ties with Sri Lanka. She longed to have some conversation with whom she can discuss some common features of her homeland. She felt that all these trivial reliefs made some remarkable difference in the country that is too brittle. It is this desire to develop some intimacy with her countrymen that drives her to the smoke of a bad marriage. She interpreted her husband's irrepressible behaviour "as sexual jealousy, then she saw it as an attempt to limit her research and studies. It was the first handcuff of marriage, and it almost buried her" (144). She realises that she begun to love him because of her loneliness but when she found it difficult to get along with him, she decided to end their relationship. Ondaatje speculates that her decision to drop the relationship with him parallels her intention to subjugate Eastern cultural identity in favour of the West.

Ondaatje exposes Anil's conflict between the dichotomies of Eastern and Western cultures. He apprehends the anarchy involved in following one's tradition in alien lands. He reiterates that in homeland, one is surrounded by family order and values. There is no anonymity in one's homeland but when they migrate to the foreign lands they escape the vigilance of the customs and manners. They live a freewheeling life with no respect for their cultural heritage. He substantiates that "we take our clothes off because we shouldn't take our clothes off. And we behave worse in other countries . . . . What is that quality in us? Do you think? That makes us cause our own rain and smoke?" (138).

Ondaatje explores the effect of acculturation on individual identity. He accentuates the influence of Western countries on Anil's perspectives and life style, "[t]he island no longer held her by the past. She'd spent the fifteen years since ignoring that early celebrity" (11). Her distance from her homeland helped her in interpreting her homeland with a panoramic vision. The surfeit of violence that has taken place in Sri Lanka after her departure has in turn numbed her desire to return. "She was appalled by the blood that flown through the bridges since the war. She felt that the island has become "a more complicated world morally" (11).

Anil assimilates herself to the Western virtues of individuality and does not associate with the communal culture of Sri Lanka. She courted foreignness during her European and North American education. She loses the sense of her original self and feels at ease on Bakerloo line or the highways around Santa Fe. She is alienated from Sri Lanka to the extent that instead of coming to Sri Lanka as a return home, she sees it as an unfortunate temporary leave of absence from the West. She feels baffled when she was sent by the International Human Rights Investigation to investigate the widespread murders carried out in the island. She muses, "Oh—what do I like? Most of all I think I like that I can do things on my own terms. Nothing is anonymous here, is it. I miss my privacy" (72). She finds it difficult to work in sparse high-tech areas of Sri Lanka as she could not locate half the equipments that she needed.

Anil notices a stark contrast between the advanced environment of the adopted land and the low-tech native country. The sense of detachment from the homeland coupled with the adopted culture of the new environment results in hyphenated identities. Abhijit Gupta in his review entitled "Unearthly Beauty" reiterates that in expatriate writings, "The overwhelming theme is that of separation, of human beings fenced apart from each other, each inhabiting their personal island of pain. Cut off from the nourishing roots of family and community, all of Ondaatje's characters seem to live in a state of numbness, a shell shock of the mind" (23-24) He avers that the aloofness from the homeland discerpes them from their roots – language, history, culture. The sense of rootlessness and uncertainty shared by the expatriates affect the sense of integrity of the self.

Anil had many relatives in Sri Lanka, but she did not wish to rebuild an intimacy with them. She felt very glad to be alone in her own world. She had adopted Western style of dressing and manners. Her absence from the homeland in fact distances her from her mother tongue. She avers that she can speak "just English. I can write some Sinhala" (36). During her meeting with her ayah, Lalitha, she experiences a loss of language between them. She could not speak fluently in Sinhala, instead sought the help of Lalitha's granddaughter to translate the English she spoke. She is even further separated from Lalitha, the symbol of her Sri Lankan past, when the granddaughter starts talking to Lalitha in Tamil, a language which she never knew. Anil finds it difficult to speak with any non-English speaking Sri Lankans. Antoinette Burton insinuates in the article "Archive of Bones: *Anil's Ghost* and the Ends of History" that "Anil is a stock character in postcolonial fiction: the Europe-or America-returned professional woman struggling to maintain her hard worn status against all odds" (41).

Ondaatje denies the possibility of the fixity of identity or identification by drawing attention to the ambiguity behind the transition of Anil's name. She was known throughout her life by two different names. She disliked the two entirely inappropriate names that she had been given during her childhood days, and so she desired to adopt her brother's unused second name. She tried to buy the name from him when she was twelve years old by offering to support him in all family arguments. She thereby got her name Anil from her brother and became to be known within her close circle as Anil Tissera. Her intense sense of contentment and determination to maintain her newly adopted name does not diminish over time, as "[e]verything about the name pleased her, its slim, stripped-down quality, its feminine air, even though it was considered a male name. Twenty years later she felt the same about it" (67). The inclusion of a male name with her own signifies the complex nature of her identity that manifolded with her migrant experience.

Anil's investigation in war torn areas of Sri Lanka enables her to acquire a panoptic view of the predicament of the people in her homeland. She realises that during the civil war, millions of people were found missing and hundreds of them were dead, "people just started disappearing, or bodies kept being found burned beyond recognition. There is no hope of affixing blame. And no one can tell who the victims are" (42). She gets repulsed by the civil war that has torn the country apart and fostered an aura of fear, suspicion and almost impalpable evil on the citizens of Sri Lanka.

Anil mediates her understanding of the traumatic condition of the country, "the darkest Greek tragedies were innocent when compare with what was happening here" (11). Her investigation made her to realize that the accumulating horrors connote an insane sense of delirium that had enveloped the country. She longs to utilise all her skills to resolve the extensive murders that is carried out in the island, "She believed that meaning allowed a person a door to escape grief and fear, but she saw that those who were slammed and stained by violence lost the power of language and logic" (55).

Ondaatje demonstrates the personal experience of trauma and the way trauma is experienced both as a physical and psychological event that affects the psyche of the individual. Anil had worked in several wary places like Oklahoma but her stay with the Sri Lankan victims gives shock to her intimate knowledge of self and world. The political trauma that she witnessed since her entry to Sri Lanka disorients her. She had her food along with the exhuming bodies and gradually she became much thinner as she gets more and more involved in her work. She was exhausted by the widespread murders and the physical condition of the survivors who are affected by various diseases like dysentery, hepatitis, dengue fever.

Anil realises that she was besieged by the uncertain laws and fear that was everywhere. She was not able to have any solid ground to which she can hold onto with one arm, "Truth bounced between gossip and vengeance" (54). She struggles to have a definite path leading to the source of mysteries around her. She avouches to bring out some changes in the island instead of composing a political writing that would give her financial gains but her hyphenated identity in turn creates distrust in the minds of the natives like Sarath and Gamini, "'You know, I'd believe your arguments more if you lived here,' he said, 'you can't just slip in, make a discovery and leave'" (44). Ondaatje posits that the unassailable love that Sarath and Gamini felt for their homeland inspite of the massacres that is carried out in the island, epitomises the love that natives had for their land.

Anil's dislocation and sense of being out of place in her mother country is overcome when she is finally able to identify the victims of civil war not as strangers, but as her own people, "I think you murdered hundreds of us. *Hundreds of us.* Sarath thought to himself. Fifteen years away and she is finally us" (271). Her life in Western countries has influenced her customs and manners, but when she witnessed the trauma experienced by the people of her homeland, she once again identifies herself as a citizen of Sri Lanka. Silvia Albertazzi in her review on the novel observes that "her progressive awareness of the political situation of the island coincides for her with the emergency of a new sense of identity, in which her Asian past is no more at odd with her Western present" (74). The physical displacement of the emigrants does not repress their love for their nation. They are emotionally and psychologically attached to the social conditions of the country and consequently advocate for the welfare of the nation at the time of crisis.

Ondaatje ascertains that Anil's experience in her homeland has changed her attitude towards the country. She develops an emotional affinity with people of her homeland. She takes up the conviction to bring about peace by projecting the plight of the country to the International Human Rights authorities. She takes up the resolution to maintain the same intimacy even after leaving Sri Lanka, "if she were to step into another life now, back to the adopted country of her choice, how much would Gamini and the memory of Sarath be a part of her life? Would she talk to intimates about them, the two Colombo brothers?" (285). Her desire to identify herself as the sister of Sarath and Gamini exemplify her intention to be identified as a Sri Lankan. She rejuvenates her national identity by aligning herself with the homeland.

The emigrants' struggle to reconstruct the other half of the identity actualizes only when they develop an intimacy with their homeland. They achieve a sense of rootedness when they renew and rebuild some attachment with their homeland. Salman Rushdie in his book *Imaginary Homelands* comments that the expatriates' impulse to maintain ties with their homeland is due to their notion of being "haunted by some sense of loss, some urge to reclaim, to look back, even at the risk of being mutated into pillars of salt" (10). Ondaatje directs the migrants living in the adopted land to preserve their identities by taking pride in their ancestry and thereby achieve a sense of belonging.

Ondaatje considers that the growing interconnectedness of the various places of the world hastens the need for developing an understanding of wide variety of cultures along with the knowledge of the native culture. He accentuates that the national identity offers the characters to transcend the notions of homelessness and wilderness by achieving a stable identity. The ability to perceive one's cultural condition and the tenacity to cope with the changes will enable an individual to form a composite identity.

Works Cited

Albertazzi, Silvia. Rev. of *Anil's Ghost. Wasafiri* 32 (2000): 74-75.

Burton, Antoinette. "Archive of Bones: *Anil's Ghost* and the Ends of History." *The Journal of Common Wealth Literature* 38.1 (2003): 39-56.

Gupta, Abhijit. "Unearthly Beauty." Rev. of *Anil's Ghost. Indian Review of Books* 9.12 (2000): 23-24.

Hall, Stuart. "Introduction: Who Needs 'Identity'?" *Questions of Cultural Identity*. Ed. Stuart Hall and Paul Du Gay. London: Sage, 1996. 1-17.

Jameson, Fredric. *The Cultural Turn: Selected Writings On The Postmodern 1983-1998*. London: Verso, 1998.

Ondaatje, Michael. *Anil's Ghost*. London: Picador, 2000.

Rushdie, Salman. *Imaginary Homelands*. New York: Penguin, 1992.

20

Aporias of Formalistic Criticism: T.S. Eliot's Two Essays on Milton and Paul de Man's Rhetorical Readings

Rajesh B. Sharma

In the series of critical writings, T.S. Eliot wrote two articles on Milton, "Milton I" and "Milton II". In the first, he criticizes Milton for creating artificial, unimaginative, conventional, vague poetry. Milton is assailed for not contributing to the development of English language and literature. Eliot considers Milton less poetic as Milton prioritized the aural imagery as against the visual and tactile, which are called the essential qualities of the great tradition of English poetry. Milton is accused of disrupting and dislocating meaning in his poetry as he indulges in rhetoric. Excess of' music leads to disjunction in the sound and sense, which ultimately results in the discontinuity of the organic unity between the signifier and the referent. Shakespeare, Dante and others are called the poets of the great tradition as they achieved the perfect unity between form and meaning. Eliot reverses his stance in "Milton II" and finds Milton a great, unique poet. To the readers' bafflement, Eliot canonizes Milton, in "Milton II" for excelling in those very poetic qualities for the lack of which he was condemned in "Milton I".

The criticism as practised by T.S. Eliot in "Milton I" paradoxically leads to Milton's canonization in "Milton II". It becomes necessary that T.S. Eliot's poetic theory is re-read with a rigour to assess the causes and nature of inconsistencies in which Eliot indulges. This paper attempts to reflect upon the subjective fallacies of various kinds that T.S. Eliot committed while writing "Milton I" and "Milton II". I have taken these subjective fallacies to be the forms of de Manian blindness from which Eliot could not escape, because the inevitable faith in the truth of the materiality of sense is generated in the lived experiences of human life through pure signifiers. Eliot performs in the paradigm of aporias which are the result of his excessive faith in empty signifiers which create the delusions of essentiality.

The centrality of T.S. Eliot's argument can be situated in the binaries that he creates between grammatical, referential mode of language and the rhetorical, non-referential mode of language. The organic nature of linguistic medium is so natural with Eliot that he sees complete correspondence between the form and the content. For him language has the ability to convey what a subject intends to, and literary form, in all its manifestations of sign, structure and sound, is purposive and intentional. The idea of reconciliation between the form and the content is so attractive and powerful with T.S. Eliot that it becomes the breeding ground of false methods and models of literary interpretation. In his celebrated essay "What is Classic?" he finds maturity of language and style in the style which is enriched with maximum referentiality. A genius is one who exploits fully the riches of a language (Eliot 1956, 63). The 'common style', as he terms it, is invested with maximum semanticity. Henry James is exalted for his fluid style as it perfectly conveys his kind of meaning and his sense of reality. His 'involved syntax' represents his intentionality. But 'reality is no part' of Milton's intentionality (Eliot 1956, 142). Even Dryden is superior to Milton. Comparing Dryden with Milton, Eliot says:

> Of the two, I still think Dryden's development the healthier, because it was Dryden who preserved, so far as it was preserved at all, the tradition of *conversational language* in poetry: and I might

> add that it seems to me easier to get back to *healthy language from Dryden* than it is to get back to it from Milton. For what such a generalization is worth, Milton's influence on eighteenth century was much more deplorable than Dryden's (Eliot 1956, 142, italics mine).

James Joyce is also considered a writer of "traditional" greatness because "Joyce always maintains some contact with conversational tone" (Eliot 1956, 143). Shakespeare's permanence and universality is attributed to the fact that there is complete fusion of the form and intent in Shakespearean poetry "... the auditory imagination and the imagination of the other senses are more nearly fused, and *fused together with the thought*" (Eliot 1956, 142, italics mine). Eliot finds the same complete coherence between surface and core in Shakespeare and Dante when he says in these poets "There is no interruption between the surface that these poets present to you and the core" (Eliot 1956, 142). And that is why in these poets "at each reading all the elements of appreciation can be present (Eliot 1956, 142). The grammaticality of the language, the referentiality of the language and the form, the complete correspondence between the poetic intent and its organic form, is the type of genetic model and method which T.S. Eliot creates to judge Milton's poetry. Milton cannot be appreciated fully because his style is basically rhetorical, and, A disadvantage of the rhetorical style appears to be that a dislocation takes place, through the hypertrophy of the auditory imagination at the expense of the visual and tactile, so that *the inner meaning is separated from the surface* and tends to become something occult... (Eliot 1956, 143, italics mine).

For T.S. Eliot, fuller poetic appreciation is possible only when there is coherent relationship between the surface and the core, between the form and the content, between the word and the referent. With Milton he finds disruption between the signifier and the referent. And as Milton failed to create new meanings in the signifier, Eliot concludes "Milton writes English like a dead language" (Eliot 1956, 141). This so-called death of English language at the hands of Milton prompts Mr. Eliot to indulge in cannibalistic criticism of Milton, because he cannot tolerate the damage that Milton has done "to the English language from which it has not wholly recovered" (Eliot 1956, 145).

In "Milton II", Eliot reverses his stance and canonizes Miltonic poetry on those very points on which he denounced it. Here he finds a perfect organic relationship between the form and meaning. The music which sounded meaningless in "Milton I" becomes 'strongest' in "Milton II", deriving its nutrition from the complete correspondence between the sound and meaning. Eliot says "It (poetry) might also learn (from Milton) that the music of verse is strongest in poetry which has a definite meaning expressed in the properest words" (Eliot 1956, 160). Perhaps this is the 'properest' test that Eliot evolves for great poetry. Appropriate subject matter couched in proper words, and accompanying suitable extended structures, larger units of music, suggestive imagery, all serve the purpose of conveying the maximum meaning. It is this purposive and intentional value of Milton's poetry which canonizes him. Milton successfully passes the test of this purposiveness and Eliot raises him to the height and stature that "we must perhaps wait for a great poet before we find one who can profit from the study of Milton" (Eliot 1956, 155).

When Eliot wrote "Milton II", he must have thought the necessity of writing this to correct the mistakes that he had committed earlier. He corrects, of course, but what he corrects is incorrigible. What he considers as insights, are in fact the causes of blindness, which have afflicted the critic community of his type. The inconsistencies in which he indulges perhaps result from his mistake of taking surfaces as core and core as surfaces. When he is dealing with surfaces, he feels the effects of digging deep. True criticism is a creative practice of another type. And, as in the case of all sorts of creativity, true criticism too grows in the moments of crisis. True criticism bursts forth when there is an irresistible urgency to vent irrepressible ideas which have germinated from the extended deep reflections on the ontological status of language and literature. This is the moment of crisis because one starts questioning the meaning and medium both. One cannot avoid the crisis, it has to be faced if one wants to 'dig deep'.

In periods that are not periods of crisis, or in individuals bent on avoiding crisis at all cost, there can be all kinds of approaches to literature: historical, philosophical, psychological, etc., but there can be no criticism. For such periods or individuals will never put the act of writing into question by relating it to specific intent (de Man 18).

T.S. Eliot seems to follow Kantian aesthetics of art forms. He indulges in pleasure, as derived from the formal aspects of literature– words, sentences, rhythm, the texture of imagery, arrangement of sounds, etc. Art is contemplated as beautiful object which, even if it has some social purpose, exists mainly for pleasure. This pleasure principle pervades whatever else may happen. In other words, Eliot's model and method seems to be– do not dig deep, enjoy the form and surface, avoid the crisis which may result from reflecting on the true nature of language and literature.

Let me now elaborate the crisis which T.S. Eliot avoided. Earlier I pointed out that Eliot disparaged Miltonic poetry for its rhetoricity. Eliot finds that rhetoric causes disruption between the form and meaning. Eliot uses the term rhetoric' in the sense that Miltonic poetry is overornate and ostentatious, separated from the referential everyday language. Rhetorical language is opposed to conversational everyday language. Eliot's problems can be identified as that he takes rhetoric to be a disruptive force which separates meaning from the sign. Eliot perhaps overlooks nature of language. Language is essentially rhetorical, it does not refer to anything, it does not originate to make meanings, it is not constant and stable, its origin is temporal and existential, and it exists for its own sake. Rhetoricity does not disrupt the meaning because meaning is outside the language. Even everyday language which is considered to be referential is essentially devoid of any referent. The signifiers are mere signifiers arbitrarily meaning whatever the speaker/listener, writer/reader intends them to mean. Language is devoid of all meanings, it is we who invest meaning in it because we are condemned to what Fredric Jameson calls "the prison house of language". De man has put this damned existence more accurately:

> In the everyday language of communication, there is no priori privileged position of sign over meaning or of meaning over sign; the act of interpretation will always again have to establish this relation for the particular case at hand. The interpretation of everyday language is Sisyphean task, a task without end and without progress, for the other is always free to make what he wants, differ from what he says what he wants (de Man 11).

The language of literature is no better. It is impossible for literature to escape the rhetorical nature of language. Eliot wants Milton to do something which nobody, including Eliot, can do. You cannot make language what it is not. Eliot is blind to his own rhetoricity throughout when he composes poetry. I have just taken a few lines to illustrate it:

> Because I do not hope to turn again / Because I do not hope
> Because I do not hope to turn again / Designing this man's gift and that man's scope
> I no longer strive to strive towards such things / (Why should the aged eagle stretch its wings?)
> Why should I mourn / The vanish power of the usual sign? / (Eliot, "Ash Wednesday" 68)

This stanza sufficiently demonstrates that it is difficult to escape rhetoricity. It seems that Eliot feels assured that he is conveying what he intends to convey. But three repetitions of the same point prove it beyond doubt that the poet is not sure of presence of meanings. We repeat only when we fail in doing something. His repetitions are clear indications of his failures in conveying meanings as intended by him. He cannot avoid the rhetoricity of language. The two rhetorical questions also suggest that the expressions are rhetorical and the meaning cannot be fixed. The device of rhetorical question is used to make forceful assertions, but they can also be taken as questions seeking replies from the listener/reader. The two uses of the rhetorical question frustrate the very desire to have stable meanings. The conclusion is that language by its very nature cannot give us any stable meaning, it can only delude us, like *Maya*, into meanings. Eliot too is deluded into seeking meanings. "The fallacy of the belief that in the language of poetry, sign and meaning can coincide or at least be related to each other in the free and harmonious balance that we call beauty, is said to be a specially romantic delusion" (de Man 12). He falls prey to this "romantic delusion" in writing critical interpretations as well as in writing poetry.

Literature becomes authentic only when it discovers the mythic nature of language. But for Eliot it is through the formal devices that authentic literature can be created, which will ultimately get assimilated in the great tradition. His theory of impersonality is one such device. To him impersonality in poetry means absence of self expression, negation of personal feelings and emotions, including the psychological concerns. This theory of impersonality is afflicted with the Coleridgean concept of organic relationship between form and meaning. It seems as if literary forms are some kind of vessels in which contents can be poured from the mind who creates them. Words or other aspects of linguistic expressions are not vessels, carriers of feelings, emotions. If words are vessels, they are empty vessels. Impersonality in literature cannot be achieved by avoiding personal emotions and feelings, true impersonality can be achieved only by realizing that language which constitutes literature is neither personal nor impersonal. Language is without subject, so the question of subjectivity is misplaced. Blanchot talking about impersonality in Mallarme writes, "Language supposes for him neither a speaker, nor a listener, it speaks and writes by itself. It is a kind of consciousness without subject" (quoted in de Man 69).

As the formal aspects are not inherently meaningful, they can respond anyway to the intentionality of the interpreter. Literary forms are not objective structures, objectivity of literary forms is fictitiously created by the interpreter. All formal features including the sign are fictitious, and this fictionality is the only reality that a literary writer can aim at. Not realizing the fictional character of literary language, T.S. Eliot is gripped with the irresistible desire to create particular kinds of literary structures and forms which respond to his kind of intentionality. Contrary to T.S. Eliot, who is gripped with the referentiality of the language, Rabindranath Tagore in *Gitanjali* questions the referentiality of language and prays for silence throughout the series of 103 Songs. Tagore in song No. 42 prays for freedom from words, as words fail to convey his prayers:

> In that shoreless ocean, at thy silently listening smile
> my songs would swell in melodies, free as waves,
> free from all bondage of words. (Tagore 93)

It is Eliot's intentionality that is responsible for the denunciation and appreciation of Milton and not the meaningfulness or meaninglessness of formal devices as he conceives them to be. If the diction, the involved syntax, the long units of music are meaningless in "Milton I" and meaningful in "Milton II", it is Eliot who performs the trick, as the signifiers and other formal devices are devoid of any meaning whatsoever. Language exists in the void and literature names this void. "Poetic language names this void (the presence of nothingness) with ever-renewed understanding and, ... it never tires of naming it again. This persistent naming is what we call literature" (de Man 18). As literary language, like language in general, is devoid of any essence, it always aspires for semantic and sensorial totalizations. But it is a kind of delusion "... constituted in the mind of interpreter as the work discloses itself in response to his questioning. But the dialogue between the work and the interpreter is endless" (de Man 32).

Eliot accuses Milton for not contributing in any positive sense to the tradition of English language and literature. Eliot conceives tradition as a big classical majestic river to which tributaries contribute and from which tributaries flow. This is the so called dynamic conception of tradition. Milton is outside this dynamic conception of tradition as he is individualistic, creating his own principles of writing which respond to his kind of imagination. In "Milton I" Eliot denounces Milton for being individualistic and in "Milton II", he appreciates Milton for being individualistic. It happens because tradition as conceived by Eliot is a misplaced concept. Tradition is contingent, temporal and linguistically constituted concept, devoid of any meaning and essence, much like other concepts in this world. Antonin Atraud questions the concept of tradition as formulated by Eliot when he says "Written poetry has value for one single moment and should then be destroyed" (quoted in de Man 147). So to accuse Milton of creating harmful effects in English literary tradition or for not contributing positively to literary tradition is founded on subjective assumptions. How can we harm anything which does not exist?

Eliot's hermeneutic quest for Coleridgean organic unity between form and content leads him nowhere. Whether he speaks for Milton or against Milton, he indulges in inconsistencies which are the result of deeper malady, the malady of mistaking surfaces as core, the malady that originates in aporetic nature of language which in the last analysis is the breeding ground of such kind of poetics. It is a painful to reflect upon the reality of this phenomenal and material world or to reflect upon the reality of language and literature. The questions on origin, the questions on canon-formation, the questions on existence of tradition, the questions on the ontological status of language of literature, will lead to genuine criticism, and also to crisis like situations. And we, including T.S. Eliot, want to avoid crisis at all costs. For us the manifest, the *Vyakta*, is so attractive that the unmanifest or *Avyakta* does not make any sense to us. Eliot read the *Upanishads* in original Sanskrit where two kinds of knowledge given are *Vyakta* and *Avyakta*. It is difficult to understand that Eliot accuses Milton for lacking in conversational idiom and representational appeal. Till we are tied to the dead body of logocentric approach, it is difficult to visualize any authentic criticism. Authentic criticism has difficulties of its own. "Whether authentic criticism is a liability or an asset to literary studies remains an open question" (de Man 81). And the openness of the question is as wide as Eliot's own dilemma—the plight between empirical representationalism and ontological assertionism.

Works Cited

de Man, Paul. *Blindness and Insight: Essays in the Rhetoric of Contemporary Criticism.*, 2 ed. London: Methuen, 1983.

Eliot, T.S. *On Poetry and Poets*. London: Faber and Faber, 1956.

______ "Ash Wednesday I". *An Anthology of Modern Verse 1920-1940*. Ed. C. Day Lewis and L.A.G. Strong. London: Methuen, 1941.

Tagore, Rabindranath. *Gitanjali*. Kolkata: UBS, 2003.

21

Colonial Continuities in Postcolonial India: Interrogation of Society, Culture and Individual in *English August*

Hemang Desai

Against the backdrop of a novel that marvellously chronicles the litter of socio-political, administrative, linguistic and cultural pathologies through which a nation toddled and dawdled its tortuous way from decolonization to the threshold of globalization, the preset paper seeks to interrogate whether the phenomenon of decolonization has been accomplished to any appreciable extent at various levels of human life lived in multi-lingual and multi-cultural India. The legacy of invidious colonial apparatus comprising the magnanimous discourse of development, politics of representation, cryptic forms of otherization, politics of language and education etc. has become a powerful tool in the hands of home-grown neo-imperialist, exploitative establishment due to which the nightmare of colonial woes and wretchedness has continued for the marginalized long after the nation awoke to life and freedom. In this paper, an effort has been made to pinpoint the locations where colonial binaries are highlighted or subverted in the novel. The paper also addresses the dire need to adapt individual, social and cultural identities to historical realities and internalize and celebrate the phenomenon of hybridity which can foreclose the colonial binarism, facilitate anti-monolithic cultural exchange and liberate and empower the colonial subject. Finally the paper seeks to examine the roles of individual, society and political establishment in effecting the unfinished revolution of cultural reorientation.

Using the restless and confused life of a city-bred, westernized, pot-smoking and young IAS trainee posted in extremely hot and dusty Madna as a springboard, *English August* marvellously chronicles the litter of socio-political, administrative, linguistic and cultural pathologies through which a nation toddled its tortuous way from decolonization to the threshold of globalization. As it authentically captures the zeitgeist of one of the most turbulent decades in Indian history i.e. 1980s, the novel luminously problematizes the ambitious post-colonial phraseology of nation-building, national integration and inclusive development. As one races through a narrative that unfolds in an inimitably witty and racy style, one sullenly realizes that the idealism encapsulated in the discursive formulations surrounding multiple facets of decolonization sounds all too facile and hollow in a four-decade old country torn by abysmal poverty and underdevelopment, raging communal animosity, glaring language divide, Machiavellian polity hand in glove with corrupt bureaucracy, social stratification and cultural erosion.

Madna, "an eternally somnolent town", evolves as a disturbing microcosm of a nation that awoke "at the stroke of the midnight hour…to life and freedom" and turned a mute spectator to the nightmare of Naxalism, communalism, internal separatism and sly colonialism of home-grown neo-imperialist powers. The end result has been that the phenomenon of decolonization has been accomplished, not even in letter let alone in spirit, at various levels of human life lived in multi-lingual and multi-cultural India. The legacy of invidious colonial apparatus comprising the magnanimous discourse of development, politics of representation, cryptic forms of otherization, metaphysics of cultural identity and civilization, politics of language and education etc. has become a powerful tool in the hands of home-grown neo-imperialist, exploitative establishment in postcolonial

India to perpetuate the wretched condition of the colonized, the powerless or the underprivileged.

With Agastya Sen, who gets down at quintessential Indian hinterland of Madna, the reader starts off his journey through a virtual historiographical narrative with a distinct sense of déjà vu for the opening chapter of *Freedom at Midnight* (1975) by Larry Collins and Dominique Lapierre. Agastya evolves as a typical Indian counterpart of the young British officer of colonial ICS – which was Indianized as Indian Administrative Service (IAS) after independence – who got down at Victoria Station, Mumbai with a mix of disbelief and horror at the prospect of negotiating a scary and sorry landscape sullied with squalor and scorching heat, malaria and cholera, heathens and absolute anarchy, exotic culture and off-putting underdevelopment. Upamanyu Chatterjee brilliantly perspectivizes Agastya's urban sense of flinch and wince at Madna, "(a) shabby station where the train didn't stop…(with) incurious patient eyes and weather-beaten bicycles at a level crossing, muddy children and buffalo at a waterhole…names out of newspapers where floods and caste wars occurred and entire Harijan families were murdered, where some prime minister took his helicopter just after a calamity, or just before the elections." (*EA* 5)

Cigarette-and-paan dhabas, disreputable food stalls lit by kerosene lamps, cattle and clanging rickshaws on road, hollering trucks and overflowing drains, horrible mosquitoes less civilized than those of Calcutta, "endemic jaundice and epidemic of cholera" and unbelievable food become points of distress for Agastya who feels "he was living someone else's life" (*EA* 5). The writer's irreverent quip over the flippancy of the rhetoric of Indianness and Indianization that the officers at Madna so zealously mouth, comes in the form of marginal scribbling in Ruth. P. Jhabhvala's *Heat and Dust* which Mr. Menon, the sub-divisional Magistrate of Rameri, has been reading and spoiling. Comments read as "Not necessary these days to wear sola topee.

Relic of the Raj. The bureaucracy to by Indianized" and "An officer's wife *should* mix with others, but without jeopardizing the dignity of office." (*EA* 39)

Such a shallow and snobbish bureaucratic attitude echoes the codes of hypocritical respectability that even the wife of an ICS joint secretary so religiously observed in colonial times by not condescending to dine with someone of a lower rank than her husband. The frivolity of Menon's zeal for nativity is later laid bare when he smugly stoops his aesthetic standards over Rest House furniture in a tone that Madna can't aspire to anything better. He further reveals, "It's very good thing to join the Indian Administrative Service after a stint abroad. It's the best possible job, in the Indian context, you will realize that very soon and having been abroad gives you a better perspective" (*EA* 51). On the other hand, the power and pelf vicariously wielded by Mr. Srivastav, the Collector of Madna, ambitiously replicate the same that even a minor functionary of the East India Company so thoroughly enjoyed in the cantonments from where the British imperialism unleashed its reign of terror.

An instructive way to study the cultural imperialism that Srivastav so unwittingly disseminates is to interrogate the contexts of power that gives to human interactions across cultural divides a recognizable body language. Srivastav's neo-imperial establishment sprawls in a twenty-acre compound – a bungalow with twenty-two rooms and a battery of servants "who were actually peons from the office" and "who prefer to clean the shit of the progeny of a collector than to shuttle files in an office" (*EA* 57). The novelist deftly forges a subtle link between indigenous and exotic traditions of colonialism by saying that "their father and grandfathers had done much the same, but the skins of those Collectors had been red and the accent of their English alien" (*EA* 57). Srivastav also flaunts certain imperial intellectual arrogance when he damns the work ethics of his colleague Bajaj stereotyping him as 'a promotee' i.e. one who acquired the office on grounds of experience and not thorough national Civil Service Examination. While he haughtily keeps his poor petitioners-subjects standing in his office, he can't but entertain the gossips of the district and the politicians' groupies who rightfully guzzle away his time. He damns his predecessor Antony's courtesy of offering tea to petitioners as "a silly populist measure" and sullenly deprecates "the *culture* of the place" when the same people, whom he intentionally keeps waiting for the ghazal concert to start by arriving late, don't get up from their chairs at his entry. Befitting this body language of superior culture, Srivastava plays down the culture of Madna when he warns Agastya "...to be careful of the company you keep in Madna. A small place, people talk a lot, they don't have much else to do" (*EA* 80).

The Americanised Bhatia also becomes the unsuspecting spokesperson of the politics of representation when he decries, "Just notice the number of chemists in Madna. A clear sign of how unhealthy this place is" (*EA* 79). Agastya's neo-imperial mindset is laid bare when he admits that "Gandhi's a very nice guy, but I wouldn't've dreamed of being friends with him in Delhi. I would've said, small-towner" (*EA* 101). Such a milieu is a natural incubator for the notions of cultural, even moral, superiority and racial arrogance.

The urban-rural divide consequent upon a long colonial rule in India recurs as a powerful motif in the novel underscoring the grave socio-cultural implications of disparities in economic and non-economic spheres of human life. As per the Human Development Index which is a composite of variables capturing attainments in economic, educational and health sectors, the value for rural areas is 0.340 as against its urban counterpart which is as high as 0.511. The same is the situation in respect of the Human Poverty Index: rural 42.25 and urban 44.8 (Datta, 16).

Chatterjee categorically chastises the bland policy makers who either don't have the resourcefulness to map out the inclusive and sustainable policies of development or are too invidious and maneuvering to grant the underdog the right to life and happiness. Thus Srivastav sheepishly complains about the unavailability of time to chalk out the most efficient way of setting priorities and spending money. On the other hand, the money pushed into Jompana for tribal welfare is directed by the politician to benefit the non-tribal population of the plains as a part of vote bank politics. Chatterjee astutely subverts the culture-vulture binary by trivializing Kumar, the SP of Madna, on Delhi station who "without his entourage looked like any other fat grubby traveller." Even Kumar unconsciously whines about the culture of North India which he so brazenly revered, "All of North India is so crude. I know it, I grew up in its cities. In Madna, didn't you notice, people are much more cultured, more soft" (*EA* 145). At another occasion, while reflecting on Madna's indifference towards Mahatma Gandhi's precarious statue "with a rod coming out of his arse" (*EA* 21), Agastya muses that even in Delhi or Calcutta, he wouldn't have noticed it, that public apathy in India is almost a national religion, be it a village or a city.

Far from becoming a site for cultural clashes between the Eastern and the Western, modern and traditional, civilized and uncivilized, urban and rural, emotional and rational, the novel ingeniously depicts a chiaroscuro of forces that resist a neat categorization into either of the binaries in postcolonial Indian context. In fact, each character as an embodiment of value system and ideology, however subjective, becomes a representation of a cultural hybridity that shuttles conveniently between opposites in an endless game of power. Agastya evolves as the most acute and valid representative of this cultural hybridity which unfolds in his case at the levels of language, province, religion, lifestyle and value-system. He is born to a Bengali Hindu father who went out of his way to marry a vague Goanese Christian only to colonize her later to an early death and obscurity. Brought up in Delhi studying English literature, he reads Marcus Aurelius to slake his intellectual thirst but is positively confounded by his sporadic reading of *Bhagavad Gita* that Sathe gifts him. He enjoys listening to Ella Fitzgerald, Vivaldi, Keith Jarrett and Scott Joplin but is drawn towards Tagore and the *thumris* that his neighbour Shankar so passionately sings with even more intense and disarming fascination. He becomes self-conscious and scared over a faint realization of his being a dusty mirror-image of Bhatia, who "...would love to get AIDS just because it is raging in America" (*EA* 76). He loves Calcutta to a mad degree of fanaticism because the city "…just sounded lovely, romantic, with a past" and has never felt a passion for going or settling abroad the way Bhatia did. Conversely, he visualizes "Europe and America as madly expensive, strange …a passage through clean, beautiful places with faces looking through him" (*EA* 93). However, he has little knowledge about the richness of Indian cultural heritage and comes to Madna with extremely low and distorted imperial expectations. Mohan chides him, "Why're you always being *surprised* by Madna, by this temple, by that statue of Gandhi in the town, by the beauty of the Forest colony?" (*EA* 125). Towards the end of the novel, he slips into deep turmoil and derangement over the identity crisis that thoroughly overwhelms him, "For Shankar there had been his thumris and ghazals, he could conjure up exquisite nose-rings and eyelashes for consolation, and Dhrubo, too, had ragtime and his fashionable jazz, but his own taste had no continuities – merely a sad mongrel hybridity." (*EA* 275)

Agastya has neither known the sufferance of colonial rule, the riots of Partition, pangs of dismemberment and dislocation borne by Dr. Multani's father nor has he been particularly inquisitive, let alone deeply concerned, about it like John Avery who arrives all the way from London feeling weirdly curious about the place where his grandfather was devoured by a tiger. With an overwhelming sense of deprivation and alienation, Agastya wonders what it would have felt like, "… to wander the streets of Calcutta and not be allowed entry into the Calcutta Club, Natives keep out" (*EA* 230). Upamanyu Chatterjee dramatically traces Agastya's excruciating restlessness and sense of anchorlessness in Madna to his awakening to the ineluctable cultural hybridity of his generation, a race of "cultural cripples, in capable of appreciation". Agastya's predicament is a painful corollary of what Sathe terms, "ignoring one-half of yourself", of "living in a city and not knowing what the rest of India is like" as Tonic puts it, of being face-to-face with the other half of his cultural, historical and metaphysical identity. Christine, the American guest at Madan's house, becomes the author's mouthpiece when she scolds Madan for being blind to his own history and points out the pitfalls of cherishing bookish knowledge about the *other*'s culture. Multani's father beautifully sums it all, "...your generation is what it is, just like the English we speak, it is inevitable" (*EA* 230). Post-colonial discourse emphasizes the mutuality of the process of colonization, i.e., distinctive aspects of the culture of the colonized resist obliteration even under the most potent colonial oppression and in turn become the integral part of the new formations ensuing cultural confrontation. Such cultural hybridity builds in immense positive value in as much as it forecloses pigeonholing into the old binary categories and realizes the possibility of anti-monolithic cultural exchange. Ultimately as he heads "to discover himself", Agastya's journey through the novel evolves as nothing but an exposition of an apocalyptic process of unification of his split selves, of celebration of empowering hybridity.

The leitmotif of language in the novel forcefully foregrounds the complexity of cultural identity in multilingual Indian context. The officialdom in Madna prefers to communicate both at office and home in English and irks at the idea of learning local language for communication with local people who, much to its chagrin, do not follow Hindi. Srivastav grumbles, "And now everything from the State Government comes in the regional language. They think, this'll increase administrative efficiency...Rubbish" (*EA* 16). Srivastav's tendency to install Hindi as a standard against Madna's local language which, in turn, is constituted as insufficiency and deviation distinctly smacks of a colonial process initiated for the purpose of cultural control. However, he is frank enough to admit that the English that babus speak is 'funny' and officialese at best and bland at worst. Agastya is amused that "No officer ever left, they always took his leave. None of them ever stayed a night somewhere, they always made night-halts" (*EA* 203). The 'Babu' English, fraught with stilted, archaic and bombastic idiom that Srivastav funnily mimics marks a far cry from the post-colonial call for Indianizing it by adapting the alien language to the exigencies of native grammar, syntax, vocabulary and turns of phrase.

Alongside the agenda of Indianizing English, Upamanyu Chatterjee reaffirms the post-colonial resolve to give regional languages the respect due to them as a part of the unfinished project of decolonization. U.R. Ananthmurthy quite pertinently says, if we snap our inborn bond with our mother-tongues, "We are going to lose our memory. We need English, but not of the 'call-centre' sort. It is not a gateway to knowledge. We need to create in our own language. The English elite in India are not as cultured as the masses. English must be taught but children in schools need to create in their own languages, because we don't think in English. It's a received language" (Ananthmurthy, *The Indian Express*).

Srivastav, a student of Hindi-medium school in Azamganj, grumbles over the inevitability of English—an "unavoidable leftover"-for professional success. "That a young man in Azamgunj should find it essential to study something as unnecessary as Hamlet, that's absurd, no, but also inevitable" (*EA* 60). Srivastav here refers to the imperial policy of inevitability of knowledge of English Literature for entry into civil services and legal profession that has remained intact after decolonization, but is little inclined to wield the power of his office to subvert linguistic binary to decolonize the imagination of native subjects.

In colonial context, education was a sinister process to achieve what Gramsci calls "domination by consent", a process of manipulating the content and method of teaching and subsequently enmeshing of the educated subject into imperial machinery. Srivastav thus agrees to be a pawn in the game of post-colonial domination. Dilating upon the pathetically low standards of teaching in schools in small towns, he says "There's not a single good teacher in these schools.... How can there be ... when they themselves pass out of such schools and colleges" (*EA* 59). On the other hand, like all Collectors, he astutely ensures that his wife amasses degrees, not by the dint of academic acumen but by sheer force of his clout, from wherever he is posted and then returns "to those colleges to teach the rubbish they had learnt."

Agastya's cousin Tonic launches into a passionate and realistic tirade against the linguistic woes of education system in India. As a proprietor of a publishing house, he condemns his lot for having to publish a below-average book on E. M. Foster written in question-answer form by a Dr. Prem Kishan of Meerut University for professional reasons. He asks some pertinent and unsettling questions to Agastya: "Why is some Jat teenager in Meerut reading Jane Austen? Why does a place like Meerut have course in English at all? Only because the Prem Kishans of the country need a place where they can teach this rubbish?" (*EA* 170). "Education is perhaps the most insidious and in some ways the most cryptic of colonialist survivals, older systems now passing, sometimes imperceptibly, into neo-colonialist configurations" (Ashcroft eds., 425).

Chatterjee strongly condemns the fact that the conditions of production and consumption of education and its technologies have not changed the unequal power relations between the educational producers and the peripheral consumers. Tonic gives Agastya a dressing down for toying with the idea of leaving IAS while he is in a position to take on the challenge of reforming education in India. In Nehru's words, Srivastav and his ilk belong to that new caste or class created by the British, the English-educated class which lived in a world of its own, cut off from the masses of the population (Nehru, 23) and in Sathe's words "whose vision so far has been circumscribed by the smog of Calcutta"(*EA* 46). The novelist seems to underscore the fact that English in India has become a potent tool with serious colonial implications, an apparatus that has created and deepened the chasm between the educated and politically minded classes and the masses (*Gandhi* 16). It has become, as it is not in Brazil or China, the language of respect. An Indian who speaks only Indian languages will face inferior treatment in his own society.

Quite impressively, Upamanyu Chatterjee conceptualizes the ideas of colonization, representation, otherization and neo-imperialism by situating the binary opposites in mutual hierarchical relationships. Thus the principle of privilege fluctuates from one to another in tandem with the shifts in standpoints. The cartoonist Sathe puts things in bitter-true perspective when he scoffs at the hollow postcolonial ire at imperial exploitation by saying, "But you are a Bengali–and, no doubt, in keeping with your race, your father did to your poor mother what all of you did to Assam, but we only began to whine when the British did it to us" (*EA* 83).

It's very interesting to note that Madna which Agastya so much loathes for not being Delhi becomes a metaphor, even a euphemism, for his generation that bypassed "all that had made history and news". Though in different contexts, both Agastya and Madna have been impervious to the colonial realities of patriotism and bloodletting, to the *past* Agastya so gloriously romanticizes, and feels queerly nostalgic about, the past clutching which Dr. Multani's father wandered as a refugee after partition. While both Agastya and Madna feel the pangs of deprivation and the sense of being left-out, in the former's case the pain is self-inflicted while it is the result of apathy and egotism of a maneuvering neo-colonial establishment in the latter's case.

Historically, Madna was established by an eponymous eighteenth century tribal king and the relics of the crumbling fort sing paeans to the glory of the kingdom in its heyday. Agastya's oblique narrative about Madna that "seemed to have bypassed by all that made history and news, had remained impervious to the Mughals and 1857 and Bande Mataram and the midcentury travails of megalopolitan India" (*EA*, 45-6) insinuates towards the normative language of otherization in which the British typically played down the past and the cultural heritage of the Indian subjects. In his unconscious dehistoricization of Madna, Agastya indulges into what the British tendentiously and maliciously deployed ie. the politics of representation designed to capture the non-European subject within European frameworks which read his or her alterity as *terror* or *lack* (*Ashcroft eds.* 85).

A similar lop-sided ontology undergirds Bajaj's explanation for the skewed development of the tribal belt of Jompana when he denigrates nomadic way of tribal life as a major stumbling block in the way of their development. "So we say, here, if you group these villages together…then we'll help to develop the area, build their houses" (*EA* 242). To a certain extent, the establishment in the novel seems to justify the pathetic living condition of the tribals in and surrounding Madna as a suitable compensation for their obstinacy in not coming out of their primitive and pseudo cultural cocoons.

Chatterjee cleverly draws a parallel between the colonial hoax of "white man's burden" and postcolonial projects of development to expose the sordid underbelly of imperial gospel of liberalism and rationalism that legitimized colonization and acculturation of natives as inevitability. Bajaj, very much like John Locke and J. S. Mill, "divide human societies into 'civilized' and 'primitive', and treat each category as homogeneous and undifferentiated" (*Parekh* 95). He views tribal ways of life with contempt and makes no effort to understand it from within. But as Agastya later muses, Jompana turns out to be an "Indian oblivion" where development far from being even a superfice as it was in Madna's "skyline of a thermal power station, in the dead sapling edging the road", is just a word lost in government files which travel "from desk to desk, gathering around it, like flesh around a kernel, comment and counter-comment and irrelevant comment, till it was fat enough to be offal for the rats in the office cupboards" (*EA* 252).

A tragic antithesis to the perverted logic and apathy of the administration is reflected in the horrifying portrayal of destitute of tribal life at Rameri where mothers tie ropes to their small children and lower them into nearly dried-out wells so that they can bring up buckets of muddy water. Srivastav gives revealing insight into the post-colonial farce of development in India when he narrates the history of Madna to Agastya, "Once it was just another district, very rich forests and made to feel proud of its tribal traditions.... Then they found coal here, mica, limestone, one the country's richest industrial belts, now oil too. Factories soon surrounded this town, new ones come up almost every day...there must be something wrong with development if it creates places like Madna" (*EA* 20). Here Chatterjee visibly squares up in an oppositional stance against neo-colonialist exploitative power bases that have further colonized, historicized and reduced the peripheral other to cultural diminutives by trumpeting the mythical and hypothetical discourse of development that is manipulated to mean primarily growth, evolution and increase. Nirmal Selvamony sheds revealing light on this entire myth of development publicized by the colonizer. "Considering the negative development of the colonies, we might say that the unity of the families is imperiled, their histories and memories are obliterated by forces such as urbanization, employment abroad, expatriation and dislocation. Economic development is negative when man is isolated from his communitarian bonding with other men, nature and supernatural powers and seen as an individual with infinite potential and wants" (*Selvamony* 62).

The episode in which a group of tribals cut Mohan's hands for molesting his tribal cook symbolically serves to collapse the rhetoric of development masquerading molestation. As an efficient native alternative to the colonial model of development, Chatterjee projects Baba Ramanna's Rehabilitation Home for Lepers which not only provides emotional and medical support to the lepers but also empowers them by making them self-sufficient financially. Agastya literally staggers at the sheer monstrosity, nobility and virtue of Baba Ramanna's enterprise which carves fields, orchards and wells out of bareness.

The whole novel can, in fact, be seen as an attempt to subvert the colonial binaries operating at social, linguistic, cultural and even metaphysical levels in post-colonial India. At spiritual level, Chatterjee intensifies Agastya's spiritual despair to contextualize the disparity between the Eastern and Western epistemes about human nature and consequent ways of life. Agastya reads Marcus Aurelius and strives to derive solace out of his faith in human reason. Almost in Lockean vein, he wants his reason, not even his intuition, to tell him the implications of his act before he committed it. But his blind adherence to rationality fails to answer overwhelming metaphysical questions about inexplicable things happening in the world. Shankar's world, on the other hand, makes sense to him because he has transcended his reason and resigned himself to providence to the will of Jagadamba. Agastya passage to spiritual equilibrium towards the end of the novel should be traced to his brand new knowledge that considering monistic vision of human nature or existence universal, as did Locke to justify English colonization of American Indians in seventeenth century, is fallacious at best and political at worst. What soothes him finally is his will to cope his paramount sense of reason with the alternative view upholding feelings and passion as spiritual anchors of human life. Shankar symbolically digs it into his head that he dislikes the frog in his room only because he has never encountered one in his flat in Delhi before. So reason brands the unexpected as bad. But "A frog is a good animal, and wait and see, it'll eat up some of the mosquitoes in your room" (*EA* 98). His tendency to assimilate the other or what the post-colonial theory so passionately celebrates, the *difference* restores him to a sense of self-fulfilment, of hybridity.

Works Cited

Ananthmurthy, U. R. in the Sumitra Chishti Memorial Lecture delivered in New Delhi on March 2, 2009 and reported in *The Indian Express* on March 3, 2009.

Ashcroft Bill, Griffiths Gareth, Tiffin Helen (eds). *The Post-colonial Studies Reader*, London and New York, Routledge, 1995.

Datta, Prabhat. "The Great Indian Divide", *Frontline*, Volume 21-Issue 14, Jul. 03 2004

Gandhi, Mahatma, "Constructive Programme", *Navjivan*, 1944.

Nehru, Jawaharlal. *An Autobiography*, Bodley Head, 1936

Parekh, Bhikhu. "Liberalism and Colonialism: a critique of Locke and Mill" in Pieterse J N & Parekh, Bhikhu (eds.) *The Decolonization of Imagination*, OUP, 1995.

Selvamony, Nirmal. "Post-Coloniality and the Discourse of Development", in *Post-Coliniality: Reading Literature*, eds. C.T.Indra, Meenakshi Shivram, New Delhi, Vikas Publishing House, 1999, p. 62

22

The Study of the Concept of Exile: Re-reading Edward Said

Bilal A. Shah

The history of exile dates back old. There are instances of Ovid and others being given the punishment of exile. The punishment may be due to social, political, economic, cultural or religious reasons. Etymologically the word 'exile' comes from the Latin word 'exilum' meaning banishment. Numerous thinkers have been subjected to undergo the hardship of banishment. Exile as such has been the thematic concern for a countless number of literatures till today. It is one of the major characteristics of contemporary period yet as a concept and a condition it is hard to define owing to its complex and varied nature which subsequently invites multiple referents. Only few have come forth with clear and sound theories of exile.

In this paper I will analyze the concept of exile from the perspectives of the twentieth- century thinker Edward Said. Furthermore, I will discuss how his perception of exile has molded the formation of varied other ideas in his works. It may not be wrong to say that exile has been the central theme of many of Said's works. This thematic concern may not appear at all surprising once we take into consideration the 'uniquely punishing destiny' that he shares with other Palestinians. He spent his early life as a refugee in Egypt, "I was born in Jerusalem and had spent most of my formative years there and, after 1948 when my entire family became refugees in Egypt" (Said 2001: 556)). His *Out of Place*, which is 'a record of an essentially lost or forgotten world' (Said 1999: xi) clearly mentions the influence of exile on his life:

> an extraordinary increasing no. of departures have unsettled my life from its earliest beginnings. To me, nothing more painful and paradoxically sought after characterizes my life than the many displacements from countries, cities, abodes, languages, environments they have kept me in motion all these years. (Said 1999: 217).

His life is a life 'out of place'; always in exile which carries a sense of dissatisfaction and grief. He writes, "To this day I still feel that I am away from, ludicrous as that may sound, and though I believe I have no illusions about the 'better' life I might have had, had I remained in Arab world or lived and studied in Europe, there is still some measure of regret" (Said 1999: 223). He stays in New York after being displaced from – Palestine, Egypt and Lebanon. He was born in Jerusalem in 1935. Still there is the constant awareness of being at odds with his environment "Now it does not seem important or even desirable to be 'right' and in place (right at home, for instance). Better to wander out of place, not to own a house, and not ever to feel too much at home anywhere, especially in a city like New York, where I shall be until I die." (Said 1999: 269)

In 2000, Said pens an essay entitled "Reflections on Exile" where he delineates exiles as "the unhealable rift forced between a human being and a native place, between the self and its true home" (Said 2001:173).

There is the trace of 'regret' regarding exile in this essay. He continues that "exile is a debilitating solitude; a loneliness, a discontinuous state of being, a state of jealousy as the exile is full of resentment for non exiles and exiles are often eccentric intransigent, unpleasant..." (Zeleza 2005: 9). Despite all these negative connotations, the condition of exile, for Said,[1] lends a contrapuntal awareness of perspectives. This is all due to the fact that people in general are aware of only one culture, one perspective whereas people in exile are exposed to different cultures and perspectives. This exposure is of great value to an exiled person and his outlook as Said notes:

> There is a unique pleasure in this sort of apprehension especially if the exile is conscious of other contrapuntal juxtapositions that diminish orthodox judgment and elevate appreciative sympathy (Said 2001:168).

With this 'contrapuntal juxtaposition' an exile experiences the need to create his separate world. This world resembles the world of a fiction because it is 'unnatural'. It is a world of imagination and therefore we see that exiles generally are people from the field of literature,[2] politics and academics. Of course, thousands of people do experience exile however writers and intellectuals experience it in a totally different manner[3] which for them is paradoxically a catalyst of creative productivity. They have shown to write more in the condition of exile than while being in the comfort zone of their homeland. Nuruddin Farah[4] who has been in exile since 1970s produces a work entitled "In Praise of Exile"[5] where he empathically mentions that 'distance distills; ideas become clearer and better worth pursuing' (Farah 1990: 65). In the essay "Reflections on Exile" Said distinguishes exile from expatriate and refugees. In the case of expatriate there is the voluntary involvement from the person's side. He decides to stay abroad on his own. Refugees on the other hand are "bewildered people requiring urgent international assistance" (Said 2001:181).

Exiles alone are the cosmopolitan intellectuals having 'a touch of solitude and spirituality' (Said 2001:181). Exile, for Said, is a symbol of freedom, emancipation and liberation. It is no exaggeration that liberation as an intellectual mission has now shifted to its unhoused, decentred and exilic energies, energies whose incarnation today is the migrant (culture and imperialism 332). Thomas Tweed has discussed three concepts – locative supralocative and translocative in his *Crossing and Dwelling: A Theory of Religion*. 'Locative' in simple term is the centre, it values the belongingness to a place while 'supralocative' is associated with periphery rather than the centre and values transcending space instead of being located in one place. 'Translocation' somewhat swings between locative and supralocative i.e. it constantly moves between centre (homeland) and periphery (adopted land).

Said's notion of exile resembles Tweed's supralocation that emphasizes periphery or exiled state, and also to that of translocation (in between centre and periphery). The in-between position is the sacred space[6] for Said for it helps to acquire the contrapuntal vision which is essentially a deconstructive way of looking at things. The unique position of exile gives significance to the marginalized and ignored section of the society and the culture.

Said's experience of exile has led to see the concept of culture in a totally different mode. He sees 'culture' as "an environment process and hegemony in which individuals and their works are embedded" (Said 1983: 8).

According to Said, culture has a boundary that defines what is inside the culture and what is outside the culture. In other words, it has an environment within which it functions. Said cites the example of Auerbach. He (Auerbach) moves away from his familiar environment and goes to the alien place of Istanbul. Said also notes the dominating and authorizing position of culture.

Auerbach's *Mimesis* is written when he is exiled to Istanbul. The book deals with Europe but he himself[7] confesses the book would not have been written in the same manner if he has not been exiled. The situation of exile has lend a different perspective to Auerbach which otherwise would have been reconfigured by what Said says as "grid of research techniques and ethics by which the prevailing culture imposes on the individual scholar its canons of how literary scholarship is to be conducted" (Said 1983: 9).

In *Culture and Anarchy,*[8] Arnold speaks of 'the great men of culture' who have 'best knowledge, best ideas of their times'. Said remarks that these 'best knowledge' and 'best ideas' are in fact the privileged ones out of all other ideas in the society, which Arnold terms as 'culture'. Said highlights the fact that it is the State that promotes and safeguards the so called 'culture' and therefore culture and state are strongly linked. Edward Said writes that "the power of culture is potentially nothing less than the power of the State" (Ashcroft 1999: cited 53). Anything that harms the State is labelled as 'anarchy' and it includes strikes, demonstration and so on. Arnold writes:

> Thus in our eyes, the very framework and exterior order of the State, whosoever may administer the State, is sacred; and culture is the most resolute enemy of anarchy (Said 1983: cited 11).

The sacredness of the State is established and the culture is promoted to safeguard against any sort of anarchy. This paradigm is nothing but 'an assertion of hegemony by the State to maintain its power over the people. It is only by the hegemonic strength of the culture that Macaulay asserts that English language should be taught in India instead of the vernaculars language like Sanskrit. He does not hesitate to say that 'a single shelf of a good European library was worth the whole native literature of India and Arabia. He is speaking with a preconceived notion that European culture is superior to that of the Orient. The idea of the involvement of hegemony will be clear when we consider the fact that he is pronouncing his statement from "a position of power' where he can easily 'translate his opinions into the decision" (Said 1983:13). Said's idea of culture revolves around the notion of hegemony. It is not merely a way of life. Being in exile, Said has been able to see (from the median state) the clash of civilization – of the Orient and the Occident,[9] and the role of hegemony in determining what is ascribed as 'culture' and whose interest it is serving.

In his work *The World the Text and the Critic*, Said discusses a form of criticism which he calls 'secular criticism'. This criticism transcends the traditional literary criticisms – practical, academic, literary history, literary apprehension and interpretation and literary theory. Said argues that these criticisms have an orientation towards a doctrinaire set of assumptions and a language of "specialization and professionalization allied with cultural dogma" (Said 1983:25). These 'assumption' and 'cultural dogma' according to Said bring an end to criticism for criticism should not have any 'solidarity' beforehand. Secular criticism unlike the rest does not occupy specific position and label like 'Marxism', 'Feminism'. It deals with the texts by being in the state of median; by being in between the processes of 'filiation' and 'affiliation'. It has a sentitive response to the dominant culture with the acute awareness that the individual consciousness is but a product of the dominant culture. This sensitive response caters a capacity for an analytical distinction which is lacking in the traditional criticism owing to their solidarity. Said points out:

> These (the attribute of the secular criticism) trouble the quasi religious authority of being comfortable at home among one's people supported by known powers and acceptable values, protected against the outside world (Said 1983: 16).

It will not be wrong to say that Said accurately perceives this form of criticism (secular criticism) because of his own exiled condition where he himself is located in between two cultures experiencing 'filiation' and 'affiliation'. Said explains the two terms – filiation and affiliation. If a filial relationship was held together by natural bonds and natural forms of authority – involving obedience, fear, love, respect and instinctual conflict – the new affiliative relationship changes these bonds into what seem to be transparent forms – such as guild consciousness, consensus collegiality, professional respect, class and the hegemony of a dominant culture (Said 1983:20). The process of affiliation is important in the modern time. In fact Said asserts that it is increasingly becoming difficult to maintain filiation to one's native culture and avoid affiliation to the new values and new ideals. Said cites the example of Eliot and draws our attention to the shift in his poetry as it has occurred in course of his life. In the poem like "Prufrock, Geriontion," and "The Waste Land", Eliot has expressed the failure of man to regenerate. This failure is starkly the characteristic feature of the modern time which Eliot depicts in his poems through the images of aridity sterility wastefulness and alienation. The phase up to the writing of *The Waste Land* is a painful period for Eliot both psychologically and emotionally. John Xeros Cooper writes that *The Waste Land* was written by a man who seemed on the edge of a breakdown'[10] (Cooper 2006:80). Gradually, it becomes too hard for Eliot to continue with these filial values. He therefore seeks new affiliation in the Church of England. He calls the English Church as "something representative of the finest spirit of England of the time" (Said 1983: cited 17).

The Church of England seems to have consoled his ailment. He begins with a new series of poems after "The Waste Land". In poems like "Ash-Wednesday[11]" and "Four Quartet", Eliot is seen taking a totally different direction which his earlier readers have least expected. "Ash-Wednesday" and "Four Quartet" are religious poems. They reflect the affiliation of Eliot to new values and ideals which are found within the English Church. It is in the English Church that Eliot has found "the lost family mourned in his earlier poetry" (Said 1983: 18). Speaking about this shift of Eliot, Said says that it is publicly completed in *After Strange Gods* whose almost belligerent announcement of a credo of royalism, classicism and Catholicism form a set of affiliations achieved by Eliot outside the filial pattern given him by the facts of his American birth (Said 1983: 18).

The movement from the process of filiation to affiliation characterizes the worldliness of texts according to Said. Before going into the details as such it would be good to know how the 'text' is perceived by him. The text as used and understood by him is somewhat different from that of Roland Barthes. Barthes views text as a form of structure having syntagmatic and paradigmatic elements.[12] Said however goes further to take into account the involvement of culture in the production of text. For him, it is a 'cultural act' what Barthes has done is the separation of the text from the world by giving it an autonomous identity. He on the other hand speaks of the worldliness of the text by locating it in the world. He writes: "A text in its actually being a text is being in the world" (Said 1983: 33). Regarding the relation of the text and the world, the classicists view that the world exists outside while the text simply represents it. Structuralist on the other hand sees the world as being constructed by the text. The world as such does not exist. There cannot be any non texual experience of the world. These two views are balanced by Said. According to him, The text does not exist outside the world, as is the implication in both the realist and structuralist positions, but is a part of the world of which it speaks, and this worldliness is itself present in the text as a part of its formation (Ashcroft 1999:39). Thus text plays a significant role in the ways we perceive the world however the existence of the world as such is not denied by Said. Coming to affiliation, it is (as a critical approach towards text) is of crucial importance for Said because it breaks the text from its filiative connection with other texts and is replaced by affiliation to the world thus establishing the worldliness[13] of the text. A reader is liberated to see the text as a phenomenon in the world with all sorts of affiliation – non-canonical, non-traditional and non-literary able of Contents

Bill Ashcroft explains: "Affiliation, then is a feature of the text's worldliness. While filiation suggests a Utopian domain of texts connected serially, homologously and seamlessly with other texts [...] The affiliation of the text constantly leads us back to its worldliness, for we are drawn to ask the question: 'Where is the text taking place?'; 'How is it taking place?" Affiliation draws us inexorably to the location and the locatedness of the text's production (Ashcroft 1999:43). Perhaps it will not be wrong to say that Said's ideas generally involve location and its association to culture. His views are embedded in the 'worldliness' which we can attribute to his state of exile.

In the essay entitled "Intellectual Exile: Expatriates and Marginal" Said brings forth the concept of Intellectual Exile. According to him, an intellectual exile is comparable to the person who has suffered a shipwreck and has landed on an island, thus compelling to live 'with the land, not on it.' The image of Robinson Crusoe might have come to the reader's mind. However, Said observes that an intellectual exile does not try to 'colonize his little island' like Crusoe. An intellectual exile is more akin to Marco Polo who is always on move from one place to another,[14] and never settles down. The condition of the homelessness which is the destiny of an intellectual exile gives 'certain rewards and yes privilege' (Said 1994: 44).

According to Said, an intellectual exile carries in him both what is left behind and what is present in front of him now. He is provided with a double vision which does not allow him to see things separate. This double vision engenders a new and unpredictable component which for Said is "a better perhaps even more universal idea" (Said 1994:44). Perhaps even more important than this aspect of a double vision is the intellectual exile's perception of 'situations as contingent'.

The change in place and with it the change of culture, ideas and values make it possible for an intellectual exile to apprehend situations as human made and not natural or god given and therefore subject to change. Said writes: "What in effect is the exile standpoint for an intellectual is that you tend to see things not simply as they are but as they have come to be that way". (Said 1994: 45). The reflection on how a situation has 'come to be that way' opens the possibility for modification and change (for a better one). Undoubtedly, an intellectual exile is thus endowed with revolutionary ideas. He is "necessarily ironic, skeptical even playful" (Said 1994:45). An intellectual exile needs not to be an 'actual immigrant' observes Said in his essay "Intellectual Exile: Expatriates and Marginal". By the exercise of the faculty of imagination an intellectual can "move away from the centralizing authorities towards the margins" (Said 1994:47). This brings us to something he has said about exile somewhere around the beginning of the essay – exile as a metaphorical condition.[15] The intellectual exile in this case is very much a member of the society in which he lives. The membership is there so he is not an exile in 'actual condition' but he is at war with the society and therefore his 'privileges, power and honors' are somewhat diminished. Said writes in this context: "The pattern that sets the course for the intellectual as outsider is best exemplified by the condition of exile, the state of never being fully adjusted, always feeling outside the chatty, familiar world inhabited by natives so to speak, tending to avoid and even dislike the trappings of accommodation and national well-being" (Said 1994: 39). In the discussion of Intellectual Exile, it is importance to bring forth the notion of amateurism as given by Said. He calls the critic who follows secular criticism as amateur. The word 'amateur'[16] contrasts with 'professional'. This is significant. Said's choosing of this particular word hints at his attempt to freed the critic from the bondage of the 'narrow professional specialization' which dissociates criticism from the worldliness. The worldliness of the critic is as crucially important for Said as the worldliness of the text. Bill Ashcroft explains the importance of criticism by describing the drawback of professional expertise in criticism:

> The cult of professional expertise in criticism is pernicious because it surrenders the actual material and political concerns of society to a discourse dominated by economists and technocrats (Ashcroft 1999: 47).

It is important that we do not translate Said's concept of 'amateurism' as an easy and superficial substitution of criticism. Rather it seeks to accomplish a vital task of foregrounding the real situations and circumstances in criticism. He himself stands as a good example of an amateur. His study of a wide range of discipline is strongly grounded in the worldliness; in the politics of culture. His own works and varied pronouncements show his affiliation to the real situations. He never divorces himself from the environment which engenders both his criticisms and the texts. An exile himself he understands the impact of the worldliness most probably better than anyone else.

Said's intellectual works in a framework which is not static but dynamic in nature results from the interaction of varied cultures – the marginalized as well as the centralized culture. The intellectual while having a critical perspective on certain issue locates himself within his particular culture and then attempts to expand the horizon to include the one which is ignored. The consequence of such an attempt is the textured universalism in which one side is not neglected for the other side; in which the marginal and the central come together for a better whole. Further this attempt is a real test for an intellectual and is by no means easy. His capacity to leave or abandon his royalty to a specific vulture is put under scanner.

Generally, a person has prejudices and inclinations which establishes his 'non secular' attitude and also formulate his individual identity. Said is asserting the intellectuals to dissolve[17] their individual identities with the realities of other people instead of trying to overrule them. It may be argued that Said, being denied of any culture in particular due to his fragmented and partial situatedness, voices for in-between situations. For him it is not a matter of choice but rather a compulsion[18] subjected by his exilic condition. If he is claiming to be on one particular side, then the claim itself sounds empty and rightly so for once he has been pushed out of his inherent culture, he can never belong to any other culture. He speaks of affiliation to new values and ideas yet an exile remains somewhat aloof from all sorts of attachment. His key tenets celebrate the in-between condition which he himself occupies. Various reasons are ascribed for this exaltation —contrapuntal vision, worldliness, secular outlook, affiliation, and so on and so forth. Still this can be looked as a maneuvered or a clever attempt to valorize his unique condition which many consider as unfortunate. It will not be wrong to say that this so called 'unfortunate' has been transformed by Said to make it a blessing in disguise.

None the less, to flatly assume that he has romanticized the state of exile will be an act of overlooking on our part. Said understands the gap that one may experience in perceiving exile from the level of imagination and from the level of lived experience. While being in the mental level, a person might be charmed by it even literature is abundant with the stories of men who have admirably conquer the miserable condition of the exile. So much so for the imagination but when one actually lives it and experiences it in its harsh actuality then the terrible nature of it is revealed in full swing. 'The crippling sorrow of estrangement' remains forever with the exile.

Antonio Gramsci has discussed two types of intellectual – traditional and organic ones. The traditional one remains aloof from the social change and is conservative by nature. On the opposite pole is the organic intellectual. He is revolutionary and is well grounded in society. He strives to change tradition and bring modification for the betterment of the society. Apart from Gramsci there is another thinker whom Said discusses in *Representation of the Intellectual.* She is Julian Benda. Benda has given the notion of intellectuals as "Philosopher Kings who constitute the conscience of mankind". It echoes Plato's idea of the Philosopher King who is most apt to rule his *Republic.* Benda's Philosopher King will uphold the standard of truth, justice, and morality in the society. Gramsci's intellectual and Benda's intellectual get juxtaposed in Said's idea of an intellectual. His intellectual should have the organic nature while at the same possessing the vision of a philosopher who is concerned with justice and equality. "There has been no major revolution in modern history without intellectuals; conversely there has been no major counter-revolutionary movement without intellectuals" (Said 1994:8). Elsewhere he observes that "The intellectual does so on the basis of universal principles: that all human beings are entitled to expect decent standards of behaviour concerning freedom and justice from worldly powers or nations, and that deliberate or inadvertent violations of these standards need to be testified and fought against courageously" (Said1994: 9).

Comparable to the movement of an exile, ideas and theories move from one place to another. Said gives the example of the idea of transcendence moving from Orient to Occident. The intellectual life as such is given impetus by this circulation of ideas and therefore it is a positive condition. In his essay "Traveling Theory" he explains that we can have four levels of this circulation. One, there is the initial situation or the point of origin from which the idea engenders. Two, the idea moves from its natal location and time to another location and time. Third, there is the struggle for space i.e. the confrontation as well as the acceptance of the original idea into a new one to suit the purpose of the new users. Coming from the first level to the last one, ideas lose some of their originality and they refigure themselves into a new pattern. In Said's words, the ideas lose "their original power and rebelliousness" (Said 2001:436).

Said is influenced by Lukac's theory of reification. An idea or a theory is generated under the pressure or provocation of a 'real historical circumstances'. These circumstances fail to remain same in the later time and so the other versions of the theory do not possess the same strength and forcefulness. Said says "the theory is degraded and subdued, made into relatively tame academic substitute for the real thing" (Said 2001:436).

In the argument as to what should constitute a canon, Allan Bloom has written in *The Closing of the American Mind* that the then existing canon for an American literature student should kept unaltered in order to prevent the decline in the quality of the American literary education. This step will help the student to come into contact with better individuals who are more cultured, intelligent, educated and sensitive. Said argues against Bloom's view of canon saying that it is one sided in dealing with the plurality of cultures and therefore suggests a canon of texts where the heterogeneity and the plurality of the society are reflected. Conrad's *Heart of Darkness* should be studied but not in isolation. It should be read along with the text like Achebe's *Things Fall Apart*. The combination of such texts will provide a deconstructive reading of both the texts and a better understanding of the real scenario.

Bill Ashcroft sums up:

> So the debate about the curriculum unleashed by Bloom's book circulated around questions about the monocultural and Anglocentric character of American society. While the Bloom position advocates the confirmation of a particular Eurocentric tradition, many university teachers, along with Edward Said saw the need to adjust the traditional curriculum to the needs of a rapidly changing American population (Ashcroft 1999: 16).

In the 'curriculum debate' Said's attempt has been to seek for an inclusive and liberal canon where both the centre as well as the marginal finds a voice of their own. This perspective has come from his exilic positioning as Ashcroft writes, "the specular displaced intellectual reads the works of the Western canon because that become the site of his or her own strategic act of reading as resistance" (Ashcroft 1999: 16). Said's originality in analyzing text and critic lies in his giving importance to the location and situatedness of them. He has asserted the worldliness of the text and the critic thus, advocating the materiality of the condition of writing. This materiality has been subdued by the emergence of the poststructuralist theory. The text in the poststructuralist theory has been completely disassociated from the environment it has come forth. Said is thus reversing the poststructuralist's stand. Bill Ashcroft gives his conclusion:

> So Edward Said's originality lies in his determination, his unflappable persistence in promoting a notion of the materiality and worldliness of writing, textuality, reading, criticism and intellectual work in general (Ashcroft 1999: 24-25)

Said's lasting contribution is that he makes people see exile in a new light. He suggests that exile can be a negative as well as a positive condition. He accepts that the condition of exile is truly merciless "produced by human being for other human being" tearing "millions of people from nourishment of tradition, family and geography"(Said 2001:174). But at the same time, exile engenders critical insights, independence of thought and originality of vision. He has frequently used exile as a metaphor to describe his vision of the role of the modern intellectual who needs a critical detached perspective from which to examine his culture. His identity and worldview are shaped by his condition of exile, and therefore he repeats the act of leaving again and again. "I fabricate occasions for departure others giving rise to the fear voluntarily. The two (displacement and fear) seem absolutely necessary to my rhythm of life and have intensified dramatically during the period I've been ill" (Said 1999: 217).

References

1. It can be well observed that Said chooses the word 'contrapuntal' instead of 'dialectics'. It may be because contrapuntal is a lighter term though it also suggests dynamism between two contradictory forces.
2. Talking about the exiled community especially in Palestine and Egypt, Said says that 'these communities after all produced prominent writers like Edmond Jabe, Giuseppe Ungaretti, Constantine Cavafy' (Said 1994: 35-36)
3. 'paradoxically' since banishment is imposed to inhibit the writer or the intellectual from having his words however, the contrary is seen to be happening in the condition of exile.
4. Nuruddin Farah is a Somali novelist whose works include *From a Crooked Rib* (1970), *A Naked Needle* (1976) and *Gifts* (1993). He deals with the theme of women's liberation, and has received international acclaim for his works but at the same time, he suffers from self-imposed

exile for twenty-two years owing to the threat of arrest by the Somali government. The government finds his works politically objectionable.

5. In the conference of writers in exile held in Vienna in December 1987, he presented the paper "In Praise of Exile."
6. Please see Barbour D John. "Edward Said and the Space of Exile". *Literature and Theology* 21, no 3 (Sept 2007): 293-301. In this article he has discussed Tweed's concept in detail.
7. Auerbach writes '...it is quite possible that the book owes its existence to just this lack of a rich and specialized library. If it had been possible for me to acquaint myself with all the work that has been done on so many subjects, I might never have reached the point of writing" (Said 1983: cited 5).nts
8. Arnold, Mathew. *Culture and Anarchy*. Cambridge: Cambridge University Press, 1961.
9. He has written a well known work on the relation of the Orient and the Occident, and the involvement of hegemony in maintaining the supremacy of the West over the East. The book is entitled *Orientalism.*
10. He faces problem with his marriage, and this contributes to his traumatic condition at that time to a good extent.
11. Ash-Wednesday is written in 1930. The new series of poems that I have mentioned begins in 1925 onwards. Cooper writes that "only those closest to Eliot were aware of the spiritual struggle through which he was passing in the late 1920s. For others, it would have been difficult to understand the significance of Ash-Wednesday in Eliot's evolution as an artist" (Cooper 2006: 80).
12. Syntagmatic and paradigmatic elements are introduced by Saussure to explain his theory of language. Signs in linear sequence are syntagmatic while signs in contrast with other signs are paradigmatic. The result of this binary pair of syntagmatic and paradigmatic relation is a network of mutually defining elements, in other words, a linguistic system.
13. The idea of worldliness has been explained by Said himself in his *Reflections on Exile and Other Literary and Cultural Essays* "Worldliness' is a notion I have often found useful because of two meanings that inhere in it together, one, the idea of being in the secular world, as opposed to being 'otherworldly' and two, because of the suggestion conveyed by the French word mondanite. Worldliness as the quality of a practiced, slightly jaded savior faire, worldly wise and street smart" (Said 2001:301).
14. A good example can be had from the movie *Castaway* (200). The name itself is suggestive. In *Castaway*, Tom Hank who plays the lead role suffers a plane crash and is forced to live on an isolated island. He experiences an exilic life and struggles to maintain his social and cultural

being by speaking to a lifeless basketball named Wilson. The traumatic and heart wrenching condition of isolation from one's culture, language and society is depicted in the movie.

15. Said discusses this concept in page 39 of the text Representations of the Intellectual in the essay entitled "Intellectual Exile: Expatriates and Marginal".
16. 'Amateur' comes from the French word amateur meaning 'love of something'. Said has been inspired by this meaning of the word while coining the term.
17. Dissolving of identity is perhaps easier when a person is in exile. "Identity – who we are, where we come from, what we are – is difficult to maintain in exile" (Ashcroft 1999: cited 7).
18. He writes in *Reflections on Exile* that "exile is not, after all a matter of choice: you are born into it, or it happens to you" (Said 2001:184).

Works Cited

Ashcroft, Bill, Pal Ahluwalia. *Edward Said: The Paradox of Identity*. New York: Routledge, 1999.

Bayoumi, Moustafa, Andrew Pubin. *The Edward Said Reader*. New York: Vintage Books, 2000.

Cooper, John Xeros. *The Cambridge Introduction to T.S. Eliot*. Cambridge University Press, 2006.

Farah, Nuruddin. "In Praise of Exile" in Glad, John. *Literature in Exile*. Durham: Duke University Press, 1990.

Said, Edward. *Out of Place: A Memoir*. New Delhi: Penguin Books.1999.

______. *Reflections on Exile and Other Literary and Cultural Essays*. New Delhi: Penguin Books, 2001.

______. *Representations of the Intellectual: The 1993 Reith Lectures*. London: Vintage Books, 1994.

______. *The World, the Text and the Critic*. London: Vintage Books, 1983.

Singh, Gurbhagat. "Expatritiate Writing and the Problematic of Centre: Edward Said and Homi Bhabha" in Jain, Jasbir. *Writers of Indian Diaspora: Theory and Practice*, Jaipur: Rawat Publication, 1998.

Zeleza, Paul Tiyambe. "The Politics and Poetics of Exile: Edward Said in Africa. *Research in African Literatures"* 36 no 3 (Fall 2005) 1-22.

23

Self to Cosmic Consciousness: Transformative Journey of Shiva in *The Immortals of Meluha* and *The Secret of Nagas*

Lata Mishra

Debutante author Amish in his two novels, namely, *The Immortals of Meluha* and *The Secret of Nagas* (Shiva Trilogy- Part 1 & 2), provides an integral analysis on the modern world. Amish's potential to create myth for our modern times that makes pertinent points about the real world is marvellous. The work combines the narrative excess with the philosophical debate. Amish recreates the myth of Shiva, Ganesha, Sati and Kali through his study of all spheres of Indian life and literature. He makes Shiva myth appealing and intelligible to the modern mind. Those who still keep the oral tradition alive through chanting and singing of hymns and folk songs deserve gratitude and admiration of young generation. At the same time there is also a need to understand and reinterpret its meaning. Recitation without a knowledge of its meaning does not enlighten one. Amish insists on engaging oneself in action because actions purify as knowledge liberates. Through recreation, 'The Shiva Trilogy," becomes a living inspirational scripture capable of providing spiritual direction in the modern world.

The present paper is an attempt to explore identity, reality, knowledge and the dichotomy of the order/chaos axis in the context of a universal understanding of consciousness. The paper in its first section, analyses the childhood memory and consequent dreams of Shiva under the lens of Carl Jung's *On the Nature of Dreams* (1967). The brief introduction of the two selected novels is followed by the study of the various Vasudevs, that Shiva meets on his transformative journey to the kingdoms/cities in the novels that exist as organic entities. These cities can thrive and grow, but they also age and decline, as if they have the life of their own. The journey begins from Mt. Kailash in Tibet to Meluha and Swadeep. Shiva then marches to Brangaridai and Dandak Forests near Narmada. The second section focuses on Shiva's meeting with the second Vasudev. In the third section the Vasudev of Magadh Temple gives Shiva insight into the masculine and feminine principle operating in the universe.

The Meluhan order in the novel is perceived as a masculine attitude, that reflects the authoritative, vertical, hierarchical order of being and knowledge, and the Swadeepan chaos as feminine attitude that contains the seeds of order within. Chaos initially may mean confusion but as will be inferred it is a kind of order that is difficult to perceive as such. The Vasudevs initiate and direct Shiva in his karma. There are almost nine discourses with them. The Vasudevs are presented as scientists who live in temples which serve as transmitters from where they communicate with each other through radio waves. Here the two novels are also explored through the application of the non-linear dynamics theory and the discussion on the chaotic attractors of dynamical systems. The complexity theorists view all systems as self-organizing. As the Indian philosophy perceives, Amish too presents the individual psyche and society as a system that undergoes the process of self-creation and self-generation as opposed to a deliberate construction. As amply explicated in the paper, the society is in constant interaction with its surroundings and any attempt to block the system would be to cut it off from the interactions that maintain it, thereby likely leading to its destruction.

I

Childhood memories reside in the conscious and unconscious mind. An individual suppresses traumatic memories unconsciously and these memories are "repressed memories." Such memories are the ones suppressed beyond the realm of conscious awareness. Repressed memories are often the stuff that contains unbearable pain, fear or disgust, experienced by an individual. Shiva as a young child has suffered such an experience when one day while returning home at dusk to his native place, Mt. Kailash, he falls upon a man and woman caught in an act. Initially the young boy is excited to watch and later reports to his teenage friends but suddenly he realizes that it's a sexual assault by the man. As the victim woman notices him and cries for help, a scared Shiva flees from the spot, never turning back.

> And then came the moment that would haunt him for the rest of his life...The hairy monster turned to see who the woman was calling...The boy quickly picked up his sword and fled... He could hear the man's heavy breathing. (*IM* 221)

Carl Jung, a Swiss psychiatrist and the founder of analytical psychology, regarded the nature of dreams to be "a spontaneous self-portrayal, in symbolic form, of the actual situation in the unconscious" (Jung, 1967, Vol. 8, par.505) Our unconscious mind in our dreams expresses itself in a language of symbols, images, and metaphors. Shiva's suppressed memories of this incident diminishes his personal value and makes him feel bad about himself. Repression is an unconscious act while suppression is conscious effort. However hard Shiva tries, he finds forgetting difficult. For this he often resorts to marijuana. Jung suggests two functions of dreams. Dreams compensate for imbalances in the dreamer's psyche. They bring unconscious contents that have so far been suppressed by consciousness to the surface. Shiva's dream of the same woman calling for help keeps recurring in the novel. He moves to Meluha on beckoning of Nandi, the Meluhan captain. Meluha is a vast empire extending from Kashmir to

Gujarat, Rajasthan and parts of Uttar Pradesh. Here he meets Sati, the daughter of Daksha, the emperor, and falls in love. When Sati explains him why she would not attend yajna, a ceremonial fire sacrifice organized by the royal party, Shiva's mind revolts at the humiliation of his beloved and the injustice done to vikarmas in Meluha. He is desperate to bring dignity back to his beloved and the dream of the childhood traumatic event is back that night. He wishes to 'redeem' himself. Vikarmas are the subjugated group in Meluha. This system of labelling of vikarma is not based on caste but as Nandi explains:

> Vikarma people, my Lord are people who have been punished in this birth for the sins of their previous birth. Hence they have to live this life out with dignity and tolerate their present sufferings with grace.... They are not allowed to marry since they may poison others with their bad fate,. They are not allowed to touch any person who are is not related to them or is not part of their normal duties. (*IM* 93).

Sati is one of the vikarmas, but is privileged to live in a palace. She strictly adheres to all other rules laid down for vikarmas. Any person who touches a vikarma has to observe the *Shudhikaran* ritual.

According to Jung, when the dreamer recognizes and accepts the unconscious contents in his psyche, a greater psychological balance is achieved. He further argued that dreams unite consciousness and the unconscious in a healthy, harmonious state of wholeness. He termed this process as individuation, which is the "complete actualization of the whole human being" (Jung, 1967, Vol. 16, par.352). Amish's aim in this metanarrative seems to provide practical knowledge of consciousness, this knowledge is boundless, infinite field of wakefulness that can be explained by an individual as his/her own simplest form of awareness. Knowledge proper is obtained by ordering, connecting and synthesizing the Shiva-Vasudev meetings into some system. The discourses held in these meetings leaves readers with the hope achieving infinite creativity and fulfilment. Shiva evolves through continuous development of consciousness to become a universal human being. He cognizes and represents the universal mechanics of creation and lives the higher states of consciousness.

The other terms Jung uses for consciousness are ego or persona. Persona is the mask that one wears in society to adapt to its norms. Beneath the persona lies shadow that is all that is repressed. A self-conscious person confronts his shadow and the world of darkness. A shadow often surfaces in our dreams and is of the same gender. Shiva's dream remains the same with minor deviances. Acting upon a thought, in the waking state of consciousness, one is bound to a cycle of experience, impression, desire, action and further experience. The childhood experience leaves an impression on the mind of Shiva. Whenever in adulthood the new impressions associate themselves with similar past experience stored in Shiva's mind an impulse is created that rises to the thinking level and assumes a form of thought. Through this thought a desire emerges and in turn Shiva spurs into action.

II

The Vasudevs in the novels serve as stimulants to Shiva. The rise of self-consciousness in Shiva may be traced in his relation with all the Vasudevs in the two novels. The first Vasudev Shiva meets is in Brahma Temple at Meru. Shiva meets Sati and falls in love at this place. This Vasudev reappears in Shiva's dream. In the chapter "Attack on Mandar," Amish brings in the Derridean play between "presence" and "absence", and concomitantly dissolves their difference. The first Vasudev of Brahma Temple convinces Shiva that the existence (presence) of the world is actually constructed around its absence. In other words, it is the absence that constructs the presence, and the existence of "presence" is impossible without the conception of its "absence." The Pandit engages Shiva in a dialogue and fittingly argues:

> "What is the colour of that leaf?...It's green.".... Light falls on that an object and when it reflects back from that, you see that

> object....What normal sunlight is made of?....White light is nothing but the confluence of seven different colours...White sunlight falls on that leaf. The leaf's physical properties are such that it *absorbs* the colours, violet, indigo, blue, yellow, orange and red... It doesn't absorb the colour green, which is then reflected back, Hence I see the leaf as green... What colour it absorbs and what it rejects. Or is it every single colour in the world, *except* green?" (Amish 295).

Martin Heidegger rejects the calculative, utilitarian view of reason. To him reason is not the sole source of legitimate. The knowledge of *truth* cannot be confined to rationalized propositions about being alone but ought to encompass the knowledge of the Being of beings. Rational and scientific knowledge just give the information from one particular perspective. Therefore any one kind of knowledge of beings cannot be privileged over any other. No propositional knowledge is absolute; it is all relative. Vasudev continues his discussion:

> There are many realities. There are many versions of what may appear obvious,'... 'Whatever appears as the unshakeable truth, the exact opposite may also be true in another context. It is the context or perspective that you're looking from that moulds which particular reality you see.' (296)

In their interaction both the Vasudevs and Shiva rise to self-consciousness. The Vasudevs are informative, but Shiva is investigative. He sees things external to him. In an attempt to know them he works on them and shapes them. His interactions with Kali, Ganesh, Parashuram and societies of Meluhans and Swadeepans, in general, enables him to inwardise them. In his way he gains self-consciousness. Indian philosophy believes that at birth, an individual's mind contains past impressions (*karmasaya*). These impressions combined with hereditary constitution and social influences develop the psyche of an individual. The Vasudevs in the novels address Shiva as 'fellow traveller in *karma, karmasarthi*' (*IM* 46)

Jacques Derrida's introduction of the notion, *Différence,* suggests that without differentiation there could be no experience, meaning or being. Following this, the search for absolute truth or singular vision of self and the world seems a fancy idea. Taking this further, the absolute must rest upon the foundation of that which is different from itself. This argument leads to a respect for differences and rejection of Hegelian-like attempt to integrate all ideas. The ideas thus are integrally related to their polar opposites. The one cannot be treated as superior to the other. Jung echoes similar ideas but takes a step forward:

> ...he who accepts what approaches him because it is also in him, quarrels and wrangles no more, but looks into himself and keeps silent. He sees the tree of life, whose roots reach into Hell and whose top touches Heaven. He also no longer knows differences (301).

Amish, in accordance with Indian philosophy re-enlivens the universal field of pure consciousness. Reconciling or holding together of opposite values is the fundamental property of consciousness. This theme of opposites co-existing in the universe surfaces repeatedly in the conversation of the Vasudevs.

The second Vasudev, that Shiva meets is at Mohan Temple of Mohan Jo Daro at Meluha. To analyse the Shiva-Vasudev conversation carried here, it would be appropriate to first discuss the Dynamic Systems Theory and consider individual and society as a system. The concept of chaos is taken from the field of mathematics that studies the System. The *Oxford Dictionary* defines system as "a set of things working together as parts of a mechanism or an interconnecting network; a complex whole" (1212).

III

The Dynamical Systems Theory and the Chaos Theory deal in the long-term qualitative behaviour of dynamical systems. The study reveals that the Systems that are stable in relation to their environment can become unstable and vice versa. This theory basically studies the continuous state, the deterministic systems.

It includes both discrete and continuous time systems as well as linear and non-linear systems. The Dynamic Systems Theory was originally developed for applications to the problems arising in physics and engineering, but the complex social systems can also be well explored through the application of the Chaos Theory or as also referred to as non-linear dynamics, dynamical systems theory, or dynamical systems method by mathematicians.

Sometimes the dynamic systems may exhibit aperiodic behaviour and the linearity or cyclity is affected. This effect that may occur due to just a minor change in the system may lead to major changes in future states of the system. Edward Lorenz, while working through computer on the weather pattern, observed that in dynamical systems even rounding numbers that may be regarded as an insignificant change causes significant changes in results. This effect that triggers large changes on future results is termed as *the butterfly effect*. The world we live in does not comprise mere objects but rather is made up of a network of living and non-living complex systems. The components of the system are in continuous interacting relationships. The *Oxford Dictionary* defines chaos as "the property of a complex system whose behaviour is so unpredictable as to appear random, owing to great sensitivity to small changes in conditions" and "complete disorder and confusion" or "mayhem" (Thesaurus,137). According to Edward Lorenz (1993) chaos is a system "that is sensitively dependent on interior changes in initial conditions …within one and the same system" (Lorenz, 24).

The Oxford Dictionary defines order as "the arrangement or disposition of people or things in relation to each other according to a particular sequence, pattern or method' and "a state in which everything is in its correct or appropriate place" or "the state that exists when people obey laws, rules or authority"(816). Thus chaos and order seem to stand poles apart. In social systems also, order and chaos are often conceived of as polarized twin concepts, order referring to permanence, chaos to the opposite. The relationship between the two concepts is, however, more complicated. "Order," for instance, does not necessarily indicate the absence of chaos. In society, though the systems show a cyclical pattern—the formation, dissolution, and reformation of order— yet it is observed widely that the pattern never repeats itself completely. The social life in one cycle is never an exact replica of the previous one. Determinism is the philosophical belief that every event or action is the inevitable result of preceding events and actions. Thus, in principle at least, every event or action can be completely predicted in advance or in retrospect.

In thermodynamics, energy transfer is studied in three types of systems: isolated, closed and open ones. An isolated system is one that does not allow any exchange of energy or matter while closed system may exchange energy but not matter with an outside system. Open systems can exchange both matter and energy with an outside system. Since the two novels, *The Immortals of Meluha* and *The Secret of Nagas,* thematise the chaos theory, it may lead to an assumption that the narrative is about fractured time, lost meanings and the absurdity of human condition, but the writer, Amish Tripathi has created a narrative in which the chaos theory symbolizes precisely the ways in which human beings can gain knowledge of the world and make knowledge meaningful in their particular human context.

The structure of the novels is built around the juxtaposition of or interrelationship between the two worlds of Suryavanshis and Chandravanshis. The first novel is set in Meluha and Ayodhya, capital of Swadeep, while its sequel takes the readers to Kashi, Magadh, Brangaridai and Dandak forests. The kingdom of the Suryavanshis is Meluha and that of Chandravanshis is Swadeep. Meluha runs along the lines of RamRajya and strictly follows the Laws of Lord Rama. The Suryavanshi motto is *Satya, Dharma, Maan,*' Devagiri, the capital of Meluha, is described as:

> the city was divided into a grid of square blocks by the paved streets. There were footpaths on the side for pedestrian... all the

> buildings were constructed as standard two storied block structures made of baked bricks.... All windows and doors were built strictly on the side walls of buildings, never facing the main road... The most common backgound colour though, appeared to be blue... the city was divided into many districts.... Each district had its own markets, commercial and residential areas. (*IM* 62-63).

The Chandravanshi motto is *Shringar. Saundarya. Swatantrata.* Their capital Ayodhya is described in thise words:

> Some open grounds had been converted into giant slums... The already narrow roads had been made even narrower by the intrusion of cloth tents of the homeless. There was constant tension between the richer home owning class and the poor landless who lived in slums. The Emperor had legalised all encroachments established before 1910 BC. That meant that slum dwellers could not be removed unless the government created alternate accommodation. (*IM* 372).
>
> 'Here each house had its own individual allure. The Swadweepans... created houses that were expressions of passion and elegance. The Swadweepans had none of the restraints of the Meluhans. Everything was painted bright. (*IM* 373).

In the most ordered city of Meluha, children are also brought up in most disciplined fashion:

> all children that are born in Meluha are compulsorily adopted by the empire. All pregnant women have to travel there (Maika) for their delivery.... Once the child is born, he or she is kept in Maika for a few weeks for health reasons while the mother travels back to her own city.'...'The child is then put into the Meluha gurukul... They grow up with all the resources of the empire available to them.... When the children turn sixteen, they are allocated to the applicant parents... (*IM* 97).

Freedom for citizens is severely limited with social laws rigidly maintained by ideological means and force. Parent-child bonds are deliberately eroded with the child estranged from the mother and its identity diluted soon after its birth. Healthy children are transferred to Maika, while the deformed and disabled ones are deported from the kingdom. Thus an ideal society is maintained and prided upon. Some Meluhans however 'tired of the regimented life' have taken refuge in Kashi, "They tolerated the chaos of the Chandravanshi ways for the pleasure of watching their children grow" (*SN*77).

Melhuan society can be placed within the modernist paradigm considering its reliance on totalizing theory. At the centre, a logos is said to be at play; as in Daksha's forces of rationalization and Parvateshwar's adherence to Laws of Lord Rama. Thus the grand narrative of Mluha is replete with assumptions of homogeneity, desirability of consensus and order. Daksha rests his views on some kind of conception of tension-reduction as the operative force in the social structural development. The deformed are deployed out of kingdom. The diseased and handicapped are seggregated from the mainstream society. Order is seen as desirable without further explanation. Deviance is defined in terms of distance from assumed acceptable standard of normativity.

The liberal Chandravanshi life is described as:

> The people were living embodiments of the Chandravanshi way of life. The women wore skimpy clothes, brazen and confident about their sexuality,. The men were as fashion conscious as their women—what Meluhans would call dandies. the relationship between the men and women could only be characterized as one teetering on extremes. Extreme love coexisting with extreme hate, expressed with extreme loudness, all built on the foundations of extreme passion. (*IM*374)

The Suryavanshis regard the Chandravanshis as corrupt people:

> 'Yes,' said Daksha. 'The Chandravanshis are corrupt and disgusting people. No morals. No ethics. They are the source of all our problems. Some of us believe that Lord Ram was too kind. He should have completely destroyed them. But he forgave them and let them live. In fact, we have to face the mortification of seeing the Chandravanshis rule over Lord Ram's birthplace-Ayodhya!' (*IM*100)

Further, in Book 2, Daksha continues "The evil Chandravandravanshi way of life has to end and these people have to be brought to our pure Suryavanshi ways" (*SN*13). Handicapped people and mothers of still-born, in Meluha are *vikarmas*. Apart from vikarmas, the Meluhans are segregated into four categories: brahmins, kshatriyas, vaishyas and shudras. Only the royal class is allowed to keep track of its biological child brought up in Meluha. Meluha is beset by desperately low fertility rates following strict rules prohibiting a mother from reaching out to her child, almost immediately after birth. As a result, the privileged return to their parents after education while the rest, according to their talents and knowledge, are allotted parents of a particular class. The patriarchal order of Meluhan society manages to keep broadly under control practices, such as caste discrimination and violence. However, soon readers realize that Daksha has been faced with the false choice of accepting and implementing such a social structure, for it is a form of totalitarianism.

Chapter 2 of Book I, 'Land of Pure Life', reveals the anxiety of king Daksha, as his kingdom that so far seemed an impenetrable and safe haven for its citizens is under threat by treacherous Chandravanshis. Apart from the occasional attacks, the kingdom figures as a model of empiricism and order. The entire kingdom, in fact, looks like a microcosm of the universe with all in perfect order. However this rationality and empiricism soon seem to be destabilized. Swadeepan society which initially seems to be a critique of Meluha, has found grounding in the insights of the chaos theory and Lacanian thought. They privilege disorder rather than order. Their starting point is paralogism: privileging instabilities (Lyotard 1984). This model of society begins with far-from-equilibrium conditions as being the more "natural" state, and places a premium on flux, non-linear change, chance, spontaneity, intensity, indeterminacy, irony, and orderly disorder. No permanent stable order is possible or even desirable. No centre or foundation exists. They consider the search for an overall, all-encompassing totalizing theory as an illusory exercise.

Shiva meets the third Vasudev in Ayodhya at Rama Janmabhoomi. Shiva fights a war against Chandravanshi on being convinced by the Meluhan emperor of their being evil. Later in a despondent and remorseful mood he ponders over the war and the defeat of the Chandravanshis, whom till now he had thought to be evil. The Vasude enlighten Shiva that the universe is a manifestation of the illusion of duality. The dynamics of existence of the masculine and feminine principles is the most fundamental concept in life consciousness. He says:

> Yes, a duality that is one of the many perspectives of the universe-the masculine and the feminine. The Asuras and the Suryavanshis stand for the masculine. The Devas and the Chandravanshis speak for the feminine. The names change, but the life forces they embody remain the same. They will always exist. There is no way that either can be destroyed. Otherwise the universe will implode. (*IM* 392)

Vasudev's discourse on duality in universe finds its analogy in the Danish physicist, Niels Bohr's Principle of Complementarity. Bohr argued that every entity in Nature possesses pairs of contradictory characters, such as corpuscular property and wave property. He found that the contradictory characters are complementary to each other rather than being exclusive. In order to integrally comprehend the entity as a whole, both the contradictory characters need to be taken into consideration.

Nagas are introduced as evil force in Book 1 by Nandi, the Meluhan captain as:

> They are cursed people, my Lord,.. are born with hideous deformities because of the sins of their previous births. Deformities like extra hands or horribly misshapen faces. But they have tremendous strength and skills. The Naga name alone strikes terror in any citizen's heart. They are not even allowed to live in the Sapt Sindhu.'...
>
> Our land, my Lord, the land of seven rivers. The land of Indus, Saraswati, Yamuna, Ganga, Saryu, Brahmaputra and Narmada. This is where Lord Manu mandated that all of us, Suryavanshis and Chandravanshis, live. (*IM* 59)

These Nagas, who are dreaded terrorists in Meluha and as reported, have allied with Chandravanshis, in Book-I, as readers come to know in Book II, have settlements in Panchavati. They parade the city once a week singing songs that reflect their emotions:

> You were my world, my God, my creator,
> And yet, you abandoned me.
> I didn't seek you, you called me,
> And yet, you abandoned me.
> I honoured you, lived by your rules, coloured myself in you-colours,
> And yet, you abandoned me.
> You hurt me, you deserted me, you failed in your duties,
> And yet, I'm the monster
> Tell me Lord, what can I.... (*SN* 147)

The appropriated modified discourse on the Chaos theory can be applied to the examination of the novels. Kellert defines chaos theory as "the qualitative study of unstable aperiodic behaviour in deterministic nonlinear dynamical systems" (2). A determinist linear thinking of Suryavanshis over-simplifies reality. Their life and its working is as predictable as the movement of pendulum, a simple example of a dynamical system. Dynamical systems theory is the branch of mathematics devoted to the motions of systems which evolves according to simple rules. Man as well as society, as a system, are complex in nature and thus cannot be studied as an isolated system. An isolated system in physics is one where there can be no exchange of matter or energy. Every complex system is also a *dissipative structure,* as explained by Prigogine, as it takes on and dissipates energy when it interacts with its environment. Man constantly interacts with his ever-changing environment. Thought processes are generally non-deterministic in nature, more like a maze, but the Meluhan rules do not realize that disorder, confusion, uncertainty, or instability prevail all the time. This is "the butterfly effect", a term used in the Chaos Theory to explain how a minor change may cause drastic and unexpected results. Each Meluhan who seems to be so stable in relation to his environment on deeper inspection seems to contain seeds of chaos and suppress the unstable in him. The forced orderliness of Meluhans is seen in their Maika and vikarma system.

On the other hand, the Swadeepans' life appears to be chaotic on the surface but there exists some kind of order within their inner self, as reflected to Shiva, when he meets a beggar at the temple. The Swadeepans carry the motto of 'Passion. Beauty. Freedom' (*IM*371). On the temple steps of Ayodhya, Shiva meets a beggar in torn clothes who offers a share of his food on a banana leaf. As Shiva is coaxed into eating with him:

> Shiva could not find the heart to look up anymore. As his heart sank deeper and his tears rose, he ate the portion the old man gave him quickly. The food was over in no time.
> *Freedom. Freedom for the wretched to also have dignity. Something impossible in Meluha's system of governance* (*IM* 386).

The Meluhan life is limited to a single culture and locality. The rest of the world is known dimly, if at all, and only then through the distorting filter of their own local society. Models of one-directional change assume that change in a certain direction induces further change in the same direction; models of curvilinear or cyclical change, on the other hand, assume that change in a certain direction creates the conditions for change in another direction. More specifically, it is often assumed that growth has its limits and that in approaching these limits the changed curve will inevitably be bent, but the human race, as a whole, is a true dynamical system that follows the principles of the Chaos Theory.

Swadweep is 'a confederacy of aligned kings' (*SN* 15), where each king pays tribute to the Swadeepan Emperor and rules independently. In a debate with Dilipa, the Swadeepan Emperor Daksha concerning rights to subjects, states, "Then there will be chaos," (*SN* 15). Kashi has given refuge to Brangas. This is the place open to all kinds of social, cultural and commercial transactions. Many Meluhans have fled to this city. Brangaridai has Nagas as his allies. Shiva, the hero of the novel, undergoes archetypal-imaginative journey of transformation. The hero in the novel does not fight the villain but the writer elevates the action in his fiction, as the task of Shiva is not to trounce evil individual but to confront the evil that attaches man to itself. Shiva and Sati who set out on their journey, reach the stage of maturation in Swadweep when they confront the cultural other. They gain self-control in Kashi and then set out in search of an answer to the mystery of truth versus deception/perception versus reality.

Advaita Vedanta accepts the pluralistic nature of the world. It is neither monism nor non-dualism. It believes Reality to be Pure Consciousness. All the diverse areas in the empirical universe are connected at the deeper level.

IV

In Indian mythology, while Sati or Parvati represents marriage and motherhood, Kali stands for destruction. She is also the one who protects and sacrifices for her children (devotees). Shiva's destruction opens the path for the new creation. In the selected texts, before meeting Shiva, Sati has no identity of her own. Her identity, nature and actions are defined and acted out vis-a-vis her father, Daksha. The much doting father but equally manipulative, King Daksha keeps Sati ignorant of the truth that she has given birth to a deformed son and misinforms her of the still-born birth. Shiva succeeds in luring her into remarriage and thus into the wider circle of worldly life. In, Book 2, however, it is Sati who introduces Shiva to Kali and thus extends his circle of activity. At this point, Shiva involves in the act of destruction/creation which is actually an act of arranging and producing order from chaos.

While Sati provides a traditional model for women in their relationship with men by being calm, approachable and docile, Kali's wrath and retribution presents her as aggressive and fiercely independent goddess. In the novel Sati is brought up in a civilized, orderly and refined Meluhan Kingdom while Kali's abode is the wild, raw and chaotic forest of Dandaka. Sati in the novel is described as beautiful, but it is her devotion and asceticism that attracts Shiva to her. Anandmayi, on the other hand, is portrayed as a seductive princess of Ayodhya. Anandmayi is an embodiment of female beauty and the instigator of desire. She not only sexually attracts the celibate Parvateshwar but also impresses him with her intelligence and warrior skills. She capably breaks the order (vow and Suryavanshi Laws) and creates chaos in the life of Parvateshwar. To Parvateshwar, Suryavanshi way had 'been the bedrock of life' and he had found this 'predictability *quite* (added) comforting' (SN,256). Anandmayi as a 'strange attractor' turned his, 'world upside down'. She represents the rhythm of physical world who impels creation.

In Chapter 16 of Book 2, "The Opposites Attract", Shiva embraces Parashuram, Sati unites with Kali and the upright Meluhan General Parvateshwar accepts the Chandravanshi, Anandmayi. This union of opposites leads them to a state of chaos that self-organises and thus becomes the ideal basis for creativity. Such "attractors" of disorder, in the theory of chaos, are equations that predict the long-term behaviour of complex systems. Just as a butterfly flapping its wings causes a hurricane in another part of the world so are the lives of Shiva, Sati and Parvateshwar affected by the entry of these 'strange attractors', also termed as 'the butterfly effect'. Kali, who as Naga Queen, seemed quite angry and erratic earlier, finally succeeds in bringing Shiva to the wilds of, the Dandaka Forests. Sati, the most obedient daughter, produces Kali before Daksha, and in this way exposes the king's conspiracy. Parashuram, as an strange attractor, leads Shiva to Brihaspati in Panchavati. Ganesha in Indian mythology is the son of Shiva and Parvati. He is known to remove obstacles from the path of devotees. In the novel, Ganesha is Lord of the people. He strongly draws Shiva towards himself in an attempt to abduct Sati and thus is the most important 'strange attractor'. The entire plot in the novel is the outcome of Ganesha's actions. The Lord of the People and the turbulent conditions that create him, draws ordered complex systems into disorder. The state of non-equilibrium of the system is exposed by Ganesha and this non-equilibrium sets out in turn to reveal the hidden potential concealed by equilibrium.

V

In the Chaos Theory, in a system multiple agents interact to generate strange attractors. The complexity approach to chaos believes in a tight relation between chaos and order. This interaction leads one to another in a dynamic process. Chaos, in this approach, is not avoided but utilized to organise the system, through an "attractor". Shiva's uncle tells him, "My child, your destiny is much larger than these mountains. But in order to realise it, you will have to cross these very same massive mountains" (*SN*145).

The application of the Chaos Theory to the study of these novels discusses the existence of multiple variables in a society that prevents predictability. A real world system is complex and thus, the study in its pattern, would be more desirable, rather than studying it in parts. Just as a weather pattern is drastically affected by slight changes, changes in society due to minor variations also creates a chaotic pattern. Societies as a complex system are an *open* and *dissipative* structures. "Dissipative structures" are offered as relatively stable societal structures that remain sensitive and responsive to their environment. This concept implies both relative stability as well as continuous change. Contrary to modernist Meluhans, Swadeepans as postmodernists consider ongoing flux and continuous change as desirable. In society, clashes may occur, resulting in fall from equilibrium, but the dynamics can bring the society towards a new emergent structure. Besides this, the paper more importantly exposes and explores the patterns within a social system, which, in turn, may give a greater understanding of the system. The novels seem to suggest a need to perceive the interactions occurring within a structure, on the basis of which reframing and consequently progress may take place. Society is a living entity and thus it is also realized that it self-creates and self-constructs itself.

While the conversation with the mundane characters remains at the expressed level of speech, the discourse with Vasudevs is carried out at subtle and transcendental level of pure consciousness, without sounds. Their minds send radiowaves to each other, thus eliminating the possibility of a gap between sound and meaning. Vasudev of Ayodhya temple urges Shiva to let his thoughts flow freely in order to discover the truth. Vasudev of Magadh Temple explains:

> Everything needs balance, Neelkanth. The masculine needs the feminine.The energy requires the mass. (*SN*113)

At Kashi Vishwanath Temple Shiva gains insight into:

> There is a god in every single one of us. And there is evil in every single of us. The true battle between good and evil is fought within. And the great evil connects itself to the evil within us. (*SN*114)

Vasudev Pandit, Gopal discusses with Shiva:

> Lord Manu had said it's not people who are evil. True Evil exists beyond them. It attracts people. It causes confusion amongst its enemies. But Evil in itself is too big to be confined to just a few. Shiva frowned. *You make it sound like Evil is a power as strong as Good. That it doesn't work by itself, but uses people as its medium.* (*SN*276)
>
> So why does Evil exist? Why can't it be destroyed once and for all?...but Evil does rise and will keep rising again and again Why?...Because Evil serves a purpose...
>
> That is what Lord Manu believed. And the institution of Mahadev acts as the balance, the control for that purpose. To take Evil out of the equation at the correct time (*SN* 277)

Plurality of truths contained in scriptures formed by blend of history, folklore and empirical knowledge is limited by finiteness of human mind as well as culture of the time. Amish Tripathi delves deep into this great Shiva myth of India and employs it as a vehicle of a new vision and interpretation. There is order in creation and system in nature. Shiva gains Knowledge of Supreme Creativity, that can hold universe in one wholeness. The initial order of the world that gets derailed in course of time, creating chaos is restructured and aligned with the cosmic structure by Shiva, bringing a new evolved order into existence. Thus the cyclity continues. For the non-dualists philosophers the pureconsciousness exists below the surface of all the micro-entities of the phenomenal world. It is this Reality that Shiva, the man, strives to achieve through his *karma* and perseverance. The paper may be concluded after the study of the two novels and with some presumptions regarding the second sequel of Trilogy, *The Oath of Vayuputras*, yet to be released, with the words of Carl Jung on the subject of cognizance:

> All science however is a function of the soul, in which all knowledge is rooted. The soul is the greatest of all cosmic miracles, it is the *conditio sine qua non* of the world as an object. It is exceedingly astonishing that the Western world (with few exceptions) seems to have so little appreciation of this being so. The flood of external objects of cognizance has made the subject of all cognizance withdraw to the background, often to apparent non-existence. (Qtd. Schrödinger, 129)

Works Cited

Hornby, Turnbull ed. *Oxford Advanced Learner's Dictionary*, O U P,1996.Print

Kellert, S.H. *In the Wake of Chaos: Unpredictable Order in Dynamical Systems*. 1993. Chicago: The University of Chicago Press, 1993. Print.

Lorenz, E. *The Essence of Chaos*. Seattle WA.: University of Washington Press, 1993. Print.

McHale, Brian. *Postmodernist Fiction*. 1987. New York: Methuen, 1987.Print.

Nicolis, G., Prigogine, I. *Exploring Complexity: An Introduction*. 1989. New York: W.H. Freeman and Co., 1989. Print.

Oxford English Dictionary. USA; Oxford University Press. 1989. Print.

Schrödinger, Erwin.What Is Life?: with "Mind and Matter", Cambridge, Cambridge University Press, 1992. Print

Soanes, Spooner, Hawker, ed. *The Oxford Thesaurus of English* Delhi: OUP, N.Delhi. 2009.Print.

Tripathi, Amish. *The Immortals of Meluha.2010.* Chennai: Westland ltd. 2010.Print. (Abv.as IM)

______. *The Secret of Nagas.* 2011 Chennai: Westland ltd. 2011.Print.(Abv. as SN)

Index